LIBERALS, INTERNATIONAL RELATIONS AND APPEASEMENT
The Liberal Party, 1919–1939

Richard S. Grayson

FRANK CASS
LONDON • PORTLAND, OR

First published in 2001 in Great Britain by
FRANK CASS PUBLISHERS
Crown House, 47 Chase Side,
Southgate, London, N14 5BP

and in the United States of America by
FRANK CASS PUBLISHERS
c/o ISBS, 5824 N.E. Hassalo Street
Portland, Oregon, 97213-3644

Website: www.frankcass.com

British Library Cataloguing in Publication Data

Grayson, Richard S., 1969–
    Liberals, international relations and appeasement: the
    Liberal Party, 1919–1939. – (British foreign and colonial policy)
    1. Liberal Party – History – 20th century 2. Great Britain –
    Politics and government – 1910–1936 3. Great Britain –
    Politics and government – 1936–1945 4. Great Britain –
    Foreign relations – 1910–1936 5. Great Britain – Foreign
    relations – 1936–1945
    I. Title

ISBN 0-7146-5092-7 (cloth)
ISBN 0-7146-8133-4 (paper)
ISSN 1467-5013

Library of Congress Cataloging-in-Publication Data

Grayson, Richard S., 1969–
    Liberals, international relations, and appeasement: the Liberal
Party, 1919–1939 / Richard Grayson.
        p. cm. – (Cass series: British foreign and colonial policy, ISSN
1467-5013)
    Includes bibliographical references and index.
    ISBN 0-7146-5092-7 (cloth) – ISBN 0-7146-8133-4 (paper)
    1. Great Britain–Politics and government–1910–1936. 2. Great
Britain–Politics and government–1936–1945. 3. Liberal Party (Great
Britain–History–20th century. 4. Liberalism–Great
Britain–History–20th century. 5. Great Britain–Foreign
relations–1910–1936. 6. Great Britain–Foreign relations–1936–1945.
7. Great Britain–Foreign relations–Germany. I. Title. II. Cass
series–British politics and society.
    DA578 .G73 2001
    324.24106'09'042–dc21

                                                                2001032493

Typeset in 10.5/12.5 Zapf Calligraphic by Vitaset, Paddock Wood, Kent
Printed in Great Britain by
MPG Books Ltd, Bodmin, Cornwall

H 4762369 2.

Contents

Illustrations

Series Editor's Preface

FOREIGN POLICYMAKING in opposition is never easy. There is not only the obvious problem that, at some point, wider loyalties are likely to constrain oppositions, but also the question of what is the purpose of policymaking in opposition anyway? This is a particular problem for a dwindling minority party, as the Liberals were in the process of becoming in the years covered by this book. Their moments of influence during the inter-war years – the two minority Labour governments of 1924 and 1929–31 and the initial phase of the National Government in 1931–32 – were brief and problematic. In such circumstances, Liberals could not hope directly to shape policy. Despite holding the balance in the Commons in 1924, for instance, they nevertheless could do little more than oppose the naval estimates. Rather, Liberals had to seek to shape the environment in which policy was made and to promote particular principles from which policy might be elaborated.

In some ways, the climate of the period was not inimical to this endeavour. Liberalism survived as an ethos, if not as a political programme. Moreover, it furnished an electoral battlefield which both the major parties sought to colonise. It could not be ignored. Indeed, at the start of the period, objectives and institutions peculiarly associated with the Liberal Party, such as free trade, to a declining extent, and the newly established League of Nations, enjoyed a status almost as political shibboleths, although in both cases the situation was to change rapidly in the 1930s. Even then, however, the idea of collective security through the League retained the potency to shape the way in which the National Government approached the 1935 election. Liberal ideas on international affairs, in other words, enjoyed a constituency well beyond the formal boundaries of the party.

These ideas, Richard Grayson demonstrates, had a number of key components. Central to these was the importance of international cooperation. Both the League of Nations and free trade, in their different ways, were seen as devices to promote this. Whilst nation states were seen as necessary expressions of community, policies to limit their absolute sovereignty were seen, not least in the light of the carnage of the First World War and the flawed peace that followed, as eminently desirable. The key concept, as Grayson shows, was that of interdependency, the expression in the international arena of the utilitarian object of securing the good of each through the good of the whole. The Empire, for instance, was seen throughout this period by most Liberals as a force for good in which this principle was realised.

How interdependency was to be achieved elsewhere during these years was, however, more problematic. In the 1920s, the League of Nations was too readily seen as sufficient. During the following decade, in contrast, most Liberals turned to ideas of collective security and international police action. These were rejected by others, notably Lord Lothian, as incompatible with the ideas of interdependency for which Liberals stood – rather, they seemed to threaten a return to the dangers of the pre-1914 alliance system. He was of course right, in a sense, but for the concept of interdependency to work a sense of mutual benefits, equity and easy redress was required, none of which factors, as Keynes warned, was secured by the post-1918 settlement. By the 1930s, it was too late. Liberals instead had to join with the other parties in groping towards responses to the international storm clouds of the decade.

In this the Liberals seem to have occupied a middle position: more belligerent than the government in the face of aggression, and more prepared than Labour to support increased arms spending. Their position, however, only shifted slowly and was not fully apparent until the end of the decade. For instance, as Grayson points out, until 1938 they continued to favour non-intervention in Spain; not, admittedly, on the same grounds as the government, but because they were unconvinced that intervention in a civil war was consistent with Liberalism. The relationship between interdependency and the projection of power was no less of a problem. Collective security, ultimately, required the latter, even if an attempt was made to keep with the earlier faith by reference to tempering it by recognition of the just grievances of the aggressor powers. Realising this in practice is, however, never an easy balancing act.

In the period covered by this book, Liberals were never called upon to perform this balancing act in government. However, this does not mean that their ideas were unimportant. In particular, the concept of interdependency has continuing value for a rapidly globalising world, combining as it does the ideas of flexibility, shared benefits, accountability and international cooperation. Richard Grayson's work therefore, is not just a contribution to the history of the British Liberal Party, or even to the understanding of the diplomatic difficulties of the inter-war years. Through that prism, it addresses issues of international security and economic order of enduring relevance.

Peter Catterall
Series Editor

Preface

A T THE END of July 1938, several hundred Liberals gathered in Oxford for the annual Liberal Summer School. For many there, it was an annual holiday, quite distinct from anything organised by the other parties. It was also entirely separate from the party's formal conference, the Liberal Assembly, which would meet later in the year. Unlike the Assembly, the summer school did not take time for votes on resolutions and its debates were not governed by standing orders. It was simply a chance to debate ideas in a way that is so often impossible during the day-to-day grind of party politics. It was one of the things that kept the inter-war Liberal Party vibrant and relevant.

In the summer of 1938, post-*Anschluss*, pre-Munich, foreign affairs were uppermost in the minds of Liberals. Those at the summer school heard a debate on the issues between two giants of inter-war Liberalism: the party's former leader, Herbert Samuel, and the leading Liberal intellectual, Ramsay Muir. Over the course of a debate which extended over two days, Samuel put the view that with the League of Nations finished, and other international alliances problematic, Britain should make it a priority to meet Germany's legitimate grievances. He was particularly keen that Britain should not act against Germany simply because it disapproved of the Nazi regime.

Ramsay Muir took a different view. Muir said it simply was not possible to disregard the Nazi regime, because it kept on demanding more, whatever it gained. To stop this, Muir said,

> Liberals believe the right way to avoid a universal war is quiet firmness in upholding the right, and on the other hand a generous readiness to proclaim to the world that we are ready to remove the evils which have contributed to the present situation.[1]

It was this latter view that summed up Liberal foreign policy in the late 1930s. It was the view put forward by the party's leader, Archibald Sinclair, and was the view articulated by the vast majority of Liberal activists at every available opportunity. This view was based on two policies. One involved making concessions on issues such as colonies to countries such as Germany, which Liberals called 'economic disarmament'. But the second policy, 'collective security', involved ensuring that all concessions were backed up by the threat of force should international agreements or law be broken.

This twin-track approach meant that the Liberal Party was a distinctive voice against appeasement as Britain drifted towards war in the late 1930s. That should not be surprising. Liberals were seldom away from the cutting-edge of radical thought on international affairs in the twentieth century. Often dismissed by many as crackpot theories, this radicalism would sometimes later become the consensus viewpoint, a case in point being the importance of international bodies in peace-keeping. Throughout the century, Liberals consistently pushed debate forward by offering programmes for solving the world's problems. The roots of Liberal policy lay in a moral belief in the goodness of human action and intentions, and a view that nations could be made to behave in the same way as individuals: the doctrine of 'interdependency'.

This has been dismissed as unrealistic by some,[2] but it can be portrayed also as an ambitious attempt, perhaps even revolutionary, to change the way nations behave. Nobody could argue that Liberals thought that nations did behave in a moral fashion – that would indeed be naïve – but they knew that nations should behave morally, if the goals that all democrats professed to seek were ever to be achieved. Difficult to achieve? Yes. But impossible? No, and not to be dismissed lightly, unless one rejects any role for visionaries and idealists and argues that they never have any influence.

That radical vision was never more visible than in the inter-war years. During the 1920s and 1930s, Britain faced many challenges in the international arena, and alternative policies were hotly debated not only in parliament but also in wider political circles. These two decades constituted one of the few periods in British history when the country experienced three-party politics. However, as yet there is no major study of the Liberal Party's central role in party political debates on inter-national policy. The present study fills that gap by documenting and assessing the party's views on foreign and imperial policy.

In so doing, this book demonstrates the importance of analysing the 'low' politics of areas that traditionally have been dominated by 'high' politics. The role of bodies such as the Liberal Summer School and the Women's Liberal Federation are examined, along with the work of key thinkers such as J.M. Keynes and Ramsay Muir. Meanwhile, the author has had access to a new source on grassroots activism: the minutes of a Liberal debating society, known as the '8.30 Club'.

This book makes two major contributions to our knowledge of the role of international relations in British politics in the inter-war years. First, by analysing the Liberal Party's principles and policies on international relations, it offers a new perspective on British Liberalism. Second, by exploring the Liberal Party's alternative to the Baldwin–Chamberlain policy of appeasement, it enters the lively historical debate on the options open to Britain in the 1930s. In doing so, the book shows that in the mid-1930s the Liberal Party had a clearly defined policy based on economic disarmament and collective security through the League of Nations. From 1938, after the League of Nations had clearly failed, they put forward the view that collective security could only be secured by alliances between nations outside the League. In so doing, they recognised what Chamberlain did not see until at least March 1939, and in conjunction with anti-appeasers from other parties, they offered a clear alternative to government policy.

NOTES

1. *Manchester Guardian*, 4 Aug. 1938, p. 8. 'Comments', *New Statesman & Nation*, 16, 398 (new series), 6 Aug. 1938, p. 206.
2. Michael Freeden, *Liberalism Divided: A Study in British Political Thought, 1914–1939* (Oxford: Clarendon, 1986), p. 365.

Acknowledgements

THIS PROJECT began when I completed my doctorate on Austen Chamberlain's term of office as foreign secretary. During my research on that subject, I had become interested in how political parties tackle international policy, and how the issue plays a part in party politics. This is far from being well-trodden ground, and I sought much advice before pursuing my interest. I am particularly grateful to John Charmley (University of East Anglia), John Dunbabin (St Edmund Hall, Oxford) and Alastair Parker (The Queen's College, Oxford), for encouraging me to proceed with the research. They have not been involved in this project as it has unfolded, so they share no responsibility for its faults, but their encouragement was crucial at an early stage. I would also like to thank Peter Hennessy (of Queen Mary and Westfield College, London) who was equally encouraging when it looked like the research might extend into the post-war period.

Although it is a history of Liberal internationalism, this book is obviously informed by the author's involvement in the development of contemporary Liberal thought. In the past few years, I have had the privilege to work with many of the people who are currently grappling with the application of Liberal thought to both international and domestic politics, including John Alderdice, Vince Cable, Ralf Dahrendorf, James Gurling, Charles Kennedy, Robert Maclennan, Dick Newby, Clive Parry, Conrad Russell, Margaret Sharp, Matthew Taylor, William Wallace and Shirley Williams. Although none of them has had any involvement in this project, I hope that it is all the better for representing even more of a dialogue between past and present than is usual for a work of history.

I am very grateful also to Mrs Nelia Penman for agreeing to be interviewed, and for providing access to the minute book of the '8.30 Club'. Her subsequent generous deposit of the minutes at the University of Bristol Library will ensure that this fascinating resource is available to a wide audience for generations to come.

I must also record my thanks to Andrew Thompson of the University of Leeds, who both as a friend and as a colleague read early drafts and provided invaluable questions to test my arguments. His involvement has greatly improved the work that has finally appeared in print.

Finally, I would like to thank my parents, Jannat and Don, and my wife, Lucy, for their love and support while this book was being produced. The work was written under two different governments, and unfortunately life for young academics has shown no sign of improving over this time. In these circumstances, family and friends make all the difference.

COPYRIGHT

Liberal Party policy statements and photographs are reproduced by permission of the Liberal Democrats. On finding that permission to quote is usually granted by the party's Director of Policy, I was rather perturbed as to whether I could grant myself permission to quote, so I am grateful to Ben Stoneham, then the party's acting chief executive, for signing the matter off.

The current Viscount Thurso has kindly granted permission to quote from the papers of his grandfather, Archibald Sinclair, which are deposited at Churchill College, Cambridge. The Lloyd George Papers are in the custody of the House of Lords Records Office and copyright permission has been granted by the Clerk of the Records who acts on behalf of the Beaverbrook Foundation Trust. The Stansgate Papers are in the custody of the House of Lords Records Office and copyright permission has been granted by the Clerk of the Records.

Abbreviations

CPGB	Communist Party of Great Britain
CR	*Contemporary Review*
DC	*Daily Chronicle*
DN	*Daily News*
FR	*Fortnightly Review*
FV	*Forward View*
HCLF	Home Counties Liberal Federation
LFNA	League of Free Nations Association
LGLM	*Lloyd George Liberal Magazine*
LNS	League of Nations Society
LLF	London Liberal Federation
LNU	League of Nations Union
LPO	Liberal Party Organisation
LSS	Liberal Summer School
MG	*Manchester Guardian*
MLF	Manchester Liberal Federation
NLF	National Liberal Federation
NO	*New Outlook*
NC	*News Chronicle*
NLF	National Liberal Federation
NS	*New Statesman*
SWG	*Saturday Westminster Gazette*
UDC	Union of Democratic Control
WCLF	Western Counties Liberal Federation
WLF	Women's Liberal Federation
WNLF	Women's National Liberal Federation
WW	*Weekly Westminster*
WWG	*Weekly Westminster Gazette*
WG	*Westminster Gazette*

1. Left to right: Sir Herbert Samuel, Walter Layton, Hubert Henderson, David Lloyd George and J.M. Keynes at Churt, 1927.

2. Ramsay Muir.

3. Sir Archibald Sinclair.

4. Violet Bonham Carter meeting Paisley milliners in 1921.

—1—

Introduction

Only by understanding the Liberal Party's ideological inheritance, and the political context of the 1920s and 1930s, can we adequately assess the importance and nature of its policies on international affairs. So this chapter sets the scene. It does so first by surveying key background material, and then by discussing the legacy of Liberal internationalism as it existed from the middle of the nineteenth century to the end of the First World War. It also discusses the electoral progress of the Liberal Party in the inter-war period, and surveys the international situation of the time. The chapter concludes with an outline of current historiographical debates on British foreign policy in the 1930s.

LIBERAL INTERNATIONALISM

Background material

As an introduction to general Liberal thought, there is nothing better than Conrad Russell's *An Intelligent Person's Guide to Liberalism* (1999). An excellent starting point when studying political thought on international relations is Martin Ceadel's *Thinking About Peace and War* (1987). In contrast to the traditional 'idealist' and 'realist' categorisations, Ceadel elaborates a more sophisticated framework which it is useful to understand in order to place Liberals in an appropriate ideological position. Ceadel divides those who have thought about peace and war into five major categories: militarism (war is inherently good); crusading (aggression can be contemplated for the sake of peace); defencism (aggression is always wrong, but defence is always right); pacific-ism (war can be prevented and eventually abolished by reforms, with defence justified as a way to protect reforms); and pacifism (war is never permissible). In most important cases, Liberals have fallen into Ceadel's category of pacific-ism. There are also sub-divisions of pacific-ism formulated by Ceadel: internationalism to 1914, confederalism from 1914 to the 1940s, federalism from the late 1930s to 1950s.[1] The application of this to the Liberal Party will be returned to in the Conclusion.

If Ceadel's work offers an ideological framework, two historical overviews are provided by Michael Howard and A.J.P. Taylor. Specific British Radicals are covered by A.J.P. Taylor, *The Trouble Makers: Dissent over Foreign Policy, 1792–1939* (1957). Although this book is now over 40 years old, the pages still fizz with Taylor's enthusiasm for a diverse range of dissent in foreign policy from the late eighteenth century to the 1930s. A general study of liberal (rather than Liberal) attitudes to war is found in Michael Howard, *War and the Liberal Conscience* (1981), which traces the roots of liberal attitudes to international relations back to three thinkers: Erasmus, Thomas Paine and Jeremy Bentham. Erasmus put forward the idea that war was evil; Paine saw links between war and social problems; while Bentham emphasised the need for nations to abandon colonialism and accept free trade in his *Plan for a Universal and Perpetual Peace* (1789). Howard argues that by the end of the eighteenth century there existed a distinctly liberal view of the world, based upon a belief that war was the root of most social problems, and that if intercourse between nations was left to merchants rather than governments, all would be well. By the 1830s, a commitment to 'nationalism' had also been taken on board by many liberals, influenced by the enthusiastic advocacy of the cause by people such as Giuseppe Mazzini in Italy.[2] The definitions of 'nationalism' and 'nation' have been hotly debated (see, E.J. Hobsbawm, *Nations and Nationalism since 1780: Programme, Myth, Reality* (1992).

But in its simplest sense, nationalism as historically supported by liberals can be defined as the idea that nations have an ethnic and/or linguistic basis. Liberals further believed that each distinct group should rule itself as a nation state, rather than being part of an empire (as with the subject nations of the Ottoman Empire), or being divided into smaller political units (as with the pre-unification German states).

Moral legacies: c. 1850–1919

However, no distinctive liberal view of international affairs was associated with any particular party in Britain until the middle of the nineteenth century. By then, Liberal foreign policy was closely linked with Richard Cobden, a Liberal MP in 1841–65. He saw a moral and legalistic element to foreign policy, arguing that 'the intercourse between communities is nothing more than the intercourse of individuals in the aggregate'.[3] Perhaps Cobden's influence should not be overestimated, as some writers have argued that at least in the 1860s ideology was less important in foreign policy than were straightforward prudence and caution. John Vincent points towards a willingness to partake in power politics in the East as indication of the lack of moral content in Liberal foreign policy at the time.[4] However, foreign policy had the capacity to excite some Liberals. The Crimean War, the Italian Risorgimento and the American Civil War, all focused radical attentions on worthy causes abroad. In the first case, they were enthusiastic about war against despotic Russia, and in the second two, they found heroes to admire – Garibaldi and Lincoln.[5] Such enthusiasm for causes to some extent contradicted Cobdenite inaction and disengagement. This was partly based on the strength of Protestant dissent in Liberalism, which believed that God intended an era of peace between nations, and that such a time was close at hand.[6]

If Cobden articulated moralism as the basis of the Liberal world-view, he basically favoured inaction over any active role in international affairs – this was, in essence, no foreign policy. With W.E. Gladstone, everything changed.[7] He brought a new positive direction to foreign policy, defined by his Midlothian campaign of 1879–80 and by his attacks on Disraeli's position on the Bulgarian atrocities. These atrocities took place in May 1876, with 12,000 Bulgarians killed by Turks. Gladstone urged an inquiry, but Disraeli dismissed his calls, saying that reports were exaggerated. This position was opposed to Gladstone's desire to protect minorities and sprang from his growing belief in 'the public law of Europe'. Taylor has argued that Gladstone sought positive action, rather than simple Cobdenite inaction.[8] In the Midlothian campaign, Gladstone outlined six key principles: (1) just laws and economy; (2) preservation of peace; (3) concert in Europe; (4) avoidance of needless and entangling alliances; (5) love of freedom; (6) equal rights of all nations. Some of these points were matters of consensus – there were no Conservative governments gleefully pursuing war or profligate spending. However, Gladstone's rejection of alliances, combined with the pursuit of concert in Europe, was distinctly different from the policy on offer from the Conservatives. Indeed, the belief in Concert did much to undermine the earlier Liberal commitment to nationalism, which Gladstone's 'equal rights of all nations' at least paid lip service to.

Yet even more important than that was the moral tone of Gladstone's foreign policy. It remained a feature of Liberal foreign policy long after its author's death, and, crucially, it was even more influential than some of his Midlothian principles. Thus, despite his warning against alliances, many pre-1914 Radicals were closely tied to the entente with France. They were deeply opposed to Prussian militarism, and believed that an alliance with Europe's other great 'liberal' state was the best way to resist it.[9]

Gladstone died in 1898; his legacy to Liberal Party foreign policy was a strong belief in international law (which was gradually becoming more dominant than the party's belief in nationalism), combined with a moral fervour about its implementation. None of this, however, provided the Liberal Party with specific foreign policies. Thus, in the period before

1919, it became deeply divided over international policy. One extremely divisive issue was the Boer War of 1899–1902, during which 'pro-Boers', such as David Lloyd George, were highly critical of the government's record. It is clear from this period that Liberal Imperialists such as Edward Grey believed that continuity was vital in international affairs, thus limiting any possible distinctiveness of Liberal foreign/imperial policy. However, many Liberals did believe that a moral international policy was possible, and many Liberals, notably Lloyd George, took up the Boer cause in the House of Commons.[10] Other anti-imperialists in the Liberal Party were hostile to the Empire for a range of different reasons: these included the belief that empire was morally wrong, and concerns for financial retrenchment, but also the view that Africans were lazy and dishonest and should be left to rule themselves. However, except for the work of J.A. Hobson discussed below, Liberal anti-imperialism was principally a phenomenon of the 1890s. Although significant issues such as Chinese slavery exercised Liberals, and although there was consistent pressure for retrenchment, the Empire was far less divisive by 1906. By that time, there were fewer Little Englanders in parliament, and vigorous imperialists were less vocal. Liberals had come to terms with the Empire. As a general principle, they were less concerned about ending it than with fair treatment for native peoples.[11]

For the 1905–14 period, Edward Grey (as foreign secretary) was in control of British foreign policy, and to the consternation of some Radical Liberals, he did not pursue any distinctively Liberal policy, other than self-government for the Transvaal and working closely with Europe's other great liberal power, France.[12] However, even the relationship with France had been initiated by his Conservative predecessor, Lansdowne, in April 1904. Grey merely continued that policy. For the Liberal Imperialists, who effectively controlled policy through Grey, such continuity was much valued. They thus played the same balance of power games that their Conservative predecessors had done. Grey differed from the Conservatives in charge at the turn of the century, only in his fear of Britain's 'splendid isolation' – thus Russia (and therefore its ally, France) became the object of diplomacy. As Grey's first biographer claimed, his policy was to avoid war through diplomacy, but to ensure that if war broke out, the United Kingdom would not be isolated.[13] In defence policy, the Liberal Imperialists had nothing distinctive to offer except an extension of their domestic concept of efficiency to naval matters.[14]

It is also true that by 1906 fewer Liberals were preoccupied by international issues. Inspired by New Liberalism, the party was zealously pursuing the domestic social reforms that laid the foundation of the welfare state. However, New Liberals did make some contributions to thought on internationalism, especially the Liberal intellectual, J.A. Hobson, who argued in the *Nation* on 1 August 1908, that 'the problem of peace is nothing less than the problem of democracy, in its political, industrial, and moral aspects'.[15] Hobson primarily applied this to imperialism, in his most famous work, *Imperialism: A Study* (1902), in which he argued that the driving force behind imperialism abroad was poverty at home, which drove manufacturers to search for markets abroad due to the problem of 'underconsumption' – that is the inability of poor people in a domestic market to buy its products. If all at home were adequately paid, Hobson argued, they would be able to afford their own country's products, and imperialism, and thus much aggressive international competition, would become unnecessary.

Apart from Hobson's view of imperialism, New Liberalism gave little thought to international relations, and thus made no impact on the Liberals who were in control of government foreign policy. This did not prevent some backbenchers from criticising policy. A key episode was the 1911 Agadir Crisis, when the United Kingdom stood out against supposed German expansion in Morocco. Two radical Liberal MPs, Noel Buxton and J.H. Whitehouse, visited Germany and found that German attitudes towards Britain had been damaged by this; on their return, they urged the government to make it clear that Britain was not hostile to Germany. Although in 1904, many Radicals saw the Anglo-French entente as a Liberal policy (representing support for cultured liberal France against the dangers of Prussian militarism), the desire for Anglo-German rapprochement was shared by many Radicals, and anti-German sentiments were seen as largely unjustified. In particular, Grey's personal fear of Germany was blamed for stirring up hostility to that country. It was said to have led to an illiberal foreign policy, not only regarding Morocco but in other parts of the world where Grey placed emphasis on not alienating countries who might support Britain against Germany in the future. Examples cited included Persia (appeasing Russia), Tripoli (appeasing Italy) and the Congo (appeasing Belgium).[16] Continuity with Tory foreign policy, as practised by Grey, was also specifically criticised by Josiah Wedgwood, the MP for Newcastle-under-Lyme.[17]

If New Liberalism had provided no clear path for Liberal international policy, that did not prove a significant problem while the main challenges in politics came from within British shores. In 1914 all that changed, and neither Grey's diplomacy, nor radical opposition to it, could do anything to prevent the outbreak of war in August of that year. With their hands on the levers of power, Liberals had to come up with methods of running Britain's war effort. But, having brought Britain into the war, Liberals were again divided, as they were uneasy about fighting it. This was especially a problem when it came to the issue of conscription, which seemed necessary if the flow of soldiers to the

Western Front was to be maintained, but sat uneasily with Liberal ideals of individual freedom.[18]

Such tensions had dire results for the party, with splits and defections taking place at all levels. A coalition formed with the Conservatives in May 1915 eventually led to severe discontent within the new government over Asquith's leadership, and his replacement with Lloyd George in December 1916. Some recent work has sought to argue that Asquith laid the foundations for Lloyd George's reputation as the 'man who won the war', and there may be some truth in this. It remains undeniable, however, that Asquith was uncomfortable as war leader, whilst Lloyd George was in his element after replacing him.[19] Some Liberals, on the other hand, distanced themselves from the Liberal Party in 1914, by forming the Union of Democratic Control (UDC) with Labour politicians such as Ramsay MacDonald. This organisation blamed 'secret diplomacy' for the outbreak of the war, and as its name suggests, it called for democratic parliamentary control of foreign policy. As a recent work on the UDC argues, even today its ideas seem Utopian, as some secrecy is a hallmark of all foreign policy.[20] Nevertheless, the UDC's effects on the Liberal Party were marked; by 1918, figures such as E.D. Morel, and the MPs C.P. Trevelyan and Arthur Ponsonby, had all joined the Labour Party. They had found it impossible to work within the Liberal Party as they opposed its foreign policy, and through their work in the UDC, they found that Labour's policies were an attractive alternative.[21]

This is not to say that nobody who remained in the Liberal Party had any new ideas on foreign policy. Grey himself, having ceased to be foreign secretary on the formation of the Lloyd George coalition, became one of the most prominent advocates of the idea of a League of Nations.[22] He believed that such a clear framework of international law and obligations would be a firm barrier against war. But overall, the state of Liberal internationalism at the end of the First World War was indicative of the rest of the party's programme – strong on basic principles and moral fervour, but vague in terms of specific policies.

ELECTORAL FORTUNES OF THE LIBERAL PARTY, 1918–45

The years immediately following the 1914–18 war marked a rapid and decisive end to the Liberal Party's tremendous record of success over the previous 70 years.[23] Yet although the party was far from holding office for much of the 1920s and 1930s, it still represented and spoke for a significant section of public opinion, which ensured that the UK enjoyed one of its rare sustained periods of three-party politics.

The Liberal Party emerged from its wartime turmoil much weakened. At the 1918 election, Liberals favouring the maintenance of the wartime coalition with the Conservatives had continued to follow Lloyd George, and these Coalition Liberals gained 133 seats in the 1918 'Coupon' election (see Appendix 1 for election figures). The Liberals who remained loyal to Asquith fared less well, gaining a similar percentage of votes to Lloyd George's followers, but being reduced to only 28 MPs. The effects of this split at parliamentary level were very damaging to many local Liberal associations;[24] it is the wartime split, and its continuation at the 1918 election, which is often blamed for the decline of the Liberal Party. However, many historians argue that the expansion of the electorate in 1918 to include a larger number of working-class people, meant that Labour was in a better position than the Liberal Party to be the main progressive party.[25]

There can be no resolution to this contentious debate here, but in either case, when Conservative MPs decided to end the coalition in October 1922, the National Liberals (as the Coalition Liberals were now known) were almost without a cause. They had based their existence on support for a coalition which was now rejected by the Conservatives. So Lloyd George's following slumped to 62 seats, whilst the Asquith Liberals revived to 54 seats. Andrew Bonar Law now led a Conservative government with a substantial majority. For many Liberals, some kind of reunion of the two factions seemed to be the only alternative to a bleak future. In any case, their hand was forced by the decision of the Conservative prime minister, Stanley Baldwin (who had replaced Bonar Law, who was terminally ill, in May 1923), to call an election in December 1923, with the Conservatives basing their campaign on protection of British industries through tariffs.

If there was one point on which all Liberals could agree, it was the virtue of free trade; they had no problems opposing the Conservative scheme, and the reunited Liberal Party recovered dramatically to win 159 seats. However, the party was soon to be squeezed between Labour and the Conservatives when Labour formed a minority government in 1924 under Ramsay MacDonald. The government lasted only ten months, but it was enough to make voters believe that the only real choice in politics was between the socialism of MacDonald, or the order and moderate reforms of Baldwin's Conservative Party. There was thus a marked decline in Liberal support between the 1923 and 1924 general elections, when Liberal seats in the House of Commons were reduced from 159 to 40.

Lloyd George took over from Asquith as party leader in 1926, and the Liberals recovered slightly in 1928. In that year, the party won many friends with the publication of its ambitious report, *Britain's Industrial Future*, more commonly known as the *Yellow Book*, which proposed a reflationary financial and fiscal policy, aimed at reviving the British economy. It was not a moment too late: before the *Yellow Book*, the party had struggled to put forward a distinctive view on domestic policy, other than linking their ideas on economic recovery to a commitment to free trade. The *Yellow Book* remained the basis of Liberal policy for years to come,[26] but the Liberal revival at the 1929 general election, winning 59 seats, was not enough to prevent Labour forming a second government – again, as in 1924, without a majority, but now as the largest party. This balanced parliament soon caused the Liberal Party to split again, in 1930–31, over whether to support Labour or the Conservatives. Lloyd George favoured Labour, but John Simon favoured the Conservatives, and the followers of Simon were soon calling themselves Liberal Nationals. In fact, the Liberal Party did not need to make a decision of one party over another, as in August 1931, the National Government was formed because of Britain's dire financial crisis. This government consisted of Conservatives, Liberals and some of the Labour leadership (although not the mass of Labour MPs) – notably MacDonald as prime minister. The two Liberals initially in the Cabinet were Herbert Samuel (as home secretary until September 1932), and the Marquess of Reading (briefly, as foreign secretary until November 1931, when he was replaced by John Simon). Reading thus stands as the only Liberal to control Britain's foreign policy in 1919–39, but his term of office was little more than a stop-gap, and his biographer concedes that he 'had next to no impact on British foreign policy'.[27] Having introduced a series of emergency measures to reduce government expenditure, the members of the coalition agreed to fight an election together, gaining a massive total of 554 seats against Labour's 52.

Lloyd George had not taken part in the discussions over the formation of the National Government as he was ill, and in November 1931 he was replaced as leader by Samuel. Although Samuel did not wish the coalition to fight an election so soon, he continued to support all government measures until it imposed tariffs in March 1932. The Liberals remained in the government, but voted against this measure as part of an 'agreement to differ'; however, when these tariffs were extended in the Ottawa Agreements later that year, Samuel and his followers resigned from the government. John Simon's Liberal Nationals remained with MacDonald. Though Samuel's Liberals remained on the government benches (moving to the opposition benches a year later), they were now completely out of power. What was even more damaging than a lack of power, was that the Liberals seemed to be completely divided, even though the Simonites were very much an elite group, with little support in the country, whilst the Samuelites were supported by the mass of Liberal activists. This meant, as Archibald Sinclair wrote to Samuel,

> We suffer badly from our press and from the fact that we present the appearance of hopeless disunity. The fact that the Liberal organisations all over the country support you is not appreciated by the public who

are only impressed by the dissensions between Samuelites, Simonites and Lloyd Georgeites.[28]

After losing his seat at the 1935 general election, Samuel was succeeded by Archibald Sinclair in 1935. In addition to losing their leader, the Liberals had fared badly at the election, gaining a mere 20 seats, having stood only 161 candidates. The Liberal Nationals, however, gained 33 seats from only 44 candidates, although these were elected without Conservative opposition, and psephologists usually include them in the Conservative figures for that election. The government was now almost entirely Conservative, and led by Baldwin, who took over from MacDonald a few months prior to the 1935 general election. Baldwin remained as prime minister until he was succeeded by Neville Chamberlain in May 1937. Later, in 1947, the Woolton–Teviot Pact saw Liberal National cooperation with the Conservatives formalised, with their gradual merger completed in the 1960s.

Following the 1935 election, the Liberal Party discussed how it might reorganise itself in order to become more effective. This resulted in the replacement of the National Liberal Federation (NLF) with the Liberal Party Organisation (LPO), and the annual meeting of the NLF replaced by the Liberal Assembly. The new LPO aimed to create a broad umbrella for a diverse range of Liberal organisations, such as the Liberal Publications Department, which had sometimes lacked coordination with each other.[29] For the rest of the 1930s Liberal support remained weak. Reunion with the Liberal Nationals was discussed in 1937–38, but Liberal support for free trade was a serious barrier. There was, therefore, no Liberal recovery in the late 1930s, and during the Second World War, the three main parties adopted an electoral truce, in which only the party which had previously won a seat would stand if a by-election in that seat occurred. At the 1945 general election, only 12 Liberals were elected; the low point came in the 1951 general election, when the party gained only 2.5 per cent of the votes, and only six seats in the House of Commons. The Liberal Party remained far from any prospect of office until its recovery under Jo Grimond in the 1960s. With the Lib–Lab Pact of the late 1970s, and the heady days of the Liberal/SDP Alliance to come, more optimistic days lay ahead for British Liberals.

INTERNATIONAL AFFAIRS, 1919–39

Aside from the domestic political and electoral context, Liberal policy was also formulated within a broader international framework. The agenda for much of the inter-war period was set by the treaties which concluded the First World War, the most important being the Treaty of Versailles (June 1919). Under the treaty, in the infamous 'war-guilt clause', Germany was declared to have been responsible for the war, and was required to make reparations payments to the countries it had fought. Territorial matters were also dealt with: Alsace-Lorraine was returned to France, while substantial portions of Germany were given to Belgium, Denmark, Poland and Czechoslovakia. All German colonies were taken away, and placed under the authority of the League of Nations as mandates, administered by the allies. The German army was limited to 100,000 soldiers, and Germany was prevented from having tanks, military aircraft and submarines. The Rhineland was demilitarised, and British, French and Belgian troops were to occupy it for 15 years. In Germany, the treaty was described as a 'Diktat'. Even outside Germany, it was widely seen as a harsh peace, most notably by J.M. Keynes, in his *The Economic Consequences of the Peace* (1919), which argued that reparations would wreck the German economy, and lead to the collapse of central Europe.

A series of other treaties were made between the allies and the other defeated powers. Under the Treaty of St Germain (September 1919) Austrian territory was given to Poland, Czechoslovakia, Romania, Italy and Yugoslavia, and any union between Germany and Austria was prohibited. The Austrian army was reduced to 30,000 soldiers, and Hungary was made into a separate country. Similar measures were taken towards Bulgaria in the Treaty of Neuilly (November 1919), and Hungary in the Treaty of Trianon (June 1920). Turkey was a more complicated problem: initially, in August 1920, the Ottoman government agreed to the Treaty of Sèvres, in which they made substantial territorial concessions. However, the treaty was not ratified: Mustafa Kemal had established a rival government in Ankara in April 1920, and he soon gained control of the whole country; the allies were therefore forced to renegotiate with Kemal.

In the meantime, Britain nearly became embroiled in another war with Turkey, during the Chanak Crisis of August–October 1922. This arose from the Greek retreat of 1921–22, in the face of Turkish advances which threatened Constantinople (held by the allies since the war under the Treaty of Sèvres), and Lloyd George's decision to authorise British troops at Chanak to reinforce the Greeks. A stand-off ensued, with the Turks agreeing to recognise the neutral area around Constantinople until a new peace was formulated. This was achieved in July 1923 in the Treaty of Lausanne, when Turkey agreed to surrender the non-Turkish parts of the Ottoman Empire, and accepted the demilitarisation of the Straits, but regained parts of Turkey lost at Sèvres. Though this seemed finally to end the war, one issue remained, that of the Mosul vilayet – a former Ottoman administrative district forming the northern third of Iraq, and managed by Britain as a League mandate. At Lausanne, the Turks had surrendered the other two vilayets, Baghdad and Basra, but they still claimed Mosul. This remained controversial, and some even believed that an Anglo-Turkish war might take place, until the Turks gave up their claim in June 1926, probably out of fear that Mussolini was about to attack them.[30]

Following the treaties: three major issues needed to be resolved in the 1920s: the settlement of 'inter-allied debts' (debts between the former wartime allies); the question of French security; and the precise amount of the reparations owed by Germany. Britain's principal debt was to the United States: this was resolved by Stanley Baldwin in 1923, and throughout the 1920s Britain managed to pay the Americans by collecting the war debts owed to it by France and Italy, and by collecting reparations from Germany.[31] However, the issues of reparations and French security were much more problematic and destabilising. A number of attempts were made to resolve the questions in a series of conferences in 1920 (at Boulogne in June, Spa in July and Brussels in December), 1921 (London in March) and 1922 (Cannes in January, and Genoa in April).

But it was not until the Locarno Treaty of 1925 that the Franco-German border was settled. 'Locarno' was actually a series of international agreements, including non-aggression treaties between, for example, Germany and Poland; but the main Locarno agreement involved German recognition of its border with France and Belgium as specified in the Treaty of Versailles, along with German acceptance of the demilitarised status of the Rhineland. This treaty was guaranteed by the United Kingdom and Italy, and it was hoped that it would remedy the insecurity which had been felt by the French ever since the US Senate failed to ratify the Anglo-American guarantee of French security agreed at Versailles in 1919.[32]

With inter-allied debts and French security the subject of major agreements, only reparations remained. Two schemes addressed this problem: the Dawes Plan of 1924 and the Young Plan of 1929, which lowered German liabilities to a level which German politicians found more easy to accept. Germany's original reparations burden as established in 1921 was 132 billion marks (approximately £6.5 billion). The Dawes Plan of 1924 did not fix Germany's total liability or the duration of payment. However, it did establish a payment plan, in which Germany agreed to make fixed annual payments of 1 billion gold marks in the first year, and 2.5 billion thereafter, financed out of taxation, and accompanied by international loans to stabilise the economy. The Young Plan dramatically reduced both the annual payments, and the total liability, with Germany due to make 59 instalments, adding up to 37–40 billion marks. Following the collapse of the world economy, however, payments were suspended temporarily by the Hoover Moratorium of June 1931, which was formally accepted by Germany and the West at the Lausanne Conference of June 1932.

There is some debate amongst historians over the extent of British involvement in Europe in the 1920s. Until recently, historians tended to see Locarno as a limit to British involvement in continental affairs, after which Britain declined involvement in European affairs. This writer however, has argued elsewhere[33] that Locarno represented the first part of a two-stage policy, in which Austen Chamberlain planned first to calm French fears through a British guarantee of the Franco-German border, and then to assist the moderate German leader Gustav Stresemann in his attempts to revise aspects of the Treaty of Versailles, such as the presence of foreign troops on German soil. Whatever one makes of this argument, Austen Chamberlain was somewhat isolated in his desire to commit Britain to a European role (even if he managed to do so successfully). For many people in Britain, the Empire was of much greater interest than Europe, and throughout the inter-war period, the British Empire underwent considerable changes.

Following the First World War, Britain had gained control of a number of former German and Turkish mandates from the League of Nations. This meant that the Empire was at its greatest ever size, with over 600 million people ruled from London. However, many of the older established parts of the Empire, with large white populations, were increasingly assertive. At the 1907 Imperial Conference, Australia, Canada, New Zealand, South Africa and Newfoundland had been recognised as self-governing 'Dominions', which meant that they had control over their domestic affairs. During the 1920s and 1930s, these Dominions (which also included the Irish Free State after the partition of Ireland) continued to assert their independence from Britain, by seeking greater control over their foreign policies. This was made clear by the Dominions at Imperial Conferences in 1921 and 1923, and at the 1926 conference, the Balfour Report established the equality of all members of the 'Commonwealth' – a term which was increasingly being used instead of 'Empire'. More importantly, though, the 1931 Statute of Westminster recognised the right of Dominions to control their own foreign affairs, and with this the Dominions effectively gained their independence.

Aside from the Dominions, many parts of the British Empire were pressing for greater control of their own affairs. For many years, Britain had ostensibly managed the colonies on the basis of 'trusteeship' – the idea that Britain was guiding native peoples towards the day when they would be able to rule themselves. This meant that when colonial nationalist movements argued for independence, it was difficult for Britain to resist. In Egypt, Britain was forced to abandon control over domestic affairs in 1922, and in 1936 it agreed to withdraw its troops from the country over a period of 20 years. Iraq (a League of Nations mandate) gained its formal independence in 1932.

However, the greatest imperial problem for Britain in the inter-war period was that of India. Indians too wanted the power enjoyed by the Dominions, and British rule faced strong opposition from the Congress movement. This campaigned for Indian self-government, and the British were forced to pass two parliamentary acts which aimed to give Indians greater autonomy within the overall framework of the Empire. The first of these acts, the Government of India Act (1919) established the plans put forward in the 1918 Montagu–Chelmsford Reforms: a system of 'dyarchy', in which Indians were represented in a bicameral legislative parliament, and provincial assemblies. This left the British viceroy with a Council for executive purposes (with three Indian members), which in the last resort could take emergency control over the whole system. A Royal Commission under John Simon was established in 1927 to examine the workings of the 1919 Act. Meanwhile, in 1929, the new British viceroy of India made the 'Irwin Declaration', in which he declared that Dominion status should be the logical outcome of India's quest for self-government. The Irwin Declaration, and the report of the Simon Commission, led to the 1931 Round Table Conference, in which leading Indian politicians such as Gandhi put their views to British leaders. These consultations led to the passage of the Government of India Act (1935), in which the Indian provincial assemblies were given greater powers. This act did not satisfy the leaders of Congress, however, and they continued their struggle for independence throughout the 1930s and into the war years. Despite widespread belief in Conservative ranks that the act would answer the Indian question, it proved to be largely stillborn.

If the Empire was gradually adjusting and affairs in Europe seemed to be relatively stable in the 1920s, one issue that was certainly not solved was that of disarmament,[34] and as we shall see later, this was a major concern for Liberals. Under Article 8 of the Covenant of the League of Nations, members of the League had pledged to reduce their armaments to 'the lowest point consistent with national safety and the enforcement by common action of international obligations'. Since Germany had been made to surrender its air force and its submarines, and reduce its army to 100,000 men, and since it had been told that this was consistent with its defence needs, German politicians were consistently pressing the leaders of other nations to disarm to similar levels. Pressure for disarmament also came from within Britain, where many in politics believed that a major cause of the First World War was the pre-1914 arms race, and that if disarmament did not take place, there would eventually be another war of a similar scale. Some steps towards naval disarmament were made at the Washington Conference of 1921–22, where Britain, the United States and Japan agreed a 5:5:3 ratio for battleships. Even so, this did not settle all naval questions between

Britain and the United States, and the question of limiting cruisers was a contentious one for the rest of the 1920s.[35]

In simple terms, Britain's interest was in having large numbers of small cruisers with 6-inch guns, whilst the United States possessed larger 8-inch gun cruisers, and persistent objections from the navies on both sides prevented agreement being reached. Meanwhile, the French were not particularly interested in naval questions, but would not sign up for any agreement unless they could ensure that their possession of a large army was recognised. A notable failure was the Geneva Naval Conference (sometimes known as the Coolidge Conference) of 1927. Meanwhile, one attempt was made to solve the problem in 1928, when France accepted the British view on cruisers, with Britain endorsing the French view on military matters. However, the Anglo-French Naval Compromise was widely perceived as a piece of disreputable secret diplomacy, and it achieved nothing.[36] Cruisers remained an issue until the Washington ratios were extended to British, US and Japanese cruisers in the London Naval Treaty of 1930. Yet even this agreement did not lead to disarmament, as the agreements were actually focused on setting limits to future building, rather than reducing the levels of ships already in existence.

Apart from these naval agreements, little progress was made on disarmament, and the period was one of dashed hopes. From May 1926, the League of Nations Preparatory Commission for the Disarmament Conference met in Geneva, to frame an agenda for a world disarmament conference. Progress was slow, not least because those participating could not agree on how to measure the size of a country's armaments, but a conference of 60 nations did eventually meet under the League's auspices in 1932–34. This, however, failed, partly due to the unwillingness of most nations to surrender any of their most important national defences at a time of growing international instability, but also because of Germany's withdrawal from the conference in October 1933. Throughout the whole of the inter-war period, with the exception of the Washington Conference, the only way in which disarmament ever took place was when a government wanted to reduce its public expenditure. This was an important factor in the development of the Ten-Year Rule, which was originally established in 1919, and authorised Britain's defence planners to assume there would be no major war for another ten years. This was placed on a rolling ten-year basis for Japan only in 1925, and for all countries in 1928,[37] although it was essentially abandoned in 1932 in the face of Japanese expansion in the Far East. This was formally approved by the Cabinet in November 1933, at a meeting held shortly after Germany left the World Disarmament Conference, though the rule was not publicly dropped until 1936. As A.J.P. Taylor points out, the lowest arms estimate put forward between the wars in Britain was in Neville Chamberlain's April 1932 budget, and this owed far more to the desire for economy than to progressive agitation.[38] After 1932, the trend in UK arms expenditure was steadily upwards.

In addition to the lack of progress on disarmament, British governments were also slack in pursuing collective security through the League of Nations. As a signatory of the League of Nations Covenant, the British commitment to internationalism was, in theory, very great. Under Article 10 of the Covenant, all signatories had undertaken 'to respect and preserve as against external aggression the territorial integrity and existing political independence of all Members of the League'. Given that the United States and the Soviet Union (until it joined in 1934) were not in the League, the only League members with military forces powerful enough to carry out League obligations were Britain and France. Yet Britain was not prepared, in advance and in all circumstances, to commit itself to carry out the League's will. This was a major problem for the League as under any violation of Article 10, the Covenant only provided for the League Council to 'advise upon the means by which this obligation [stated above] shall be fulfilled'. Throughout the 1920s and 1930s, Britain resisted all attempts (often French-inspired) to define more rigidly the obligation to act, most notably the Geneva Protocol, which the second Baldwin government rejected in 1925.[39]

This is not to say, however, that Britain completely ignored the League. Historians have often argued that the late 1920s saw Britain adopting a detached position with regard to the League, preferring instead to conduct diplomacy through 'Geneva tea-parties' – meetings between Austen Chamberlain and his French and German counterparts, Aristide Briand and Gustav Stresemann. These meetings are said to have undermined the League by discussing matters which should have been tackled in public at official meetings of the League.[40] However, this writer has argued elsewhere that the 'Geneva tea-parties' rarely discussed League business, and when they did, they usually helped save the League from an embarrassing failure to deal with a problem.[41] Despite this, Chamberlain certainly did not believe that the League could develop quickly, and he was only interested in its long-term development. In the short term, as one Conservative backbencher commented, because of strong public opinion in favour of the League, governments always had to 'be polite about the League and try and believe that it really can do what its supporters urge'.[42] This strong public opinion was reflected in the strength of the League of Nations Union (LNU), which was probably the most important non-party pressure group of the inter-war years. In 1934–35, 11.5 million people in Britain took part in the 'Peace Ballot', a survey of public opinion organised by the LNU. They overwhelmingly supported the view that 'collective security' through the League of Nations was the best way of maintaining peace.[43] As we shall see later, Liberal Party activists made important contributions to this pro-League public opinion.

Despite this lack of commitment to expanding the League's formal mechanisms, the inter-war years did witness some official British involvement in the spread of internationalism. First, in 1928, Britain was one of 62 nations who signed the Kellogg–Briand Pact. This pact renounced war as an instrument of policy, and, although it lacked any teeth, it captured the mood of the times. More practically, in 1929, the new Labour government signed the 'Optional Clause' of the Protocol of the International Court of Justice – which had been established under Article 14 of the League Covenant. This clause had originally been framed in 1920, and as its name suggests, it was not compulsory. However, having signed the clause, nations were obliged to accept the jurisdiction of the court on any question involving international law, or the interpretation of a treaty.[44] This represented a major advance for the idea of internationalism, although it was to have few practical consequences for British foreign policy.

The British lack of interest in the League of Nations symbolised a broader interest in maintaining sovereignty, and this manifested itself in the responses of the British political parties to the economic crisis of 1929–31. As we saw earlier (p. 8), when Ramsay MacDonald failed to persuade his Labour colleagues to implement a series of dramatic cuts in public expenditure over the summer of 1931, he was forced to form a National Government with Conservatives and Liberals, in order to get the measures through parliament. When the National Government decided to fight a general election as a coalition they achieved a huge majority, and set about implementing other measures in order to tackle Britain's economic problems. In relation to international policy, the most important measures were the March 1932 Import Duties Act and the Ottawa Imperial Economic Conference in September of the same year. The March act imposed a 10 per cent general duty on all imports, and this was increased to as high as 33 per cent on some goods a month later. The Ottawa Conference, via a series of individual agreements between Britain and the Dominions, established a system of imperial preference, either by reducing tariffs on trade within the Empire, or by imposing new tariffs on trade with foreign countries in order to encourage trade between different parts of the Empire. The effect of the imposition of tariffs was to show the rest of the world that Britain intended to deal with its economic problems at worst alone, at best within the Empire. Economic cooperation with foreign countries was out of the question. This was a major attack on the Liberal principle of free trade, and Liberals blamed this 'economic nationalism' for many of the world's problems.

More important than the formation of a National Government in Britain, was the fact that the economic crisis led to the collapse of the Weimar Republic in Germany and the rise of Nazism. Hitler came to power as chancellor in January 1933, and almost immediately set about revising the Treaty of Versailles in stages. One of Hitler's first steps was to withdraw from the disarmament conference in October 1933. More significant was the announcement of German rearmament: this had been taking place secretly since the 1920s,[45] but it was made public in March 1935, when Hitler formally announced the introduction of universal military conscription in Germany. A year later, in March 1936, German troops entered the Rhineland, which had been demilitarised under Versailles; almost exactly two years later, Germany established an *Anschluss* (union) with Austria, when German troops entered the country under the guise of restoring order after internal political disputes. Later in 1938, Hitler demanded the Sudetenland, which was part of Czechoslovakia but prior to the post-war peace treaties had been Austrian territory and contained 3 million German-speaking people. At the Munich Conference of September 1938, Hitler was granted the territory, and his conquest of Czechoslovakia was completed in March 1939 when he occupied the rest of the country. Finally, in September 1939, Hitler attacked Poland, partly in an attempt to gain back territory lost to the Poles in 1919, but also as a first step in his mission to obtain *Lebensraum* (living space) in eastern Europe.

The British response to the rise of Hitler is now labelled with the general term 'appeasement', which essentially means making concessions for the sake of peace. This is an oversimplification, for the British government also rearmed in the 1930s, fearing the growing strength of Germany. In fact, the British government made rearmament an important part of its policy from 1934, when the chiefs of staff warned senior politicians about the growth of German strength. This resulted in the publication of the 1935 White Paper *Statement Relating to Defence*, signalling the start of rearmament, with a particular focus on strengthening Britain's air defences.[46] However, rearmament was only ever an insurance policy. Appeasement was the policy on which the greatest hopes were placed. The policy arose partly from a sense that some of Germany's demands were legitimate, based on the view that Versailles had been a harsh peace. But appeasement also stemmed from a profound sense that Britain's main European interest was avoiding involvement in another continental war, particularly in the light of overwhelming military advice stressing Britain's inability to fight such a conflict.

One aspect of the definition of appeasement is particularly problematic. It is the question of Neville Chamberlain's personal role, and, in particular, whether he believed Hitler could be trusted. There is certainly evidence to show that Chamberlain did not trust Hitler implicitly. Only a few months before the Munich Crisis, Chamberlain told his sister, Ida, 'how utterly untrustworthy and dishonest the German Government is'. Yet there is also equivalent evidence that when the Munich Agreement had been signed, Chamberlain believed he had bound Hitler into a deal that provided the basis of peace. His statement that he had brought 'peace for our time' was the public face of this.[47]

As we shall see in the next section, the debates among historians on the merits of appeasement are vigorous and controversial. Some argue that appeasement was a realistic assessment of Britain's power and interests, while others argue that appeasement was a misguided policy, whose practitioners were extremely gullible in trusting Hitler's declarations of peace.[48] This book makes a contribution to this debate by analysing how far there was a Liberal alternative to appeasement; clearly, appeasement may be seen to have been more of a mistake if practical alternative policies were available. Despite the heat of the debate, all historians are agreed that the most important episode in the policy of appeasement was the Munich Conference of September 1938, when Neville Chamberlain met with Hitler, Mussolini and the French premier, Edouard Daladier. Fearing the outbreak of war if Hitler did not gain the Sudetenland, Chamberlain agreed to allow Hitler to occupy the area. The Czechoslovak leader, Eduard Beneš, had very little say in these events, and resigned immediately. Hitler claimed that he had no more territorial demands in Europe, and with war seemingly averted, Chamberlain returned to Britain a hero, having brought 'peace in our time'. By March 1939, however, when Hitler invaded the rest of Czechoslovakia, his pledges seemed worthless, and with attention now focused on Poland, Britain and France guaranteed Poland's security. It was in honour of this guarantee that the two countries went to war with Germany in September 1939.

One alternative attempt to limit Germany had been made in April 1935, at the Stresa Conference, when Britain, France and Italy issued a strong protest against German rearmament, and agreed to cooperate against future German aggression. However, this 'Stresa Front' was soon undermined. First, only a few months later, Britain made a naval agreement with Germany, in which Hitler agreed to limit the German Navy to 35 per cent of the Royal Navy, with submarines at 45 per cent, or parity in the event that the Soviet Union threatened Germany. This effectively meant that the British had endorsed Germany's naval rearmament. More important though, in terms of undermining the Stresa Front, was Mussolini's invasion of Abyssinia in October 1935. A month later, the League of Nations imposed a limited range of sanctions on Italy, which crucially did not include an oil embargo. In December 1935, in the Hoare–Laval Pact, Britain and France considered proposing that Abyssinia should cede a large proportion of territory to Italy. This plan was roundly condemned by public opinion and politicians in France and Britain, and Samuel Hoare, the British foreign secretary, was forced to resign. In May 1936, Mussolini took control of the whole of Abyssinia, a point which the British formally accepted in the Anglo-Italian Agreement made in April 1938 and in force from November of that year. Abyssinia showed that Italy was now clearly an expansionist power. The Stresa Front had been broken, and there was a new threat to Britain's position in the Mediterranean. British politicians had even more reason to try to pacify Germany.

The Spanish Civil War also made it clear that Mussolini would not be an ally against Hitler. This conflict began in July 1936, when Franco's fascist Falange attempted to overthrow the elected Popular Front government, which was dominated by those on the left. It took nearly three years for Franco to take control of the whole country, during which time he was aided by military support from Germany and Italy, especially the German Luftwaffe. Even though Franco was receiving outside aid, the British government resolutely opposed intervention on behalf of the Republicans, on the declared basis that it was a domestic Spanish conflict. Official British involvement was also impossible because many in Britain did not feel that there was much to choose from when given a choice between fascism and socialism. It has also been argued (by Enrique Moradiellos) that anti-revolutionary sentiments were so strong in the British government that there could never have been any question of aiding the Republicans, and that, in fact, the policy on non-intervention was effectively hostile to those fighting Franco. However, over 2,000 individual Britons joined the volunteer Inter-national Brigades fighting for the Republican cause,[49] which provided an important anti-fascist rallying point for the left in Britain, and focused attention on the ambitions of the fascist powers.

Aside from Italy and Germany, Britain was also concerned about the threat from Japan.[50] Throughout the 1920s, Japan was seen as an ally of Britain, and it was a respectable and stable force in world politics in that decade. However, in 1931–32, Japan invaded and gained control over Manchuria, and established the puppet state of Manchukuo. The League of Nations was unable to take any effective action against the Japanese. The Lytton Report, the outcome of its inquiry into the Japanese action, certainly recognised Chinese sovereignty over Manchuria, but it also stated that Japan had legitimate interests in the province, and urged Japan and China to reach an agreement. Japan would not agree to this however, as it regarded Manchuria as Japanese, and in 1933 it left the League in the face of toothless condemnations. As a result of this Japanese expansion, the Ten-Year Rule was abandoned, and work on the Singapore Naval Base was resumed, having been abandoned in 1929. The Japanese threat became all the more real in July 1937, when it launched all-out war on China. There was little that Britain could do about this, but it did mean that there were further reasons for pacifying Germany, due to the threat to Britain's interests in the Far East.

One concrete outcome of Japanese expansion was that Britain and the United States held staff talks on possible naval cooperation in the event of a war against Japan.[51] This signalled a growing US interest in affairs beyond the United States, but for the earlier part of the inter-war period, Britain had had little to do with the United States. Neville Chamberlain, writing privately at the end of 1937 to the effect that he believed the United States was close to involvement in the Far East, prefaced his comments with the view that, 'It is always best and safest to count on *nothing* from the Americans except words.'[52] This was a view that dominated inter-war Britain: the United States was powerful, but having refused to join the League of Nations, it was pursuing an isolationist foreign policy, and could not be relied upon to do anything to assist British aims. Other than involvement with inter-allied debts and naval questions, the United States was not a major factor in British foreign policy in the inter-war years.

Similarly on the edge of world affairs, but more threatening than the United States, was the Soviet Union. In Britain, at least amongst the Conservative politicians who were in power for most of the inter-war period, there existed a perception that the Soviet Union was orchestrating a world-wide plot to undermine capitalism and democracy. A result of this view was that many people saw the Soviet Union as being as great a threat, or even more of a threat, than Nazi Germany. When the communists had initially taken over in Russia, the British made clear their hostility to the new regime by sending troops to assist the 'White' Russians against the Reds in the Russian Civil War in 1918–19. From 1921 to 1924, there was an improvement in Anglo-Soviet relations: in 1921, the two countries made a trade treaty, and full diplomatic recognition of the Soviets was given by the first Labour government in 1924. However, anti-communism was a major issue in the 1924 general election, when the 'Zinoviev Letter' was published. Allegedly written by the president of the Third International, it encouraged the Communist Party of Great Britain to foment revolution, and prompted allegations that Labour was soft on communism. When Baldwin won the election, there was pressure on him for a diplomatic breach with the Soviets. Though this was resisted by the foreign secretary, Austen Chamberlain, who believed that it would destabilise European diplomacy, pressure grew for ending diplomatic relations. Following the 1926 General Strike, and the Arcos Raid of 1927, the right of the Conservative Party was able force a breach in May 1927.[53] Labour resumed diplomatic relations in

1929, but the Soviet Union was still perceived as a potential enemy by those in power throughout the 1930s.

So, fear of the Soviet Union, Japan and Italy, gave British politicians good reason not to provoke Germany by opposing Hitler's revision of Versailles. However, there were also many opponents of appeasement. Some in Britain viewed the Soviets as a potential ally against the Nazis – not only socialists, but also Conservatives. Surprisingly, given his anti-Bolshevik stance in the early 1920s, one of the most prominent advocates of cooperation with the Soviet Union was Winston Churchill. He also advocated 'Arms and the Covenant', in which nations would commit themselves to maintaining 'collective security' through the League of Nations. In popular mythology, Churchill stands out as a 'Prophet of Truth' in the 1930s, warning of the dangers of appeasement, yet ignored by political leaders. Much work has now shown that there were significant problems with Churchill's anti-appeasement case.[54] For example, his planned alliance with the Soviet Union at the time of the Munich Conference assumed that the Poles would be happy to allow the Red Army to march across Poland to defend Czechoslovakia; meanwhile, the view of Churchill calling for rearmament and being ignored overlooks the important point that Britain was already re-arming from 1935. Meanwhile, Churchill was not the only critic of appeasement: others in the Conservative Party included Duff Cooper, Leo Amery, Anthony Eden (from 1938) and Austen Chamberlain (until his death in 1937); their role and that of Labour figures has not been fully explored.[55] But the role of Liberals in putting forward an alternative to appeasement has not. It is by doing this that this book makes a contribution to the debate on alternatives to appeasement.

An important issue when defining Liberal Party foreign policy is to define it in relation to the policies put forward by the other two parties. However, for the Conservatives, this is rather difficult to do, as they were in office for all of the inter-war period except for the Labour governments of 1924 and 1929–31, and thus Conservative foreign policy was closely linked to that of government policy. We may assume, therefore, that appeasement was essentially a Conservative policy, as it was pursued by a largely Conservative National Government; but to understand the impact of Conservatives on policy, it is worth noting three areas of particular concern for Tories in the inter-war years. First, many Conservatives were far more concerned about the Empire than they were about Europe, and believed that Britain's foreign policy should simply aim at avoiding any role in Europe. This view was not always influential in shaping government policy: Austen Chamberlain, as foreign secretary in 1924–29, was outnumbered by Cabinet colleagues who were hostile to Europe, but he still managed to ensure that Britain played a diplomatic role on the continent, particularly through the signing of the Treaty of Locarno. The attitude of the Conservatives can help explain why Britain involved itself in Europe at all in the 1930s through appeasement, and conversely, why Neville Chamberlain refused to make any military commitment to the continent until 1939. The second Conservative concern in the inter-war years was for Britain to look after its own interests first when it came to international trade, through the establishment of protection. This cause took a beating at the polls in 1923, but it helps explain why the National Government was so quick to adopt tariffs in 1932. The third Conservative concern regarding foreign policy was that Britain should not make any concessions on its national sovereignty, and so Conservative concerns were fairly consistently hostile to the type of 'collective security' advocated by Churchill in the 1930s. All of these issues gave plenty of grounds for the Liberal Party to criticise the Conservative Party over foreign policy.

The Labour Party's position on foreign affairs was very different from that of the Conservative Party. In the 1920s, the party was strongly influenced by pacifist sentiments, and was therefore hostile to rearmament. It was largely supportive of the League of Nations, especially through the figure of Arthur Henderson, although the extreme left of the party was suspicious of the extent to which the League existed to defend the status quo in international relations – a status quo which was seen as favouring capitalism. At the 1935 Labour Party conference, though, it was conceded that British forces might have to be used in military sanctions initiated by the League; in 1937, the party endorsed rearmament as an aid to the provision of collective security.[56] It remained the case, however, that support for the League was never pursued as enthusiastically in the Labour Party as it was by Liberals, and as we shall see, this was to be one of the Liberal Party's unique selling-points in the inter-war years.

Aside from the two main parties, Liberal international policy must also be placed in a further context: that of activism on the far left, focused on the Communist Party of Great Britain (CPGB). Although the party made no significant impact on electoral politics, it was a constant background factor, influencing as it did so many intellectuals. At times, the CPGB also seized the front pages of the popular press: over the Zinoviev Letter; after the Battle of Cable Street in 1936; and during the Spanish Civil War, when the party recruited from the broad left for the International Brigades. Liberal contact with communists was minimal – there was, after all, significant conflict between the fundamental values of Liberalism and communism. However, they shared a foe in fascism, and briefly, post-Munich, there would be a greater convergence of interest between Liberals and communists.[57]

HISTORIOGRAPHY OF APPEASEMENT

One of the major historiographical debates on Britain's international policy in the 1920s and 1930s is how far British policy was a cause of war. This debate has focused on the British response to the dictators from the mid-1930s, and the pros and cons of appeasement. One aim of this book is to feed into debates on alternatives to appeasement, and so it is necessary briefly to outline the main issues at stake.

The first contribution to the debate was made by 'Cato', a group of journalists including Michael Foot, the future Labour Party leader. In Cato's *Guilty Men* (1940), the practitioners of appeasement were denounced as having been incompetent, and having deceived the British people over the intentions of the dictators. This view, with politicians such as Neville Chamberlain seen essentially as foolish cowards, became the dominant view in Britain for over two decades. History is, after all, usually written by the winners, and while there were many who wanted to associate themselves with Churchillian anti-appeasement in the late 1930s, nobody was desperate to defend Neville Chamberlain. It developed little, except with A.J.P. Taylor's *Origins of the Second World War* (1961), which argued that, far from being a uniquely evil German leader with a plan for world domination, Adolf Hitler was an opportunist who exploited weaknesses in British and French diplomacy. This provoked a storm of criticism from those who wished to place a large part of the blame for the war on Hitler, but it also helped to strengthen the view that Hitler had only been able to gain early successes because appeasement was weak and misguided. In the late 1960s, however, the government papers became available to historians, and they were persuaded, that in many cases, the politicians had adopted perfectly understandable courses of action, given that Britain was militarily and economically very weak. A number of studies made these points powerfully, including Michael Howard's *The Continental Commitment* (1972). A more recent statement of this case was John Charmley, *Chamberlain and the Lost Peace* (1989), a controversial study which defends Chamberlain's view that even a victorious war would undermine the foundations of British power and hand Europe over to Soviet domination. We have reached the stage now where historians accept that there were understandable reasons for Neville Chamberlain to act as he did at Munich, on the basis that Britain was weak; they are now trying to establish whether the course of action open to Chamberlain was the only one.

This is an important historiographical issue because appeasement becomes far less defensible if one can argue that there were other options open to Britain. That need not involve proving that another strategy would definitely have worked, which would be beyond the capacity of even the most devoted counter-factual historian. It simply involves proving that other politicians and parties had an alternative which was cohesive, practical and given serious attention by contemporaries. The most effective recent attempt to look at alternatives is R.A.C. Parker, *Chamberlain and Appeasement: British Policy and the Coming of the Second World War* (1993). Parker describes himself as a 'counter-revisionist', and argues that 'Chamberlain and his colleagues made choices among alternative possibilities and that so far as Chamberlain decided them, and he had great power within the government, they were choices for conciliation rather than resistance.'[58] In an important chapter of the book, he outlines some of the alternatives open to Britain, concentrating on how far policies of resistance might have been adopted. He argues that despite their numbers in parliament, Liberals were particularly important because the Conservatives were consistently seeking to gain Liberal support for their foreign policy throughout the 1930s.[59] Other than this treatment by Parker though, accounts of alternatives to appeasement tend to focus on renegade Conservatives (as Parker himself has done in *Churchill and Appeasement* (2000)), and to some extent, the Labour Party. The Liberal Party, even though it was very prominent in all debates in the 1930s, has been seriously neglected. It is at this point, that this book enters historiographical debates on appeasement.

CONCLUSION

The diverse challenges faced by Britain in the 1920s and 1930s created considerable opportunities for Liberals to discuss international relations, and to formulate policies. The Liberal Party did this in several ways: the writings of Liberal intellectuals; discussions at the Liberal Summer School; and debates within the National Liberal Federation (Liberal Assembly from 1936). This book analyses the contributions of each of these three groups, before examining the role of the parliamentary party, both in formulating policy, and in acting as a mouthpiece for the wider Liberal Party. What, then, did Liberals have to say on international relations?

NOTES

1. Martin Ceadel, *Thinking About Peace and War* (Oxford: Oxford University Press, 1987), pp. 4–6, 109–13.
2. Michael Howard, *War and the Liberal Conscience* (Oxford: Oxford University Press,

1981), pp. 13–14, 29–30, 32–3, 49–50; A.J.P. Taylor, *The Trouble Makers: Dissent Over Foreign Policy, 1792–1939* (London: Hamish Hamilton, 1957; 1993 Pimlico edn).

3. Alan Bullock, *The Liberal Tradition from Fox to Keynes* (Oxford: Oxford University Press, 1967), p. 76. The most recent biography of Cobden is Wendy Hinde, *Richard Cobden: A Victorian Outsider* (New Haven, CT: Yale University Press, 1987), and he is also discussed in Miles Taylor, *The Decline of British Radicalism, 1847–1860* (Oxford: Clarendon Press, 1995).

4. John Vincent, *The Formation of the British Liberal Party, 1857–1868* (Hassocks: Harvester, 2nd edn, 1972 (1st edn, London: Constable, 1966)), pp. 247–9.

5. Eugenio F. Biagini, *Liberty, Retrenchment and Reform: Popular Liberalism in the Age of Gladstone, 1860–1880* (Cambridge: Cambridge University Press, 1992), pp. 372–7.

6. Bernard Semmel, *The Liberal Ideal and the Demons of Empire: Theories of Imperialism from Adam Smith to Lenin* (Baltimore MD: Johns Hopkins University Press, 1993), p. 53.

7. Further details on Gladstone can be found in modern biographies, such as Roy Jenkins, *Gladstone* (London: Macmillan, 1995), and in H.C.G. Matthew's two books, *Gladstone, 1809–1874* (Oxford: Oxford University Press, 1986), and *Gladstone, 1875–1898* (Oxford: Clarendon, 1995).

8. Taylor, *The Trouble Makers*, p. 71.

9. Ibid., pp. 126–7.

10. Michael G. Fry, *Lloyd George and Foreign Policy, Volume One: The Education of a Statesman, 1890–1916* (Montreal: McGill-Queen's University Press, 1977); Stephen Koss (ed), *The Pro-Boers: The Anatomy of an Antiwar Movement* (Chicago, IL: University of Chicago Press, 1973); H.C.G. Matthew, *The Liberal Imperialists: The Ideas and Politics of a Post-Gladstonian Elite* (Oxford: Oxford University Press, 1973); Bernard Porter, *Critics of Empire: British Radical Attitudes to Colonialism in Africa, 1895–1914* (London: Macmillan, 1968); John Wilson, *CB: A Life of Sir Henry Campbell-Bannerman* (London: Constable, 1973).

11. Porter, *Critics of Empire*, pp. 85–7, 294, 307, 328–9.

12. For Grey, see, G.M. Trevelyan, *Grey of Falloden* (London: Longman, 1937); Zara Steiner, *The Foreign Office and Foreign Policy, 1898–1914* (Cambridge: Cambridge University Press, 1969); Keith Robbins, *Sir Edward Grey: A Biography of Lord Grey of Falloden* (London: Cassell, 1971); F.H. Hinsley (ed.), *British Foreign Policy under Sir Edward Grey* (Cambridge: Cambridge University Press, 1977). For the Radicals, see, A.J. Anthony Morris, *Radicalism Against War: The Advocacy of Peace and Retrenchment* (London: Longman, 1972). New Liberals, such as J.A. Hobson, are covered in Peter Clarke, *Liberals and Social Democrats* (Cambridge: Cambridge University Press, 1978).

13. Trevelyan, *Grey of Falloden*, pp. 108–9.

14. Matthew, *The Liberal Imperialists*, pp. 196–8, 203–10, 216–18.

15. Clarke, *Liberals and Social Democrats'*, pp. 164–5, 178–9.

16. Morris, *Radicalism Against War*, pp. 10–11, 260, 275.

17. Bullock, *Liberal Tradition*, p. 246.

18. Trevor Wilson, *The Downfall of the Liberal Party, 1914–35* (London: Collins, 1966), is still an invaluable account, although conscription is covered in more detail in R.J.Q. Adams and Philip P. Poirier, *The Conscription Controversy in Great Britain, 1900–18* (London: Macmillan, 1987).

19. George H. Cassar, *Asquith as War Leader* (London: Hambledon, 1994), pp. 234–6.

20. Sally Harris, *Out of Control: British Foreign Policy and the Union of Democratic Control, 1914–1918* (Hull: University of Hull Press, 1996), p. 255.

21. Marvin Swartz, *The Union of Democratic Control in British Politics During the First World War* (Oxford: Clarendon, 1971), pp. 209–12.

22. Edward Grey *et al.*, *The League of Nations* (Oxford: Oxford University Press, 1918).

23. For surveys of the Liberal Party in this period, see, Chris Cook, *A Short History of the Liberal Party, 1900–88* (London: Macmillan, 1989); Wilson, *Downfall of the Liberal Party*; and G.R. Searle, *The Liberal Party: Triumph and Disintegration, 1886–1929* (London: Macmillan, 1992). For more detailed treatment, see, Michael Bentley, *The Liberal Mind,*

1914–1929 (Cambridge: Cambridge University Press, 1977), and Michael Freeden, *Liberalism Divided: A Study in British Political Thought, 1914–1939* (Oxford: Clarendon, 1986).

24. For details of the internal politics of the Liberal Party in this period, see, Roy Douglas, *The History of the Liberal Party, 1895–1970* (London: Sidgwick & Jackson, 1971), pp. 108–87.

25. For reviews of this debate, see, Keith Laybourn, 'The Rise of Labour and the Decline of Liberalism: The State of the Debate', *History*, 80, 259 (June 1995), pp. 207–26; Searle, *Liberal Party*, pp. 120–64.

26. Its importance can be seen in, for example, Ramsey Muir [Foreword], *The Liberal Way: A Survey of Liberal Policy Published by the Authority of the National Liberal Federation* (London: George Allen & Unwin, 1934).

27. Dennis Judd, *Lord Reading* (London: Weidenfeld & Nicolson, 1982), p. 256.

28. Samuel Papers, A/155(IX)/17: Archibald Sinclair to Herbert Samuel, 4 May 1935.

29. Douglas, *Liberal Party*, p. 238.

30. Richard S. Grayson, *Austen Chamberlain and the Commitment to Europe: British Foreign Policy, 1924–29* (London: Frank Cass, 1997), pp. 225–30.

31. A.J.P. Taylor, *English History, 1914–1945* (Oxford: Clarendon, 1965; 1976 edn), pp. 202–3.

32. See Jon Jacobson, *Locarno Diplomacy: Germany and the West, 1925–29* (Princeton, NJ: Princeton University Press, 1972); Grayson, *Austen Chamberlain*, pp. 31–75.

33. Grayson, *Austen Chamberlain*, pp. 32, 117–20.

34. For a useful study of British policy, see Dick Richardson, *The Evolution of British Disarmament Policy in the 1920s* (London: Pinter Publishers, 1989).

35. B.J.C. McKercher, *The Second Baldwin Government and the United States, 1924–1929: Attitudes and Diplomacy* (Cambridge: Cambridge University Press, 1984).

36. Grayson, *Austen Chamberlain*, pp. 153–6, 161–2.

37. Ibid., p. 173.

38. Taylor, *English History, 1919–1945*, p. 331.

39. Grayson, *Austen Chamberlain*, pp. 33–7.

40. F.P. Walters, *A History of the League of Nations* (Oxford: Oxford University Press, 1952; 1960 edn), pp. 341–3; Jacobson, *Locarno Diplomacy*, pp. 69–70.

41. Grayson, *Austen Chamberlain*, pp. 94–104.

42. Stuart Ball (ed.), *Parliament and Politics in the Age of Baldwin and MacDonald: The Headlam Diaries, 1923–1935* (London: Historians Press, 1993), p. 59: 19 April 1925.

43. Donald S. Birn, *The League of Nations Union, 1918–1945* (Oxford: Clarendon Press, 1981). Martin Ceadel, 'The First British Referendum: The Peace Ballot, 1934–5', *English Historical Review*, 95 (1980), pp. 810–39.

44. McKercher, *Second Baldwin Government and the United States*, p. 198.

45. Hans W. Gatzke, *Stresemann and the Rearmament of Germany* (New York: Norton, 1969; first published, Baltimore: MD, Johns Hopkins University Press, 1954), pp. 113–14. See also, Marshall Lee and Wolfgang Michalka, *German Foreign Policy, 1917–1933: Continuity or Break?* (Leamington Spa: Berg, 1987), pp. 74–81.

46. A useful overview is J.P.D. Dunbabin, 'British Rearmament in the 1930s: A Chronology and Review', *Historical Journal*, 18, 3 (1975), pp. 587–609.

47. Iain Macleod, *Neville Chamberlain*, (London: Frederick Muller, 1961), p. 232; Graham Stewart, *Burying Caesar: Churchill, Chamberlain and the Battle for the Tory Party* (London: Weidenfeld & Nicolson, 1999), pp. 308–10.

48. For a good overview of the main events and issues, see, P.M.H. Bell, *The Origins of the Second World War in Europe* (Harlow: Longman, 1986). Important protagonists in debates on British policy are R.A.C. Parker, *Chamberlain and Appeasement: British Policy and the Coming of the Second World War* (London: Macmillan, 1993, 2000); and John Charmley, *Chamberlain and the Lost Peace* (London: Hodder & Stoughton, 1989).

49. Enrique Moradiellos, 'Appeasement and Non-Intervention: British Policy during the Spanish Civil War', in Peter Catterall and C.J. Morris (eds), *Britain and the Threat to*

Stability in Europe, 1918–45 (Leicester: Leicester University Press, 1993), pp. 94–104. Tom Buchanan, *Britain and the Spanish Civil War* (Cambridge: Cambridge University Press, 1997), p. 122.

50. The best survey of events in the Far East is Akira Iriye, *The Origins of the Second World War in Asia and the Pacific* (Harlow: Longman, 1987).
51. Ibid., pp. 49–50.
52. Quoted in, Parker, *Chamberlain and Appeasement*, p. 106.
53. Grayson, *Austen Chamberlain*, pp. 263–6.
54. See, Donald Cameron Watt, 'Churchill and Appeasement', in Robert Blake and Wm Roger Louis (eds), *Churchill: A Major New Assessment of His Life in Peace and War* (Oxford: Oxford University Press, 1993), pp. 199–214; John Charmley, *Churchill: The End of Glory, A Political Biography* (London: Hodder & Stoughton, 1993); Martin Gilbert, *Prophet of Truth: Winston S. Churchill, 1922–1939* (London: Heinemann, 1976).
55. Neville Thompson, *The Anti-Appeasers: Conservative Opposition to Appeasement in the 1930s* (Oxford: Oxford University Press, 1971), covers the Conservatives. A useful review is the chapter on Parker, 'Alternatives to Appeasement' in Parker, *Chamberlain and Appeasement*, pp. 307–27.
56. Kenneth Harris, *Attlee* (London: Weidenfeld & Nicolson, 1982; 1995 edn), pp. 116–18, 136–7.
57. See below, p. 72. For an introduction to the CPGB, see, Francis Beckett, *Enemy Within: The Rise and Fall of the British Communist Party* (London: John Murray, 1995).
58. Parker, *Chamberlain and Appeasement*, pp. 343–7. A useful review of the literature is Robert J. Caputi, *Neville Chamberlain and Appeasement* (London: Associated University Presses, 2000).
59. Parker, *Chamberlain and Appeasement*, p. 312.

—2—

Liberal Thinkers

IF THE LIBERAL Party was not blessed with electoral success in the 1920s and 1930s, it was still fortunate to be supported by a number of Britain's leading intellectuals. Most notable were figures such as J.M. Keynes, Walter Layton and William Beveridge. Two of these men, Keynes and Layton, made important contributions to British thought on international relations in the inter-war years, and this chapter considers their influence on Liberal thought in particular, combined with that of three other leading Liberal thinkers. Two, Gilbert Murray and Lord Lothian (formerly Philip Kerr) are still well known amongst historians today. The other, Ramsay Muir, is less well known now, but, in the 1920s and 1930s, he was prominent in Liberal circles, and was extremely influential both as a publicist and an innovator of ideas. In 1933–36, he was president of the National Liberal Federation.

This is not to say, of course, that these figures were the only people who influenced Liberal thought. Clearly, ideas were able to traverse party boundaries and, in any case, not all thinkers were attached to parties. So it is worth noting that other thinkers were influential in the Liberal Party's international thought, as they were writing on issues similar to those concerning active Liberals. Most important, perhaps, was Norman Angell, in his famous work *The Great Illusion* – he believed that war was irrational as it was against the interests of all states to fight. Though published in 1910, it still had the capacity to inspire Liberals in the 1930s,[1] and Angell's profile was high throughout the inter-war years both as a tireless campaigner for peace, and in 1929–31 as a Labour MP.[2] Another influential Labour figure was Philip Noel-Baker, a prominent Quaker and a Labour MP in 1929–31 and 1935–70, but also a widely respected writer on disarmament and the need to govern international relations by law.[3] More enigmatic was David Davies. He was a Liberal MP from 1906 to 1926, an Independent in 1926–29 and a peer from 1932, but was not seen as a party figure, and was best known for his advocacy of an international police force.[4] However, his detachment from the party means that he does not quite earn special space here. There were also a number of figures involved in the Liberal Party who do not merit separate consideration, but whose influence is covered in other chapters. These include Arthur Salter, who was a regular speaker at the Liberal Summer School, and F.W. Hirst, who was a supporter of Lord Lothian in the Liberal Party Council (see below p. 92). As we shall see later, the ideas put forward by non-Liberal figures were influential on the Liberal Party, if only by influencing the intellectual climate of the times. This chapter, however, deals with the figures who were both thinkers, and prominent Liberal activists at a national level.

J.M. KEYNES

The most prominent Liberal thinker in inter-war Britain was John Maynard Keynes. His seminal work, *The Economic Consequences of the Peace* (1919) made a major impact on all political parties, and stands today as a devastating and far-sighted criticism of the Treaty of Versailles. Keynes was born in Cambridge on 5 June 1883 into an academic family, and went to Eton, where he shone as a mathematician. He continued to study this subject, and classics, at King's College, Cambridge, but became interested in wider political issues. Taking an active role in politics at Cambridge, he became president of both the Liberal Club and the Union Society. In 1906, Keynes entered the civil service (at the India Office), but he returned to Cambridge in 1908 as an economics lecturer. He gradually rose to national prominence as an economist and, in 1915, he joined the Treasury, where he became head of the department dealing with the external financing of the war effort. He attended the 1919 Paris Peace Conference as the official Treasury representative, but he resigned in June of that year, in disagreement with the heavy reparations imposed on Germany. He noted his fears in *The Economic Consequences of the Peace* (1919), which forms the substance of this section as it provided the intellectual foundation of Liberal proposals for revising the economic settlement of Europe in the 1920s.

Keynes made contributions to thought on international relations throughout his life,[5] but this work was Keynes' major contribution to Liberal international policy, and he continued to put forward his views on the impact of financial matters on international affairs throughout the 1920s. As we shall see, he made important speeches at the Liberal Summer School, and throughout the 1920s he was closely connected to the Liberal Party, especially in the development of the Liberal *Yellow Book* on industrial policy. He was also chairman of the Liberal periodical *Nation and Athenaeum*, in 1923–31, and a regular contributor. However, during the 1929–31 parliament, Keynes was an adviser to MacDonald's Labour government, and he ceased to be active in Liberal politics. In any case, as somebody who had embraced protectionism as a short-term measure in 1929–33,[6] he would have found few friends in

Liberal ranks. In the 1930s, Keynes was associated more with his seminal works *A Treatise on Money* (1930), and *The General Theory of Employment, Interest, and Money* (1936), which were to form the basis of Keynsian economics. Keynes was forced to cut his workload in 1937 when he was seriously ill, but in 1940 he again worked as a Treasury adviser, and played a leading part at the 1944 Bretton Woods Conference, which helped to establish the World Bank and the International Monetary Fund. He became Baron Keynes of Tilton in 1942, and died on 21 April 1946.[7]

Keynes' key work, *The Economic Consequences of the Peace* (1919), emerged from his long-held view that there were economic causes of war. He believed these could be beaten by combining free trade with international action on economic issues. This was vital in Keynes' view because he saw Europe as an interdependent economic unit which would collapse if Germany was economically damaged.[8] In the short term, as his biographer says, the work stemmed from the anger and pessimism he felt about the outcome of the Paris Peace Conference.[9] Keynes was a Treasury adviser at this conference, which opened in January 1919; he had spent the previous two months working on Germany's ability to pay reparations. He also argued that inter-allied debts should be scaled down or abandoned in order to reduce the amount of money that the allies were trying to collect from Germany – the rationale being that the allies were trying to make the Germans pay for what the allies owed each other. Having said that Keynes was a Treasury adviser at the conference, this did not mean that he, or the Treasury, exerted a great deal of influence on the British delegation. Prior to the conference, the Imperial War Cabinet had appointed a committee to report on Germany's ability to pay. This committee consisted of hardline figures such as the Australian prime minister, William Morris Hughes, and it demanded that Germany should be made to pay for all the damage it had caused during the war. This report was rejected by the War Cabinet, but in the midst of the 1918 election campaign, Lloyd George agreed that Hughes and other hardliners should be the British representatives on the Reparations Commission in Paris. This meant that at the conference, Keynes and the Treasury were confined to marginal roles, such as discussions on the allies providing Germany with 270,000 tons of food in return for the surrender of the German merchant marine.[10]

In *The Economic Consequences of the Peace*, Keynes outlined his objections to the Treaty of Versailles. Much of the book was a study of the Paris Peace Conference, and it portrayed some of the major figures in a very unfavourable light. The work also examined in detail the clauses of the Treaty of Versailles, but the most substantial single section dealt with Germany's capacity to pay reparations.[11] In concluding here that

Germany's capacity was no more than £2,000 million, Keynes laid the foundation for the proposals (or 'Remedies', as Keynes called them) on revising the post-war settlement which were by far the most important aspect of the book.

The main proposals were on reparations. Keynes wanted to fix the cost of reparations (and the cost of the allied armies of occupation) at £2,000 million. He said that the surrender of German merchant ships should be recognised as fulfilling £500 million of this, and the other £1,500 million should not carry interest, and should be paid in thirty instalments of £50 million, to be paid annually from 1923. To manage this system, Keynes wanted the Reparations Commission disbanded, and its work taken over by the League of Nations, of which Germany should be a member. Keynes added that Germany should be able to pay these debts in any manner it saw fit, which meant that there should be no further expropriation of German interests abroad, other than for the payment of private obligations. Keynes' final recommendation on reparations was that Austria should not be required to pay any. On coal and iron, Keynes recommended that allied options on coal should be surrendered, but that Germany should make coal payments to France, for no more than ten years, to cover the damage inflicted by Germany on French mines. Keynes also placed some emphasis on the value of free trade, arguing that a Free Trade Union should be established, to include Germany, Poland and the successor states to the Austro-Hungarian Empire. He wanted this union to prohibit all tariffs between its members, who should be required to join for at least ten years. Other states could join voluntarily, and Keynes hoped that the United Kingdom would do so from the outset.[12]

In addition to his proposals on reparations, Keynes also argued for the settlement of inter-allied debts. Keynes' overall belief was that there was a ridiculous position in which 'The war has ended with every one owing every one else immense sums of money.' These 'vast paper entanglements' meant that the peoples of Europe would be spending 'an appreciable part of their daily produce' on paying debts to others. This could only lead to resentment.[13] Most importantly, Keynes wanted all inter-allied debts cancelled, which he said would be an 'act of far-seeing statesmanship'. Overall, this would result in losses by the United States of about £2,000 million, and by the United Kingdom of £900 million; France would gain £700 million, and Italy £800 million. However, as Keynes pointed out, large parts of these debts could probably never be collected in any case, as they had been taken out by Russia, and were unlikely to be honoured by the Soviet government. But with the debt question settled, Keynes believed that it would be easier to settle reparations, as the people of most allied countries were trying to extract reparations from Germany in order to pay their debts.[14]

Cancellation of debts, and the fixing of reparations, would loosen some constraints on economic development, but it would not necessarily provide a stimulus to growth. To provide this, Keynes argued for an international loan to Europe, mainly from the United States, to allow European industry to recover from the effects of the war. Combined with the cancellation of inter-allied debts, and the fixing of reparations, this would help to restore European stability. Unlike the inter-allied debts, this loan could be placed on strong securities, and clear arrangements for repayment could be made at the outset, as it would be certain that the loan would be repaid in full. To accompany this loan, economic development could also be aided through Germany taking a lead in encouraging enterprise in its eastern and southern neighbours.[15] These proposals combined amounted to a plan for restoring the central European economy, with Germany as a key player. Keynes said that by setting reparations levels, 'we make possible the renewal of hope and enterprise' in Germany; by moderating the requirements relating to coal, 'we permit the continuance of Germany's industrial life'. The proposed Free Trade Union, Keynes said, would minimise the dangers of economic nationalism, made more likely by the emergence of new states. It might, he claimed, 'do as much for the peace and prosperity of the world as the League of Nations itself'.[16]

The work proved to be a best-seller, far beyond Keynes' expectations. He had originally arranged for the production of 5,000 copies, for a publication date of 12 December 1919. By the middle of 1920, however, it had run to numerous reprints, selling over 100,000 copies world-wide, with over 18,500 sold in the United Kingdom, and about 70,000 in the United States. The work was widely hailed as a major achievement. Some critics (a few of whom were Liberals) said that it overlooked the positive aspects of the treaty, especially the creation of the League of Nations, and the implementation of the principle of national self-determination in the redrawing of Europe's frontiers. However, the Liberal and Labour press applauded the work, as did the Conservative chancellor of the exchequer, Austen Chamberlain – although he did say that the criticisms, coming from such an important figure as Keynes, might damage Britain's position abroad. Significantly, Asquith, who was close to Keynes at the time, made favourable comments to Keynes on the book prior to publication. Overall, as Robert Skidelsky points out, the significance of the work was that it gave a clear expression to the sentiments already felt by Liberal and official opinion in Britain. It argued persuasively that the Treaty of Versailles was far too harsh on Germany in economic terms and that it must be revised, or there would be a political catastrophe in central Europe, threatening the stability of the entire continent.[17]

Most importantly, the book gave Liberals a solid intellectual base, throughout the 1920s, for their argument that reparations should be revised. He repeated his case in a sequel to *The Economic Consequences of the Peace*, entitled *A Revision of the Treaty* (1922). As Keynes freely admitted in the book's preface, it contained little that was new on fundamental issues, although he did call for the allied armies to withdraw from Germany as part of a reparations settlement. Keynes was to repeat this call at the Liberal Summer School of 1922 (see below, p. 64), but it was not primarily associated with him.[18] This though, was largely the end of Keynes' contribution to Liberal international policy. He was certainly close to Asquith until the General Strike of 1926, when he came to believe that Lloyd George, in his criticism of the government, better represented the Liberal view. Thereafter, as stated earlier, he worked with Lloyd George as a member of the Liberal Industrial Inquiry, particularly in 1927–28, and during the 1929 general election. However, all of this was as an acknowledged expert on domestic economics rather than as an authority on international economics.[19] With the failure of the Liberal Party to make an electoral breakthrough in 1929, Keynes concentrated on trying to influence the Labour Party through government committees. Finding that this too failed, and finding that he had fewer opportunities for involvement in the Liberal intellectual world (especially because the *Nation* had merged with the pro-Labour *New Statesman* in 1931), Keynes ceased to play an active role in politics in the 1930s.[20]

WALTER LAYTON

If Keynes was the Liberal Party's economic guru in the 1920s, that mantle belonged to Walter Layton in the 1930s. Walter Thomas Layton was born in London on 15 March 1884, the son of a schoolmaster. He graduated from University College, London, in 1903, with a third in history, but subsequently gained a double first in economics at Trinity College, Cambridge. He became an economics lecturer at Cambridge, and then at University College, London. During the First World War, he worked at the Ministry of Munitions. Following this, he was a member of the Consultative Economic Committee of the League of Nations, and then the director of the Economic and Financial Section of the League. By the 1920s, Layton had become involved in Liberal Party politics, standing for parliament three times (Burnley 1922, Cardiff South 1923 and London University 1929). Unlike Keynes though, he did not return to academia after the war: from 1922 to 1938, he was editor of *The Economist*, and from 1930 until 1960 he was editorial director of the *News Chronicle* and the *Star*. Like Keynes, Layton was influential in the *Yellow Book* (see above, pp. 7–8), but it was in the late 1920s and 1930s, with his enunciation of the idea of 'interdependency' that he had his greatest influence on Liberal international policy. During the Second World War, Layton was again a civil servant, and after the war (as Baron Layton from 1947), he remained active in Liberal politics as an advocate of the United Nations, European unity and Anglo-American cooperation. He died on 14 February 1966.[21]

Even though Layton was an active Liberal, his economic expertise was still valued by politicians of other parties. As his biographer points out, he was trusted by all parties as a government economic adviser, advising the Conservatives on India in 1927–29, and giving advice on reparations to both Labour in 1929–31, and the National Government.[22] However, Layton remained a staunch Liberal, and was a regular speaker at meetings of both the Liberal Summer School and the National Liberal Federation. At these meetings, Layton spoke on a wide range of international economic issues, which he always closely linked to international politics in its broadest sense; these speeches are covered in later chapters; this chapter covers his writings on international policy in *The Economist*. Layton wrote articles in *The Economist* on a wide range of international issues: in 1922–35, he wrote 150 on the League and disarmament alone,[23] including his first editorial, in which he called for the major powers to conduct their business through League machinery, rather than conferences between nations.[24] None of this was particularly original, though, and Layton's contribution to Liberal international thought was seen mostly in two key areas: the linkage of international economic issues to those of international politics, and the idea of 'interdependency'.

On the first of these issues, an important campaign run by *The Economist* was for Britain to return to the Gold Standard. This happened in 1925, and Layton believed that the financial stability it would create would help establish political stability throughout the world. There was nothing remarkable in this perspective; neither was there in Layton's support for free trade. He was only one of many Liberals who wrote on free trade in the inter-war years, the most notable, perhaps, was F.W. Hirst.[25] The doctrine was traditionally believed by Liberals to be a panacea for many of the world's economic problems, and Layton did not dissent from this view. This leads on, though, to Layton's second contribution to Liberal international thought, for Layton believed that free trade was effective because the world was interdependent. In promoting this idea, *The Economist* was a valuable platform, and the first clear statement of interdependency came in a leader article written by Layton in April 1929. Layton was responding to recent criticisms of free trade which had claimed that it was a 'political Shibboleth', possibly relevant to the nineteenth century, but no longer valid. Layton said:

Circumstances, it is true, have changed since the nineteenth century. But the main trend of change is in the direction of the enormously greater interdependence of nations; and the trend has served, not to destroy, but to re-inforce every argument against trade restriction.

It was not new to see *The Economist* arguing the free trade case, but it was uncommon for anybody to be justifying it on the basis of an 'interdependence of nations' that went beyond economics. The implications of this for foreign policy were twofold in the eyes of *The Economist*: first, governments must maintain a tariff-free economic policy; second, the League of Nations must be developed to ensure that political interdependency was recognised. This was summarised in a special free trade supplement, in which *The Economist* claimed:

> It is only possible to develop a policy of political cooperation between nations if there is some degree of economic cooperation. Free trade in economic affairs is the counterpart of the work of the League of Nations in political matters. They stand as a joint policy against the alternatives of Protection, competition in armaments and aggressive nationalism.[26]

Layton and *The Economist* returned to interdependency in several leader articles throughout the economic crisis of 1929–31. In October 1930, when free trade still prevailed, at least in British policy, a leader article argued that the 'supreme difficulty of our generation' was:

> that our achievements on the economic plane of life have outstripped our progress on the political plane to such an extent that our economics and our politics are perpetually out of gear with one another. On the economic plane, the world has been organised into a single all-embracing unit of activity. On the political plane, it has not only remained partitioned into sixty or seventy sovereign national States, but the national units have been growing smaller and more numerous and the national consciousnesses more acute. The tension between these two antithetical tendencies has been producing a series of jolts and jars and smashes in the social life of humanity; and the smash which pushed us into founding the League – the Great War of 1914–18 – was not a unique catastrophe.

Again, *The Economist* saw a strong League as necessary to remedy this difficulty.[27] By 1931, when free trade was more under threat in Britain, a New Year editorial highlighted one of the major tasks of British policy in the coming decade as 'the substitution of economic cooperation for selfish nationalism in a world which grows day by day more inter-dependent'.[28] By August of 1931, *The Economist* could write (although without any obvious satisfaction) that its perspective on events had been proved correct all along. With the British economy collapsing in the face of the global economic crisis, and with this having dramatic effects on the political situation:

> the last bout of the crisis has done the world one service at least. It has secured public acknowledgement for certain fundamental facts, which, till recently, remained unrecognised by the world at large. The first of these facts – or may we now venture to call them truisms? – is that all the major problems of international affairs are inter-related. Financial credit is seen to be bound up psychologically with political security. Without political security there can be no financial and economic recovery for the world; and, in the second place, there can be no political security without political compromise.[29]

The idea of interdependency will be discussed in further detail in later chapters. But it is important to note Layton's contribution in providing it with an intellectual foundation, and with a solid foundation of publicity. Through the pages of *The Economist*, Layton was able to show how political and economic issues were related, and how the emergence of a global economic system had important implications for the political organisation of the world. But equally, he defined clearly the extent to which the political and economic aspects of inter-dependency differed, with the spread of free trade not being matched by adequate global political developments that could provide rules-based means for dealing with the shocks and jolts of national competition. For Liberals, and Layton was no exception, the obvious way of developing internationalist solutions to these political problems was through the League of Nations. One of the most prominent pro-League figures in the Liberal Party is the subject of the next part of this chapter.

GILBERT MURRAY

George Gilbert Aimé Murray was the Liberal Party's leading advocate of the League of Nations. He was born in Sydney on 2 January 1866, and came to Britain in 1877 after his father's death. He attended Merchant Taylors' School, and then gained a first in classics from St John's College, Oxford. In 1888, he was made a fellow of New College and soon made a name as one of the country's leading classical scholars. From 1889–99 he was chair of Greek at Glasgow University, but retired after being mistakenly diagnosed as fatally ill. He returned to New College in 1905, and three years later became regius professor of Greek.

He had, however, already developed an interest in international affairs, contributing to a book putting forward a Liberal defence of empire during the Boer War, and writing an essay in 1900 denouncing nationalism. During the First World War, he worked as a civil servant, but expanded his writing on international policy, defending Britain's meeting of German force with force; he also began to write on the need for an international body to ensure that there would never be another war. After the war, despite remaining in his Oxford chair until 1936, he was heavily involved in campaigning for the League of Nations. He was a founder of the League of Nations Union, and chaired its executive council in 1923–38. Murray was also active in the League itself, attending a number of official League meetings: the 1921 and 1922 Assemblies as a delegate for South Africa;[30] the 1924 Assembly as a British delegate; and as the British rapporteur on the Committee on Minorities in 1923.[31] He stood unsuccessfully for parliament six times (1918, 1919, 1922, 1923, 1924 and 1929, each time for Oxford University, and as a Liberal except for his Independent candidature in 1924). He was president of the League's Committee for Intellectual Co-operation from 1928 to 1939. After the Second World War, he remained a committed internationalist as a leading figure in the United Nations Association until his death in 1957.[32]

As we shall see in later chapters, Murray was prominent in the Liberal Party as a speaker at Liberal conferences, and at the Liberal Summer School. However, his activism was mainly confined to the early 1920s, as he was demoralised by the Liberal electoral disaster of 1922.[33] Though he continued to stand as a Liberal candidate in subsequent elections, and was still consulted by the Liberal leadership in the late 1930s,[34] he was primarily involved in politics as an active supporter of the League of Nations. Though this sometimes involved criticising the government, he was loathe to appear as an overtly partisan political figure.[35] It is, therefore, his published material on the League that is discussed in this section, as it was broadly representative of the views he put forward in his political activities. Overall, Murray's contribution to thought on international policy was to state the case for the League with skill and conviction, emphasising that faith in the League, almost a leap of faith, was the main policy necessary if the League was to work.

Murray's first work on international policy was a Liberal critique of imperial policy published in 1900, during the Boer War.[36] However, it was during the First World War that Murray took a greater interest in international policy. In August 1917, he contributed three articles to the *Daily News* (republished as a pamphlet) arguing that the essential elements of a peace settlement were that Germany should evacuate all the territory it had occupied, and admit the principle of reparation.[37] Earlier, in 1915, he had produced a defence of Edward Grey's foreign policy. Murray argued that despite radical criticisms of Grey as having antagonised Germany and practised 'secret diplomacy', Grey had in fact constantly worked for peace, and had regularly consulted parliament.[38] Murray remained a critic of the movement for democratic control of foreign policy. This was, Murray said, because 'in most wars of recent times you could find as much war frenzy in the Jingo mob as in the most plutocratic club or drawing-room'. Instead, he argued, 'The principle that will solve the problem of war is not Democracy, but Internationalism.'[39]

Murray believed that this principle of internationalism – the belief that nations should submit to international law and agreements to solve disputes – was to be promoted through a League of Nations, and he became involved in pressure groups campaigning for the establishment of a League. From November 1916, he was vice-president of the League of Nations Society (formed in the summer of 1915). However, Murray soon came to feel that the LNS was dominated by pacifists and was too pro-German (because it wanted Germany brought into the League immediately, regardless of its internal political situation), and he formed the League of Free Nations Association in June 1918. A few months later, in October, the two organisations merged, on the LFNA's terms, to form the League of Nations Union, with Grey as president – the new LNU accepted the LFNA position that Germany could only join the League when it had established a democratic system of government.[40] By this time, the allied governments had become convinced of the need for a League, and there was little that its supporters had to do to ensure its establishment. This marked a clear break with pre-1914 Liberal internationalist thought, in its emphasis on both universalism and institutionalism: the League stemmed from the belief that for international law to be effective, it had to be all-encompassing, and supported by institutions. The Liberal view before 1914 had been far more limited.

So, from 1918, Murray had turned his thoughts to how the League might make its will effective. In this, he led the way in arguing that it would have to utilise sanctions. He wrote, 'though it would be a mistake to introduce an element of compulsion into the discussions or recommendations of the Council, there will be the knowledge that, where the general opinion is clear, there is force somewhere in the background'. To Murray that meant that any nation going against the wishes of the League Council would be called to account by it. Such a nation could then face 'the sanction of the economic boycott, of excommunication, and ultimately of a crushing war'.[41] Murray was thus one of the first leading figures to make it clear that the League, to be effective, would have to be backed up by the use of force.

Subsequently, with the League in place, Murray became a leading advocate of its virtues: he believed that the League was an adequate system to preserve peace, if only all nations would abide by their pledges made in the Covenant. In 1920, as part of a series of pamphlets explaining how the League worked, Murray put the view that the League's guarantees would be effective in maintaining peace. He argued that, of course, a nation might try to defy the League:

> But, first, we hope that in the constant meetings and discussions of the Council and the Assembly all great grievances will be freely ventilated and, where possible, remedied, so that there will be no overwhelming exasperation or suspicion left at work in any nation to drive them into war. Secondly, it will be very difficult indeed, under the conditions laid down, for a nation with all its statistics and preparations for armament open to inspection, with its representatives regularly meeting the representatives of its neighbours round a table and asking and answering questions, to make any secret preparations for war or establish any clandestine alliance. And lastly, if the League as a whole keeps its word, the offending nation has no chance of success and is sure to receive a tremendous punishment.

Underpinning all of this was a strong belief that nations could be made to abide by international law in the same way that individual people abide by national laws. Murray continued to recognise that the League Council might have to organise military action against an aggressor, but he believed that economic sanctions 'will probably bring most offenders to reason'. Overall, it was necessary for the peoples of all nations to remind governments of their League obligations, and to promote the spirit of internationalism within countries – this would be pursued by organisations such as the League of Nations Union.[42]

Murray continued to make general statements on the League throughout the 1920s and 1930s in lectures, pamphlets and other publications. With Robert Cecil, he fulfilled the role of one of the League's 'Civic Monks'.[43] Most of his views were unspecific in terms of how the League should develop. He did not, for example, develop any ideas on how exactly the League might organise military force as a sanction, which was an omission given that he had seen it as the ultimate threat against a disobedient nation. Instead, he put his faith in the moral force of the League, believing that resolute support for the idea of the League was necessary to make it work.[44] That essentially meant that nations should take a leap of faith and throw in their lot with the League's procedures. His most specific statement on League policy was that it could have a role in the revision of treaties. He highlighted issues such as reparations and the allied military occupation of the Rhineland as issues where Germany had just grievances, but said that these had already been remedied. All that remained were the questions of war guilt, German colonies and territorial rearrangement. On the first issue, he wanted the allies to make a statement repudiating the sole guilt of Germany, and stating that the pre-war international system of competing nations unrestrained by international law made war 'almost inevitable'. On colonies and territory, Murray said that there were no obvious solutions – African colonies should only be given to Germany if it was good for Africa, and countries in Europe would be unlikely to give up territory willingly. However, the League could have a clear role in arranging open and fair discussion on German grievances, in the belief that Germany would be satisfied by equitable treatment. Backed up by the force of world opinion, the League could then 'advise' particular countries on solutions.[45]

Gilbert Murray, then, was a powerful voice in support of the League. His writings and his speeches placed support for the League on the high moral ground in British politics. His promotion of the systems contained in the League Covenant made a persuasive case for the view that the League could work, if only politicians would make the leap of faith and support it. However, from the middle of the 1920s Murray was not as prominent within the Liberal Party as another figure, who held similar views to Murray, but was more active in urging them upon the party. This was Ramsay Muir, the forgotten giant of inter-war Liberal politics.

RAMSAY MUIR

Less well known today than any of the thinkers examined so far is Ramsay Muir, yet he was one of the most prominent Liberals in inter-war Britain. He was a prolific writer and had a marked influence on the party. John Ramsay Bryce Muir was born at Otterburn, Northumberland, on 30 September 1872, the son of a Presbyterian minister. He was educated at a small private school in Birkenhead, and won a scholarship to University College, Liverpool, in 1889. He was initially funded by the Presbyterian Church, and was training to be a Presbyterian minister, but after only a year he switched to a history course, partly due to his own religious doubts. A first at Liverpool was followed by four years at Balliol College, Oxford, where he gained firsts in greats and modern history. Whilst at Oxford, he was interested in politics, but as he recalled later,

Though I was a convinced Liberal, I was also an ardent Imperialist, because the development of the British Empire seemed to me to be a supreme expression of the very spirit of Liberalism. This put me out of sympathy with the Liberalism of the 'nineties – especially when the South African controversy became acute, for I felt that in that discussion Britain was standing for equal political rights, an essentially Liberal cause.[46]

In 1898, Muir returned to Liverpool as a lecturer, and was later professor of history from 1906 to 1913. During this time he devoted much of his historical writing to a history of Liverpool, but his political awareness was awakened by the constitutional crisis of 1910, when he wrote *Peers and Bureaucrats*.[47] He travelled in India in 1913–14, before becoming chair of modern history at Manchester, a post he held until 1921, when he resigned in order to devote himself to politics. He never quite left history; as he later admitted:

> The future development of my country, and of the world, had come to seem to me far more important than the precise location of the parish pump in 1345. I was becoming a politician; perhaps I had always been a politician, in a wide sense of the word, for even my absorbed interest in the university movement had been primarily a political interest. Perhaps my work as a historian had been spoilt because I was too much of a politician. Later my work as a politician was to be spoilt because I was too much of a historian to be completely immersed in the party game.[48]

Nevertheless, during the First World War, politics became his most important activity. Having given up his post at Manchester in 1921, he was selected as the Liberal candidate for Rochdale in 1922. He was not elected in the election of that year, but was successful in 1923. This was a bad year to be elected as a Liberal in a marginal seat, however, for the parliament lasted less than a year, and by the end of 1924, Muir was out of parliament. He was to fight another five unsuccessful election battles for the Liberal Party before his death on 4 May 1941. However, within the Liberal Party he had more success, being chairman of the National Liberal Federation in 1931–33, and its president in 1933–36.[49]

It was, however, as a thinker that Muir was best known to Liberals. One of his main contributions was to participate in the foundation of the Liberal Summer School, and this is discussed in Chapter 3. His published works were extensive, although it must be noted that Muir was not only writing about international policy. Some of his most important works were on industry and the machinery of government, and he became a leading publicist for issues which particularly concerned Liberals, such as proportional representation.[50] This chapter addresses Muir's extensive published work on international relations.

Internationalism, Nationalism and Empire

Ramsay Muir entered the First World War believing that Britain was fighting not for national power, but 'for freedom, for the rights of small nationalities, for international honour, for the possibility of peaceful and friendly relationships between equal and mutually respecting states'.[51] His analysis of the war led him to the conclusion that there was a strong link between nationalism and internationalism. He endorsed the basic Liberal principle that nationalism was the way to organise the world, believing that most conflicts arose from unsatisfied national grievances where the principle of nationalism had not been effectively protected. He also believed that nationalism would promote peace, as variety promoted strength, and nationalism was the best way to promote variety. However, he also believed that nationalism needed internationalism if it was to be secured, because, 'security and freedom of the nation-states, like the security and freedom of individuals in a State, depend upon their being able to put themselves under the guardianship of law. That is to say, internationalism is necessary as the fulfilment of nationalism.'[52] This commitment to enshrining nationalist principles through internationalism was at the basis of Muir's approach to international policy in the 1920s and 1930s.

Muir also emerged from the war with his enthusiasm for the British Empire intact. Writing in 1917, responding to criticisms that the Empire was no different from German imperialism, he cited the Empire as the perfect combination of nationalism, self-government and internationalism. He said that the dominions were clearly in the Empire voluntarily. The ancient civilisations of India and Egypt, meanwhile, welcomed the order, peace and justice that the British had brought with them. Though India sought self-government, he said, 'all the best opinion in India recognises that the progress already made has been due to British rule, and that its continuance depends upon the continuance of British rule'. Meanwhile:

> Even the most recently subdued of African tribes have shown no desire to seize this opportunity for throwing off 'the foreign yoke'. On the contrary, they have sent touching gifts, and offers of aid, and expressions of good-will. It appears, then, that the subjects of this 'Empire' have, for the most part, no quarrel with its government, but are well content that it should survive.[53]

There is no sign in Muir's work of any sense of injustice in the Empire, or the fact that it should one day end. This was to be a foundation of his views on international policy, and even in the mid-1930s, he had no doubt that the Empire would survive:

Despite all the blunders and even crimes that have been committed in its name, it will survive, changing its form as the conditions of its life change, like a great banyan tree; and even if the parent-stem should shrivel and grow weak, it will remain the central shrine of the cathedral made by its living pillars. This Commonwealth of free peoples will last on as the core of that world-unity which its long and varied history has done so much to create.[54]

Only four years later, in 1939, Muir was thinking along more radical lines about the future of imperialism. He had long advocated trustee-ship, but he now wanted this more institutionalised. He said that he wanted to share more formally the sovereignty of colonies, writing that a settlement of extra-European problems 'is impossible so long as the principle of unqualified State-sovereignty is maintained by the Western peoples themselves, and is adopted from them by other peoples'.[55] His defence of the British Empire was continued to the end of his life, and it remained the most consistent part of his academic and political careers – indeed, it represented the greatest amount of common ground between the two, as much of his historical work aimed to show how the Empire was a bastion of justice, order and liberty. As he said in the context of India, 'it was British rule which gave to India, for the first time in her history, three fundamental benefits – political unity, secure peace, and equal laws … thereby saving India from the miseries which have befallen the sister land of China'.[56]

Muir in the 1920s

Muir's first clear enunciation of his views on foreign policy are found in his 1923 work, *Politics and Progress: A Survey of the Problems of To-day*. Much of this was on domestic politics, but important foreign policy issues were also tackled. In the first part of the book, Muir sought to show what the world would look like if it was established along a 'Liberal Ideal'. Unsurprisingly, he envisaged national spirit as being the basis of nation states – nations would rule themselves. These Liberal nations would then be linked with each other through the League of Nations, but Muir's portrayal of the League was surprising, for even though he was talking about an 'ideal' world, the remit of his League was surprisingly limited. It reflected the fact that Liberals had a realistic projection of the initial capabilities of the League:

It will not be a super-State. It will have no power of imposing its will upon members, except in matters to which they have voluntarily pledged themselves; it will have no power of interfering in the internal concerns of its members, or dictating their form of government; it will have no power of levying taxes upon their citizens. It will not maintain an army capable of overawing any recalcitrant State, since the commander of such an army would have in his hands the means of making himself the despot of the world; it will trust to the action of its member-States in fulfilment of their pledges, and to agreements for mutual defence among them which will require its endorsement and only become operative when the League so decrees. In the distant future the League may develop into something more than this, but, as far ahead as we can see, the States which are included within it must be in the fullest sense free States, masters of their own destinies – and all the more free because they are secure and at peace.[57]

As for the short term, Muir addressed European issues, arguing that Britain must take a leading role on the continent as it had clear interests there. He said that the major problem was that of German reparations, and a settlement was only being prevented by the French, who feared for their own security. He thus outlined a plan for Britain to make a security agreement with France (under the auspices of the League), which Germany should then join when it entered the League. Placing such agreements under the League's guidance would remove the evils of secret diplomacy and military pacts, and with these treaties in place, significant measures of disarmament would become possible.[58] Two points are interesting about this plan: first, it bore much resemblance to what was in Austen Chamberlain's mind when he became foreign secretary in 1924, and which eventually resulted in the Locarno agreements of 1925, suggesting some common ground between Liberals and some members of the Conservative Party. Second, there was nothing in Muir's plan about enforcement of agreements. This could be seen as a strength by Liberals, as the agreements would be seen to be based on the type of trust that was so vital in Muir's 'Liberal Ideal'. However, the lack of enforcement was also a sign of the major weakness in all Liberal thought about the League – until the mid-1930s, when it was probably too late, they never managed to explain what would happen if somebody disregarded the League completely. The Liberal assumption had always been that the League would only be worth the effort if every nation joined and abided by its rules. They did not appear to feel the need to wonder about what would happen if their mission failed.

Muir was also committed to free trade throughout this period, which for a Liberal almost goes without saying. Muir's commitment to free trade came not only from belief that it was morally correct, although he certainly believed that it represented 'a great moral ideal' of international interdependence.[59] Muir also believed that it was an economic necessity. In 1927, he had published some thoughts on what Britain could learn from US industry, following a lecture tour to the United

States in 1926. He argued that the extent to which the United States had anything to say to Britain was limited by the fact that the United States benefited from a huge free trade area which was protected by tariffs. For Britain to impose tariffs would be economic suicide.[60] However, free trade was not a prominent part of Muir's writing until it had been undermined in the 1930s.

Muir in the 1930s

Muir's first book entirely devoted to international affairs (as opposed to international history or general political works) was *Political Consequences of the Great War* (1930). It should be said that this was part of *The Home University Library of Modern Knowledge*, and as such, is textbookish in many places, and essentially gives no sense of Muir's solutions to problems. It does however provide insights into his world-view. First, he perceived the world to be in conflict between the forces of nationalism, industrialism, imperialism, militarism, democracy and internationalism.[61] Second, he saw the League as firmly established 'as the necessary centre of international relations, certainly for Europe, and largely for the world'.[62] The problem with the League seen by Muir was that it had created little security, and therefore little disarmament.[63]

For more detailed ideas and proposals, we have to turn to *The Interdependent World and its Problems* (1932), *The Liberal Way: A Survey of Liberal Policy* (1934), *The Record of the National Government* (1936) and *Future for Democracy* (1939). In all these books it was noticeable that foreign policy had become Muir's major concern. In books written in the 1920s, it had been relegated below industrial questions; in the 1930s, it was not only given its own book, but in general works, it was treated as the most important issue. The major themes that are apparent in these four books are as follows: interdependency; the relationship between nationalism and internationalism; the importance of limiting absolute state sovereignty. Each work will be treated in turn to show how these issues were tackled.

In *The Interdependent World and its Problems* (1932), Muir argued that the world was now interdependent in a way that it had never been before. This was due partly to the conquest of distance through technological development. However, it was also because the world was now one international political system, in which a shot fired in Sarajevo could cause a world war. This system had arisen from the energies of the European states who now dominated the world, as had Muir's third type of interdependency – culture, where Western values now dominated in areas such as trade (dominance of Western forms of commerce), films (Hollywood) and sport (the Olympic Games).[64] However, Muir said, interdependency did not mean that nations did not have their own

identities. This was not a problem for Muir, who believed that nationalism was the best basis for forming unified states, with shared values and
a sense of community. However, nationalism could be a problem for
world peace as it could lead to nations being too assertive, and thus,
dangerous. This necessitated internationalism as the true way of safeguarding independence for all nations.[65] Otherwise, the perils of interdependence would become apparent – struggles for self-determination
or domination, tariff wars, monetary instability and social revolution.[66]
But how could an international spirit be achieved? Muir's answer was
found in limiting state sovereignty.

Limited sovereignty, though, did not mean world government. This,
Muir believed, would merely perpetuate the idea that sovereignty was
always indivisible and could not be shared. World government would
also not work due to the force of nationalism. Where then, should the
lines be drawn? Muir envisaged the League of Nations having powers
to prevent war, and regulate terms of international trade.[67] At this point,
critics of Muir might have said: 'This is just idealist Liberal rhetoric; the
League has been tried and failed.' But Muir provided an answer for
developing the League. We have seen how earlier, in 1923's *Politics and
Progress*, Muir argued for regional pacts, and these formed the basis of
his case in 1932. Arguing that the Kellogg–Briand Pact was inadequate
as it had no plan of action against nations who broke it, he called for
Locarno-style agreements throughout the world's trouble-spots, under
the aegis of the League. These should be enhanced by the prohibition
of the production or use of aggressive weapons, partly in order to fulfil
pledges made to Germany in 1919. He added, 'This, by conjuring away
the nightmare of horror which the use of these weapons has created,
would create an atmosphere favourable to the establishment of a
collective system, and therefore, ultimately, to complete disarmament.'[68]
In addition to these measures to prevent war, he called for the League
to create a new monetary standard, based not on gold, but on an index
of world prices. This should also be accompanied by the gradual
reduction of tariffs through the establishment of various free trade areas.
He said that the recent agreement between Belgium and Holland
'suggests the possibility of what might be called a Free-Trade and Low-
Tariff Club of Nations'.[69] To all of this, Muir tacked on his usual plea for
proportional representation in order to make governments more
representative.[70]

Muir developed similar themes two years later, in *The Liberal Way: A
Survey of Liberal Policy*. This was written by Muir, although as the title
suggests, it was an official Liberal Party document, which was the result
of various enquiries and debates over the previous ten years. It also
represented the outcome of debates within the National Liberal Federation, and contained critiques of Labour and Conservative foreign

policies. The book was less theoretical than Muir's *Interdependent World*, but it gave more details on how the League could be made stronger. It started with the view that effective sanctions would be needed if the League were ever to prevent war. Without a clear sanctions policy, 'This encourages particular Powers to disregard their obligations, in the hope that the other nations will not take action; and it leads other nations to fear that they cannot trust to League action to defend them in case of difficulty, and therefore to be unwilling to disarm.'[71] However, the League was not said to have failed – only individual governments were guilty of failure. This meant that to make the League effective, Britain must take the lead in passing an Act of Parliament, which would automatically come into effect if other countries passed similar acts. A fatal weakness in this was that it did not define *how many* others, but the terms of the act were listed:

1. to place a complete embargo on the export of all munitions to the offending state;
2. to forbid the giving of any financial assistance, either by the government or by private concerns;
3. to put an embargo upon all imports from or exports to the aggressor state;
4. to withdraw our ambassadors and our consuls from the aggressor state.

Having such an act in place would prevent delays in acting against an aggressor. As for war, 'Should any nation be so mad as to defy the world, war might indeed result from the application of economic sanctions.' This risk would be remote though, and Britain would be bound only with others. Overall, it was said, such a policy would involve 'the recognition and acceptance of the world's interdependence'. However, it was riddled with ambiguities, especially over the length of delay before which military action could be taken against an aggressor.[72]

What else was there for the League though? There was a vague suggestion that it should be amended in any way necessary to get the United States and the Soviet Union in. There were more detailed suggestions on short-term disarmament, involving abolishing all weapons forbidden to Germany, introducing international supervision of arms manufacture and setting limits on arms expenditure. When this had resulted in sufficient disarmament, there could be an 'international police force'.[73] Furthermore, the League should take a greater role in the international economy, by promoting agreements to allow the gradual reduction of tariffs, and a return to the Gold Standard. This was a change from Muir's *Interdependent World* policy, but it was argued that it was the only sound and simple basis for stability.[74] No striking views were put forward on the Empire – Britain's record was defended, but none of Muir's schemes for international trusteeship were included.[75] They were, perhaps, too radical for the Liberal Party for the time being.

By 1936, in *The Record of the National Government*, Muir's resolve on military action had stiffened. With Abyssinia in mind, he argued:

> It is only because this is *not* made clear to the world that wars of aggression take place at all. To make it clear that Britain and other loyal members of the League will if need be fight for the maintenance of the collective system is *not* to run the risk of being drawn into frequent wars; it is to reduce the risk of war to a minimum. It is by wavering on this vital point, so that nobody has known what she will do, that Britain has been largely responsible for bringing the collective system into disrepute, and increasing immensely the danger of war.[76]

However, this book was essentially just a critique of Britain's failure to do anything right in the 1930s, especially its failure to provide a lead in international affairs. Muir's unremarkable critique of appeasement at the time of Munich chimed with that of many others, and he may have been influenced by, for example, Churchill. Muir believed that Britain should have stood up to Germany in combination with France and the Soviet Union. This view was put forward in a fairly straightforward textbook, though, and he did not articulate anything more than the general sentiment that a military threat to Germany would have been a good thing.[77] There was, for example, no consideration of how the Poles might have felt about the Red Army crossing Poland to get to Czechoslovakia.

Thus, it was not until 1939, in *Future for Democracy*, that Muir clearly outlined how Britain should take a stance against dictatorship. In this book, he recognised that the League of Nations had failed; in its place, he wanted Britain and the Dominions, if possible accompanied by the United States and France, to make a declaration against all aggressors. This would state that all disputes should be settled by discussion, with a third party (possibly the League) as judge, and that there should be 'all-round disarmament'. This would be backed up by a pledge that, 'For these principles of international policy, the signatory powers will use all their influence, and will take counsel together as to the means by which they can be enabled to prevail.'[78] This was backed up by the usual rhetoric about free trade being 'the great fosterer of peace'.[79] However, it is clear from all of this that the Liberal programme, though evolving, was far from detailed. There was no clear sense of who would fight when, and how it would be guaranteed that all aggression would be resisted by all.

Brave New World

Muir's most detailed thinking about world order was unfinished when he died in 1941, but was posthumously published in 1943 as *A Better Britain in a Better World: In the Form of Letters from an Uncle to a Nephew.* In this, Muir was very critical of the League's universalism – the belief that any security threat anywhere in the world was the interest of all nations. Muir argued, in contrast, that, 'for the prevention of war and aggression, universalism was not an advantage but a drawback ... What was everybody's business was nobody's business.' He also argued that absolute sovereignty, not nationalism, was the main cause of war: 'it has done infinite harm in the case of some big States which have pursued their own insensate ambition to the ruin of their neighbours and the destruction of peace'.[80] Thus, for Muir, world federal union was not the answer. Instead, it was necessary to organise a 'Confederation of European nations'. All disputes within the Confederation would be referred for discussion, with the last resort being a decision by the governing body of the Confederation; any dispute with a non-member to go to members for consideration; all would help each other with military aid or economic sanctions; in the event of war, forces would be under the control of the Confederation – these forces should be national forces so that, for example, Poland could have a large army, and the United Kingdom a large navy, but the minimum and maximum of each force would be fixed, and the air forces should by merged as one. If any member breached any provisions of membership, the member would be thrown out, and action taken if it also behaved aggressively. Gradually, the Confederation should gain powers over monetary and trade issues. To make this work, members of the Confederation should be of roughly equal power. So German power must be reduced, possibly by being divided into smaller states. Smaller nations could then federate, for example, the Nordic states (Norway, Denmark, Sweden and Finland), the Danubian states (Austria, Hungary, Czechoslovakia, Yugoslavia and Romania). Muir summarised this as follows: 'I conceive, therefore, of the future Europe as a region in which there will be many little states, grouped together for military and some economic purposes in a series of federations, which will all be linked in a great Confederation of Europe.'[81] The League of Nations would continue to conciliate on trade and colonies, but would only be consultative, although the international court might be under the League. It would probably not have control over colonies which would be placed under a system of international trusteeship (similar to mandates), possibly under the control of the Confederation of Europe. The Empire would remain in its existing form – Muir saw no contradictions here with regional federation.[82]

Muir's contribution to Liberal international policy can best be summed up by saying that he was the most prolific Liberal writer of the inter-war years. In his writing, he put forward a wide range of ideas drawn from numerous sources, and one can see that he was strongly influenced by people such as Layton, Keynes and Murray. He developed many of their ideas into detailed statements of Liberal attitudes, which were accessible to a wide range of people. In particular, like Layton, he developed the idea of 'interdependency', making it the basis of Liberal internationalism in the 1930s. Yet, like most Liberals, he remained committed to 'nationalism' as the basis of internationalism – this meant that nations should share sovereignty, rather than rejecting the idea of national sovereignty. This put Muir at odds with the leading Liberal federalist, Philip Kerr.

LORD LOTHIAN (PHILIP KERR)

Of all the Liberal thinkers discussed in this chapter, Philip Henry Kerr was the only one ever to hold Cabinet rank. Despite being prominent in the Liberal Party throughout the 1920s and 1930s, he was less influential in Liberal Party policy than any of the other figures so far discussed. Nevertheless, his influence outside the party remains strong today, particularly through the work of the Lothian Foundation, which among other things, promotes debate on federalism.

He was born in London on 18 April 1882 and gained a first in modern history from New College, Oxford in 1904. He immediately became a part of the 'Kindergarten' working with Alfred Milner in South Africa, where he was private secretary to the lieutenant governor of the Trans-vaal, Arthur Lawley. On returning to Britain in 1909, he helped establish the imperialist periodical *Round Table*, which sought to achieve greater union within the Empire. From 1916 to 1921, Kerr was Lloyd George's private secretary, and is thought to have been influential in the drafting of the preamble to the Treaty of Versailles, which he subsequently saw as an indefensible treaty. In 1923 his collaborative work with Lionel Curtis, *The Prevention of War*, highlighted his commitment to federalism, and in 1930, after the death of his cousin, he became Lord Lothian. From March to July 1931, he was involved in the Three Party Committee on Disarmament, with Lloyd George and Samuel, also representing the Liberals on its agenda sub-committee (see below, pp. 111–12).[83] In 1931–32, he was one of the Liberal members of the National Govern-ment, as chancellor of the Duchy of Lancaster, and then a junior minister in the India Office, but he resigned with the other Liberals over the Ottawa Agreements. In 1933, he produced a general pamphlet on Liberalism,[84] and he was most prominent in his continued advocacy of federalism throughout the 1930s; but it was as an opponent of the idea of 'collective security', and a supporter of negotiations with Hitler, that he was known in Liberal ranks. In 1939, until his death on 12 December 1940, he was Britain's ambassador to Washington.[85]

Lothian's place in a discussion of the Liberal Party's international policy is partly due to his position as a leading supporter of appeasement, even at the time of the Munich Crisis. Though few in the party endorsed Lothian's perspective on Munich, he nevertheless stands out as a prominent dissenter over the Liberal Party's belief in 'collective security'. This aspect of his career is discussed in later chapters, but in simple terms, Lothian opposed the idea because he believed that the way to preserve peace was for nations to surrender completely their national sovereignty and to participate in a world federal government. Collective security, in Lothian's eyes only prolonged the myth that peace was compatible with a world in which nations retained sovereignty, and did not pledge to abide by a wider system of international law. In this section, the subject is the federalist position taken by Lothian – he was the leading British federalist in the inter-war years, and his work was one part of a broad Liberal movement which repudiated national sovereignty as the guiding principle of international relations. Other Liberals certainly saw federalism as a possible outcome of many years of progress,[86] but few gave it the immediacy seen by Lothian, who saw federalism as the only way of ending war for good.

Lothian published a wide range of works in the inter-war years on international issues, and on general and specific issues.[87] The two most important were *The Prevention of War* (1923), and *Pacifism is Not Enough* (1935) according to one commentator on his work.[88] The former was produced jointly with Lionel Curtis, and contained six lectures given by Lothian and Curtis (three each) at the Institute of Politics in Williamstown, in the United States, in 1922–23; the latter volume was Lothian's 1935 Burge Memorial Lecture, given at Lincoln's Inn. Between 1923 and 1935, Lothian's views changed little.

The most detailed case for federalism was put forward by Lothian in his three Williamstown lectures. In the first of these, he outlined 'The Mechanical Reason for War', in which his case was summed up in the following statement:

> What is the fundamental cause of war? I do not say the only cause of war, but the most active and constant cause. It is not race, or religion, or color, [sic] or nationality, or despotism, or commercial rivalry, or any of the causes usually cited. It is the division of humanity into absolutely separate sovereign states.[89]

Lothian saw this division as a problem because it meant that in the international sphere there was nobody to define law, no court to interpret it, and 'no policeman to enforce obedience to the law'. This created anarchy as, if diplomacy failed, force was 'the only means of redress'.[90] Appealing to his American audience, Lothian added that this situation was directly comparable to the Wild West of the mid-nineteenth century, in which lawlessness prevailed.[91] Lothian developed these ideas in his second lecture, 'The Psychological Reason for War'. In this, he argued that the division of the world into sovereign states promoted 'national selfishness' in which people thought of themselves as owing allegiance to their nation, and only their nation – they had no sense of the 'general good'.[92]

What was Lothian's alternative? In his third Williamstown lecture, Lothian argued that 'The Only Road to International Peace' was a form of federal world government. He admitted that 'I am not talking practical politics. I am for the moment a political theorist. The ending of war along the lines I have been discussing is not a matter of practical politics today. Nor will it be for many years. We are still at the thinking stage.'[93] However, working towards world federalism was the only way to prevent war, as it was the only way in which international law could reign supreme, and the only way in which all people could be made to 'feel that they can be citizens in both the nation and the world, and that there is no rivalry between them'.[94] All other strategies would fail: in particular, disarmament would not work until all countries had the security of international law, while the League of Nations could only ever represent the selfish interests of sovereign nations.[95]

Nothing had changed in Lothian's views on the dangers of national sovereignty when he gave the Burge Memorial Lecture in 1935. This was published as *Pacifism is Not Enough Nor Patriotism Either*, and in it, he reiterated all the points he has made in *The Prevention of War*. However, he did focus particular attention on why the League and the Kellogg–Briand Pact could not ultimately prevent war. He claimed that both were valuable as 'intermediate educative steps', and called them 'the crude beginnings of the new world order', but fundamentally, Lothian believed that they did not end the commitment of states to maintaining their national sovereignty.[96] This view underpinned his opposition to 'collective security' at the December 1936 Liberal Council, as we shall see later (see below p. 92).

As some writers on Lothian have suggested, his work on federalism was most influential in the post-1945 period, when he was widely accepted throughout Europe, particularly in Italy, as the leading British federalist.[97] Within the Liberal Party, his own support for appeasement certainly diminished his influence in the late 1930s, and it was not the case that the Liberal Party became a world federalist party in the inter-war years. However, Lothian was still a powerful voice in the party for two reasons. First, as we shall see in later chapters, he regularly put his views forward at a range of Liberal meetings, and he was valued as a commentator on international relations in general. More important, though, he gave clear reasons in his work on federalism as to why national sovereignty needed to be limited, or even surrendered. Other Liberals also put this case, notably as we have seen, Murray, Muir and Layton; but Lothian advocated it with a passion and clarity that ensured that it was at the forefront of Liberal thinking on international policy in the 1920s and 1930s. Even if Lothian did not persuade the Liberal Party to adopt federalism in the 1920s and 1930s, he did at least severely dent the reputation of the concept of national sovereignty.

CONCLUSION

So the Liberal Party had a wide range of intellectual sources on which it could draw for interpretations of international relations. Almost immediately after the signature of the Treaty of Versailles, the treaty was denounced by J.M. Keynes who provided many people, including Liberals, with clear reasons for making treaty revisions a major plank of their foreign policy platform. That these revisions and all other important aspects of foreign policy should be conducted through the League of Nations, was made clear by a range of thinkers, especially Gilbert Murray. A federalist alternative was put forward by Lord Lothian, and although this was not adopted by the Liberal Party, it helped to persuade Liberals that national sovereignty was a false idol. Criticisms of national sovereignty were also made by Walter Layton and Ramsay Muir, who did much to put forward the idea of interdependency. As we shall see in subsequent chapters, this idea had a profound impact on the development of Liberal international policy. We now turn to how interdependency and other ideas made an impact on various Liberal forums, beginning with the Liberal Summer School.

NOTES

1. Author's interview with Nelia Penman, 6 May 1997.
2. J.D.B. Miller, 'Norman Angell, and Rationality in International Relations', in David Long and Peter Wilson (eds), *Thinkers of the Twenty Years' Crisis: Inter-War Idealism Reassessed* (Oxford: Clarendon, 1995), pp. 100–21.
3. Lorna Lloyd, 'Philip Noel-Baker and Peace Through the Law', in Long and Wilson (eds), *Thinkers of the Twenty Years' Crisis*, pp. 25–57.
4. Brian Porter, 'David Davies and the Enforcement of Peace', in Long and Wilson (eds), *Thinkers of the Twenty Years' Crisis*, pp. 58–78.
5. D.J. Markwell, 'J.M. Keynes, Idealism, and the Economic Bases of Peace', in Long and Wilson (eds), *Thinkers of the Twenty Years' Crisis*, pp. 189–213. D.J. Markwell, 'John

Maynard Keynes and International Relations: Idealism, Economic Paths to War and Peace, and Post-war Reconstruction' (Oxford DPhil., 1995).

6. Markwell, 'Keynes and International Relations', pp. 177–89.
7. *Dictionary of National Biography, 1941–1950* (Oxford: Oxford University Press, 1959), pp. 452–7. Robert Skidelsky, *John Maynard Keynes: Hopes Betrayed 1883–1920* (London: Macmillan, 1983). Robert Skidelsky, *John Maynard Keynes: The Economist as Saviour, 1920–1937* (London: Macmillan, 1992).
8. Markwell, 'Keynes and International Relations', pp. iv, 177.
9. Skidelsky, *Keynes: 1883–1920*, p. 378.
10. Ibid., pp. 354–68.
11. John Maynard Keynes, *The Economic Consequences of the Peace* (London: Macmillan, 1919), pp. 103–210.
12. Ibid., pp. 245–8.
13. Ibid., pp. 262–4.
14. Ibid., pp. 253–61.
15. Ibid., pp. 265–70, 276.
16. Ibid., pp. 248–9.
17. Skidelsky, *Keynes: 1883–1920*, pp. 381–99.
18. John Maynard Keynes, *A Revision of the Treaty* (London: Macmillan, 1922), pp. v, 175.
19. For the development of Keynsian economics, see, Peter Clarke, *The Keynsian Revolution in the Making, 1924–1936* (Oxford: Clarendon, 1988).
20. Skidelsky, *Keynes: 1920–1937*, pp. 222–4, 249–57, 264–5, 344, 436.
21. *Dictionary of National Biography, 1961–1970*, pp. 636–8.
22. David Hubback, *No Ordinary Press Baron: A Life of Walter Layton* (London: Weidenfeld & Nicolson, 1985), pp. 63–6, 102–4, 115–17.
23. Hubback, *No Ordinary Press Baron*, p. 92.
24. *The Economist*, XCI, 4090 (14 Jan. 1922), pp. 39–40.
25. See for example, Francis W. Hirst, *Safeguarding and Protection* (London: Richard Cobden-Sanderson, 1926).
26. *The Economist*, CVIII, 4468 (13 Apr. 1929), p. 783, and Supplement 'The Case for Free Trade', p. 2. Ruth Dudley Edwards, *The Pursuit of Reason: 'The Economist', 1843–1993* (London: Hamish Hamilton, 1993), p. 643.
27. *The Economist*, CXI, 4546 (11 Oct. 1930), pp. 652–3.
28. *The Economist*, CXII, 4558 (3 Jan. 1931), p. 3.
29. *The Economist*, CXIII, 4590 (15 Aug. 1931), p. 300.
30. It was common for prominent UK figures to represent parts of the Empire in an advisory category. Sometimes this depended on friendship as much as any expertise: the English cricketer C.B. Fry represented India at the behest of his Sussex colleague Ranjitsinjhi in the early 1920s. See, Iain Wilton, *C.B. Fry: An English Hero* (London: Richard Cohen, 1999), ch. 16.
31. Duncan Wilson, *Gilbert Murray OM, 1866–1957* (Oxford: Clarendon, 1987), pp. 283–94, 352–65.
32. *DNB, 1951–1960*, pp. 757–61.
33. Francis West, *Gilbert Murray: A Life* (London: Croom Helm, 1984), pp. 181–7. Wilson, *Murray*, pp. 266–8.
34. See, for example, British Library, MS Gilbert Murray, 87, ff. 72–3: Murray and Sinclair correspondence, 8 & 14 Sept. 1939; 133, ff. 83–5: Sinclair to H.A.L. Fisher, n.d. [Sept. 1939].
35. See, for example, letters to *The Times*, 4 Mar. 1939, p. 8 and 9 Mar. 1939, p. 10; MS Gilbert Murray, 119, ff. 72–6: Murray and Margot Asquith correspondence, 4 & 7 Mar. 1939.
36. Gilbert Murray, 'The Exploitation of Inferior Races in Ancient and Modern Times', in Francis W. Hirst, Gilbert Murray and J.L. Hammond, *Liberalism and the Empire: Three Essays* (London: R. Brimley Johnson, 1900), pp. 118–57.

37. Gilbert Murray, *The Way Forward* (London: George Allen, 1917).
38. Gilbert Murray, *Foreign Policy of Sir Edward Grey* (Oxford: Clarendon, 1915), pp. 8–10, 102–20, 124–6.
39. Gilbert Murray, 'The League of Nations and the Democratic Idea', in Edward Grey *et al.*, *The League of Nations* (Oxford: Oxford University Press, 1918), pp. 113–40. Quotations from pp. 122 and 138.
40. Wilson, *Murray*, pp. 247, 252–4.
41. Murray, 'League and the Democratic Idea', in Grey *et al.*, *League of Nations*, p. 133.
42. Gilbert Murray, *The League and its Guarantees* (London: British Periodicals, 1920), pp. 16–18.
43. Salvador de Madariaga, 'Gilbert Murray and the League', in Jean Smith and Arnold Toynbee (eds), *Gilbert Murray: An Unfinished Autobiography* (London: George Allen and Unwin, 1960), pp. 176–97.
44. See, for example, Gilbert Murray, *The Future of the British Empire in Relation to the League of Nations* (Sheffield: J.W. Northend, 1928); Gilbert Murray, *Cult of Violence* (London: Lovat Dickson, 1934); Gilbert Murray, *Liberality and Civilisation* (London: George Allen & Unwin, 1938).
45. Gilbert Murray, 'Revision of the Peace Treaties', in Leonard Woolf, *The Intelligent Man's Way to Prevent War* (London: Victor Gollancz, 1933), pp. 67–153.
46. Stuart Hodgson (ed.), *Ramsay Muir: An Autobiography and Some Essays* (London: Lund Humphries, 1943), p. 33.
47. Ramsay Muir, *Peers and Bureaucrats: Two Problems of English Government* (London: Constable, 1910).
48. Hodgson (ed.), *Muir: An Autobiography*, p. 109.
49. *DNB, 1941–1950*, pp. 607–8.
50. Ramsay Muir, *Liberalism and Industry: Towards a Better Social Order* (London: Constable, 1920). An Impenitent Politician [Ramsay Muir], *Robinson the Great: A Political Fantasia on the Problems of To-day and the Solutions of To-morrow, Extracted from the Works of Professor Solomon Slack, LL.D.* (London: Christophers, 1929); Ramsay Muir, *How Britain is Governed: A Critical Analysis of Modern Developments in the British System of Government* (London: Constable, 1930, and 3rd edn 1933), pp. 235–43.
51. Ramsay Muir, *Britain's Case Against Germany: An Examination of the Historical Background of the German Action in 1914* (Manchester: Manchester University Press, 1914), p. ix.
52. Ramsay Muir, *The National Principle and the War* (Oxford: Oxford University Press, 1914), pp. 4–6. Ramsay Muir, *Nationalism and Internationalism: The Culmination of Modern History* (London: Constable, 1916, and 2nd edn 1919), pp. 222–4. This was part of a trilogy, with Ramsay Muir, *National Self-Government, its Growth and Principles: The Culmination of Modern History* (London: Constable, 1918), and Ramsay Muir, *The Expansion of Europe: The Culmination of Modern History* (London: Constable, 1st edn 1917 to 6th edn 1939).
53. Ramsay Muir, *The Character of the British Empire* (London: Constable, 1917), pp. 6–7, 24–5, 37. Similar views were put forward in, Muir, *Expansion of Europe*.
54. *The Expansion of Europe*, p. 313. Muir had first developed the 'banyan' image in 1922. See, Ramsay Muir, *A Short History of the British Commonwealth: Volume II, The Modern Commonwealth (1763 to 1919)* (London: George Philip & Son, 1922), p. 790.
55. Muir, *The Expansion of Europe* (6th edn, 1939), p. xxv.
56. Ibid. (5th edn, 1935), p. 300. In 1940, Muir wrote a booklet defending the Empire, at the behest of a Rochdale businessman who had found in his travels abroad that most people believed the Empire was based on aggression. See, Ramsay Muir, *The British Empire: How it Grew and How it Works* (London: Jonathan Cape, 1940).
57. Ramsay Muir, *Politics and Progress: A Survey of the Problems of To-day* (London: Methuen, 1923), pp. 23–4.
58. Ibid., pp. 114–21.
59. Ramsay Muir, *Protection versus Free Imports* (London: Liberal Publications Department, 1930), p. 40.

60. Ramsay Muir, *America the Golden: An Englishman's Notes and Comparisons* (London: Williams and Norgate, 1927), p. 15.
61. Ramsay Muir, *Political Consequences of the Great War* (London: Thornton Butterworth, 1930), pp. 11–48.
62. Ibid., p. 188.
63. Ibid., pp. 195–6.
64. Ramsay Muir, *The Interdependent World and its Problems* (London: Constable, 1932), pp. 2–25.
65. Ibid., pp. 29–53.
66. Ibid., pp. 54–101.
67. Ibid., pp. 102–26.
68. Ibid., pp. 127–43.
69. Ibid., pp. 144–79.
70. Ibid., pp. 180–204.
71. Ramsay Muir [Foreword], *The Liberal Way: A Survey of Liberal Policy, Published by the Authority of the National Liberal Federation* (London: George Allen & Unwin, 1934), p. 34.
72. Ibid., pp. 37–9.
73. Ibid., pp. 38–41.
74. Ibid., pp. 42–61.
75. Ibid., pp. 67–88.
76. Ramsay Muir, *The Record of the National Government* (London: George Allen & Unwin, 1936), p. 200.
77. Ramsay Muir, *A Brief History of Our Own Times*, 3rd edn (London: George Philip & Son, 1940), pp. 314–15.
78. Ramsay Muir, *Future for Democracy* (London: Nicholson & Watson for the Liberal Book Club, 1939), pp. 55–9.
79. Ibid., p. 99.
80. Ramsay Muir, *A Better Britain in a Better World: In the Form of Letters from an Uncle to a Nephew an [sic] the problems ahead, and the Nephew's reactions* (London: King and Staples, 1943), pp. 25, 28.
81. Ibid., pp. 30–7.
82. Ibid., pp. 54–62.
83. CAB 16/103: Committee of Imperial Defence Sub-Committee on the Disarmament Conference (Three Party Committee), Agenda Sub-Committee.
84. Marquess of Lothian, *Liberalism in the Modern World* (London: Lovat Dickson, 1934).
85. *DNB, 1931–1940*, pp. 507–10. See also, J.R.M. Butler, *Lord Lothian (Philip Kerr), 1882–1940* (London: Macmillan, 1960).
86. Gilbert Murray, 'Revision of the Peace Treaties', in Leonard Woolf (ed.), *The Intelligent Man's Way to Prevent War* (London: Victor Gollancz, 1933), p. 130. Gilbert Murray, *Liberality and Civilisation* (London: George Allen & Unwin, 1938), p. 46. Ramsay Muir became interested in the idea during the Second World War: Muir, *Better Britain*.
87. See, for example, P.H. Kerr and A.C. Kerr, *The Growth of the British Empire* (London: Longmans, Green and Co., 1920). Philip Kerr, *The Outlawry of War* (London: League of Nations Union, 1929); Philip Kerr, *Liberalism in the Modern World* (London: Lovat Dickson, 1934).
88. Andrea Bosco, 'Lord Lothian and the Federalist Critique of National Sovereignty', in Long and Wilson (eds), *Thinkers of the Twenty Years' Crisis*, pp. 247–76.
89. Philip Kerr and Lionel Curtis, *The Prevention of War* (New Haven, CT: Yale University Press, 1923), p. 16.
90. Ibid., p. 7.
91. Ibid., p. 19.
92. Ibid., pp. 33–4, 47.
93. Ibid., p. 56.
94. Ibid., p. 69.

95. Ibid., pp. 52–5.
96. Marquess of Lothian, *Pacifism is Not Enough (Nor Patriotism Either)* (Oxford: Clarendon, 1935), pp. 10, 26–30, 39–40, 56. Quotes from pp. 10, 56.
97. John Turner, 'Introduction: Lord Lothian and his World', and Andrea Bosco, 'National Sovereignty and Peace: Lord Lothian's Federalist Thought', in John Turner (ed.), *The Larger Idea: Lord Lothian and the Problem of National Sovereignty* (London: The Historians Press, 1988), pp. 1–19, 108–23, particularly pp. 13–19, 123.

—3—

The Liberal Summer School

A MAJOR SOURCE of policy ideas for the inter-war Liberal Party was the Liberal Summer School (LSS). The LSS was established as an annual event in 1921 by a group of Manchester Liberals. It came to be a highlight of the Liberal year, providing the opportunity for party activists, thinkers and leaders to meet in an environment which was less formal than an official party conference, in order to exchange ideas on Liberalism in general, and the specific problems of the day. For some contemporaries, the LSS was the only effective thing about the party. Ernest Simon, a founder of the LSS, may have been exasperated, but still represented a common view, when he said on the eve of the 1924 general election, 'What a party! No leaders, no organization, no policy! Only a summer school! But it is still worth an effort.'[1]

Historians of the Liberal Party agree that the summer schools were an important source of ideas in the party – Michael Hart has gone so far as to claim that they were the period's 'foremost source of radical intellectual Liberalism'.[2] However, the influence of these ideas has never been fully explored, and some have claimed that although the LSS was able to discuss ideas, it was not able to transform them into political action.[3] It is argued in Chapter 4 that the LSS did have an impact on Liberal Party policy, because its debates were often reflected in the policies later passed at the National Liberal Federation. In many cases, when the Liberal Party adopted a new position on international affairs, the idea had been discussed first at a summer school. This chapter, though, focuses more on the way in which ideas on international relations where discussed at the LSS. It assesses how far they were a source of new ideas on international policy, and how far they allowed Liberals to debate controversial issues. It will be seen in this chapter that the ideas of the LSS were given detailed coverage in the Liberal press, and that therefore, the LSS was a major contributor to Liberal debates outside formal party structures. Even if policies were not adopted by the Liberal Party, this still meant that the LSS was an important dimension in political debates on foreign policy. Never before have we understood exactly how important international affairs were to Liberal Party activists outside parliament.

ORIGINS AND STRUCTURE OF THE LIBERAL SUMMER SCHOOL

The origins of the summer school movement were in Manchester. The city was a hotbed of Radical Liberalism, and in May 1919, the Manchester Liberal Federation (MLF) published its own programme, which included land nationalisation, land value taxation, disestablishment of the Church of England and the abolition of hereditary peerages. The MLF also favoured an electoral pact with the Labour Party – a desire which was not reciprocated by Manchester's Labour activists.[4] One particular group of Manchester Liberals was particularly concerned about the Liberal Party's lack of an industrial policy. Initially, this group consisted of three key figures: Ramsay Muir, Ernest Simon and Colonel F. Tweed. They sought to make their fears known at the November 1919 annual meeting of the National Liberal Federation held in Birmingham. But they found themselves almost ignored by the party establishment, and began to hold a number of private meetings at each other's houses, discussing a range of policies on industry. This resulted in the publication of a book by Ramsay Muir, calling for partnership between capital and labour in setting the aims of industry, guided by state involvement to an extent rarely contemplated by Liberals of the time.[5] In 1920, Muir, Simon and Tweed, joined by Ted Scott and Philip Guedalla,[6] met at the country home of Ernest Simon – Leadon Court, a farm near Ledbury in Herefordshire. There, they decided to hold a summer school at Grasmere the following year, in order to further discuss industrial policy. This duly assembled at the end of September 1921, for a week, and by this time, the influential Liberal economist Walter Layton had joined Muir's group. He was joined by around 90 other Liberal thinkers (among them was J.A. Hobson), although no invitations were sent to Liberal leaders or officials in order to keep it unofficial. Although the school focused on industry, aspects of international policy were discussed as we shall see later; but for now, all it is important to note is that it was decided at Grasmere that the following year, a summer school should be held in Oxford.[7] Subsequently, it met in the first week of August, although occasionally it was moved forward to the last week of July. After the 1922 meeting in Oxford, the LSS alternated between Cambridge and Oxford.

From 1922, the format of LSS days followed a similar pattern each year. In 1921, there was some discussion over whether to pass resolutions on motions. As it was generally agreed that this might limit free discussions, the idea was dropped, and subsequent meetings concentrated on open debates rather than attention to formal motions. Herein lies much of the importance of the LSS: it allowed Liberals to think about broad principles, without immersing themselves in the minutiae of everyday politics, but it also allowed them to discuss more detailed policies, without the fear of defeat in a formal party debate. This aspect of the LSS was to be important in keeping the movement free from factionalism. Instead of debates on motions, each session was set in progress by a lecture from an expert, and then members joined in with their own points. The structure of the day saw two papers given each morning, and one in the evening. There was sometimes an exchange of views between speaker and audience following each paper, but afternoons were set aside specifically for discussion.[8] Since for many the LSS was also something of a holiday, a range of non-political activities were laid on each year. At Grasmere, lakeland walks were an attraction, but in Oxford and Cambridge, punting and other river pursuits became popular. Those based in the two university cities sometimes hosted garden parties; and in 1924, the Olympic athlete Harold Abrahams, made known to a more recent audience in the 1981 film *Chariots of Fire*, organised a lawn-tennis tournament. A particularly well-reported aspect of LSS entertainment was the 'review', put on by some of the younger participants, on the final evening of the LSS, from 1922. In this review, prominent Liberals were satirised to the great amusement of attendees and reporters.[9]

The summer schools were attended by a wide range of Liberals. The 1921 event did not involve the party leadership, but this was to change before very long. Party leaders, usually *the* party leader, were subsequently invited to give an opening or closing speech at the summer school. He would be addressing a diverse audience, ranging from leading Liberal intellectuals with an international reputation, to ordinary political activists. Young Liberals were particularly encouraged to attend, aided by scholarships offered in essay competitions in Ramsay Muir's *Weekly Westminster*, and the Young Liberal journal the *Forward View*.[10] They were often joined by delegates from Liberal organisations across the world, including those from 17 countries in 1935.[11] Furthermore, although those attending to hear papers and discuss them were Liberals, those giving papers were not exclusively so; this applied particularly to foreign lecturers, but also to some Conservative and Labour politicians. Some of these attended to put a distinctive Tory or Labour view for the sake of debate; others, such as the maverick Conservative, Robert Cecil, gave talks which suggested that they had much common ground with Liberals. The numbers attending rose dramatically from 95 in 1921, to 600 in 1922 and reached 1,000 in 1924. This increase in 1924 was perhaps aided by the fact that Lloyd George and Asquith had united at the 1923 general election, which infused the Liberal Party with a new spirit of optimism. By 1931, this had declined to 400, and it slipped possibly as low as under 200 by 1934, but it was again at 400 in 1935. In 1939, however, the *News Chronicle* said that record numbers had attended, 40 per cent more than ever before – which if correct, could mean as many as 1,400.[12]

Outside the regular meetings of the summer school, there were five important ways in which its ideas were developed and diffused. First, in 1924, an LSS Research Department had been established. This worked in conjunction with other Liberal research groups, but its focus was on industrial policy, and is beyond the remit of this book.[13] Second, in March 1923, the Liberal magazine the *Nation* was bought for £12,500 by the *New Nation Company* of Ernest Simon, Leonard Cadbury, J.M. Keynes and Arthur Rowntree. Two months later, Hubert Henderson became its editor, taking over from H.W. Massingham. This magazine eventually merged with the *New Statesman* in 1931, but, until then, it was used as a vehicle for the ideas of the summer school movement, spreading them through a wide audience amongst the 'chattering classes'.[14] Third, a similar task was performed through the pages of the *Weekly Westminster*, which Ramsay Muir edited from November 1923 to January 1926, when it merged with the *Westminster Gazette*. Those who had given papers at the LSS regularly wrote articles on similar themes in the *Weekly Westminster*.[15] Fourth, the text of LSS debates was printed in volume form. In 1922, this meant a book containing the most important speeches, but thereafter, they took the form of individual *New Way* pamphlets, published by the *Daily News*.[16] Finally, and perhaps most importantly, the LSS spread its ideas through the Liberal press. From 1922, there was very detailed press coverage (even from the pro-Lloyd George *Daily Chronicle*), and this was overwhelmingly favourable, with the LSS regularly making the front page of the *Westminster Gazette*. The 1922 LSS was hailed by the *Manchester Guardian* as 'proof of a vigorous revival [of Liberalism], if proof were needed'.[17] This type of comment continued in 1923, when the papers started to run 'human interest' stories in the LSS, such as profiling a Liberal from Newcastle-upon-Tyne, John Morton, who had walked 220 miles to Cambridge in order to attend the LSS.[18] By 1928, the LSS had become a major annual event in the Liberal calendar. The *Manchester Guardian* commented that most attending were 'sound Liberals who have come to these schools from the beginning and who would as soon think of missing them as a Tory peer would of missing a meet of the hounds'.[19]

The influence of the LSS is seen most clearly in domestic policy. As stated earlier, the LSS had been set up in response to concerns over the lack of a Liberal industrial policy. When this was put to the National Liberal Federation in 1919, the Manchester Liberals were snubbed. However, by May 1920, following the publication of Muir's book on industry, and even before the first LSS, the NLF's General Committee had accepted the need for an industrial enquiry, and this was followed by the committee's adoption of policies in favour of a National Industrial Council in February 1921.[20] Subsequently, when this industrial policy was seen by Liberals to be far too limited, and Lloyd George became more interested in the issue, the summer school leaders formed the core of the Liberal Industrial Inquiry (Layton was the chairman, and Simon the vice-chairman), which eventually reported in the *Yellow Book* of 1928.[21] The 1927 summer school was exclusively devoted to the discussion of key industrial questions which formed part of the report. Herein lies the influence of the summer schools in domestic policy, but what of international relations?

The precise content of each summer school, in terms of its debates on international relations, is listed in Appendix 2. It is worth noting now that there were basically two types of presentations given at the LSS: those which were meant to inform and educate Liberals on specific international issues; and those which argued for a particular policy or course of action. It is this second category that forms the bulk of this chapter – this type of presentation was invariably the most fully reported, and the one which provoked the most debate at the LSS. However, it is worth noting the broad ranges of topics discussed in these educational presentations, for they show that those attending the LSS could become very knowledgable about foreign affairs. The 1925 LSS was the first to feature this kind of general paper, and it is perhaps a sign that the movement was trying to broaden its interests. That year saw a whole day devoted to 'Foreign Politics', during which it was addressed by prominent Liberals from Italy (Francesco Nitti, the ex-premier), France (Albert Milhaud) and Germany (Moritz Bonn), on their domestic politics.[22] In 1929, Anglo-American relations was an area of great interest, and this was reflected in the papers by Professor J.W. Garner (of Illinois University), and S.K. Ratcliffe. Garner discussed the outlook of the US Navy, whilst Ratcliffe put his view that President Hoover had a clear understanding of European issues.[23] The 1930 LSS saw consideration of imperial issues, with speeches from leading Indian politicians, Srinivasta Sastri and Ameer Ali, on the situation in India,[24] whilst in 1931 Professor E.M. Patterson of Pennsylvania spoke on American foreign policy; Lord Lothian recounted his recent visit to Russia; and G.P. Gooch assessed the prospects of democracy in Europe.[25] In 1932, R.B. MacCallum put the view that language barriers between countries were an enormous difficulty for anybody trying to promote internationalism; Frederick Whyte (a former president of the Indian Legislative Assembly and political adviser to the Chinese National Government in 1929–32) argued that the Japanese threat to leave the League of Nations over Manchuria was a bluff.[26] By 1936, the LSS was attracting very high profile speakers: in that year, the Soviet ambassador, Ivan Maisky, outlined his country's foreign policy.[27] The year 1938 saw Jules Menken (a former economic adviser to Lloyd George), discuss the role of industry in wartime; Frederick Whyte spoke on the Far East; Miss Wellington Koo talked of Chinese resistance to Japan; and Dr William

Brown (the director of the Institute of Experimental Psychology at Oxford) lectured on how crude nationalism was a dangerous psychological factor giving rise to war.[28] On the eve of the outbreak of war, the highlight of the 1939 summer school was a speech on science and art from the former Czech premier, Eduard Beneš.[29]

These speeches then, provided Liberals with a wide range of sources and viewpoints on which to ponder. However, the most important sessions at the LSS were those that dealt with the specific policies needed, and the general principles on which to base those policies. The remainder of this chapter is divided into two sections, one dealing with the 1921–30 period, and the other dealing with the years 1931–39.

THE LEAGUE, DISARMAMENT AND FINANCE: 1921–30

If the Treaty of Versailles had formally ended the First World War, it left three questions unsolved. These were: the settlement of debts between the former wartime allies; French security; and the precise amount of the reparations owed by Germany. The nature of each of these issues is outlined in the introduction of this book, and it is argued there that by the middle of the 1920s, these issues seemed to have been settled. But before that point, all of these issues were hotly debated in the Liberal Summer School, which also focused much attention on disarmament. With exception of the 1927 LSS which concentrated on discussing industrial policy, as part of the process that led to the 1928 *Yellow Book*,[30] international relations was an important part of every LSS in the 1920s.

The first LSS of 1921, as has already been said, dealt mainly with industrial questions, and it received much less newspaper attention than future events – unsurprisingly as it was only attended by 95 people. The pro-Lloyd George *Daily Chronicle* did not cover the meeting at all, even in its humorous 'The Office Window' column, but the pro-Asquith press gave it some attention. The *Nation*, the *Daily News* and the *Manchester Guardian*, all covered the LSS in at least a couple of issues, and the overall tone was complimentary as to the quality of the debate, and the value of the discussions.[31] Although the meeting concentrated on domestic policy, the economist Walter Layton did make a speech calling for Britain to cancel the war debts of its First World War allies without waiting for the United States to do likewise for Britain: this was an issue because many in Britain argued that Britain needed to collect money from its former allies in order to pay the United States, a view which had been formalised as government policy in August 1922 in the Balfour Note. Meanwhile, Layton argued that Britain should surrender its share of reparations in order to make it easier for a reparations settlement to be reached – either by France also surrendering its share, or more likely, by the French agreeing to lower payments which would be acceptable to Germany. Layton's stated aim in putting forward British debt and reparation cancellation was the overall furtherance of international financial stability, and the LSS was enthusiastic about the idea.[32] Debts and reparations continued to be raised at the LSS throughout the 1920s; this was most notable in 1922, when the LSS session which received the most attention was J.M. Keynes' call for Britain to abandon its claims for pensions as a proportion of reparations (again, as part of a process of reducing or abolishing reparations), and to end the occupation of the Rhineland. Keynes believed that the two were linked, as if Britain could reduce its claim of reparations, more could be paid to the French, who would then be willing to withdraw troops. The *Westminster Gazette* hailed this as an endorsement of the policy already argued for by Asquith (see below, pp. 101–2). The reparations issue was also tackled by Grey in the closing address, when he argued, as Layton had in 1921, that Britain should not tie its European debtors to its debt to the United States, and that it was time for Britain to be generous, by cancelling the Balfour Note and paying the United States, and by cancelling inter-allied debts. He said that the British taxpayer would not suffer as the United Kingdom would gain from the economic restoration of Europe.[33] In 1923 Asquith emphasised his view that finance was a major issue in European affairs, arguing that he still believed, as he had in his 1920 Paisley address, that Germany should have its debts set at around £2.5 billion (rather than the £6.5 billion demanded by the allies in 1921) (see above, p. 11), and that Britain should write off all its debts from its allies.[34]

International finances were also discussed in 1926, in a session led by Walter Layton, who considered Britain's role in Europe and the Empire. He argued that Britain should encourage low tariffs in Europe as this would be beneficial to British trade. However, Britain might not want to be involved in any kind of European union, due to its imperial interests. On the other hand, Layton said that Britain's European interests ruled out Britain considering itself as only an imperial power. This was an issue because the 'Pan-Europa' movement had recently been launched by the Austrian count, Richard Coudenhove-Kalergi. In the Foreign Office and elsewhere in Britain, the prospects for British membership of a federal Europe were being debated. It might have been expected that Liberals would embrace the idea enthusiastically, but they did not do so. In fact, they rarely discussed it, even when the Briand Plan was put forward, at which point Liberal MPs urged the government to consider the proposals seriously, but were not themselves especially enthusiastic.[35] There would seem to be two factors at work here. First, the simple existence of the British Empire was severely limiting on any role Britain could play in a scheme in which powers with far fewer colonies than Britain (if any) would cooperate. Even the leaders of Pan-Europa recognised this, believing that Britain's imperial role made it an unsuitable member of a federal Europe.[36] So Layton's views were certainly in line with the thinking of those on the continent who were putting forward European union through the Pan-Europa movement. But there was also a second factor which meant that in Liberal circles, Pan-Europa was a dog that did not bark. This was that Liberals were not in the market for a supranational body because they already had one: it was called the League of Nations, and it was not until after the Second World War that they would move towards European federalism (see below, p. 155).

Layton did not merely address international finances in the context of Britain's role in Europe and the Empire. He also sought to defend some of the Conservative government's record, arguing that Baldwin's debt settlement with the United States was all that Britain could get for the moment.[37] It would be fair to say then, that although Liberals at the LSS put forward distinctive Liberal positions on financial matters, they were not merely beating the party drum, and were capable of considering policies put forward by other parties in an open-minded fashion.

If financial stability was seen as a major issue by Liberals which required immediate action, they saw the long-term future of peace resting on the League of Nations. In 1922, one of the highest profile sessions was given by Robert Cecil, a renegade Conservative and one of the founders of the League of Nations. He spoke generally on the need for a new international spirit, in which powers put the League at the heart of their foreign policy. There was little new in this, and the *Manchester Guardian* suggested that Cecil was instructional rather than lively.[38] A similar view to Cecil's was put forward by Professor A.F. Pollard in a paper on the balance of power.[39] In 1923, in his opening address, Gilbert Murray made more specific proposals, arguing that Germany and the Soviet Union should be encouraged to enter the League immediately.[40] More typical, though, were repetitions that the League must be the basis of British foreign policy, such as Grey's 1926 speech on what Britain should be prepared to fight for in future; he argued that it should be made clear that the UK would fight only for the values of the League Covenant. He praised the Locarno agreements of 1925 as dealing with specific local problems, whilst avoiding the formation of hostile groupings. However, he argued that disarmament was still a major issue, and for this to take place, the Soviet Union must enter the League.[41] The view that Liberals should be more specific about the League was perhaps justified. It was put forward in 1928, when Walter Layton read a paper on the League by Wilson Harris, in which it was argued that the Liberal Party needed to be more specific about its League policy. He asked some fundamental questions: in a war-less world, how exactly would nations combine against a violator of peace? How could frontiers be revised peacefully? His answer to some of these questions was based on a view that it was necessary to establish a United States of Europe, based on a sharing of sovereignty, with a constitution involving 'the consent of the Minority to bow, in the last resort, to the will of the Majority'.[42] This may well have been taken on board by some, for the next year, more detailed proposals were made. The recently elected (at the May 1929 general election) MP for Wolverhampton East, Geoffrey Mander, spoke on disarmament, arguing that it was now time for Britain to take a lead on the issue, by signing the 'Optional Clause' (see above, p. 16) of the Protocol of the International Court of Justice – this, Mander argued, would show that Britain was truly committed to international arbitration. He also said that Britain should support the Finnish proposal for League members to give financial assistance to those who were attacked, believing that this would give the League extra teeth in providing for resistance to aggression. Finally, Mander argued that although an international police force was a long way off, an *ad hoc* force could be established now comprising contributions from member nations. It could also involve 'A League wireless station and a League aeroplane service', to ensure that broken lines of communications did not disrupt action. However, Mander went into few details, and nor did anybody else. With the exception of a later discussion in 1932, which offered as many questions as answers, this was the sum of Liberal Summer School consideration of a League military force.[43] Mander did take the case further, at the National Liberal Federation in 1934, and it was again discussed in 1935.[44] However, given the recognition that the lack of such a League military force was a major problem for the League, it was a major failure on the part of the Liberal Party that it did not put forward more detailed ideas on how to remedy the weakness.

Mander's link between the League and disarmament was a common one, and Liberals at the LSS focused much attention on disarmament. In 1922, Frederick Maurice (the director of military operations of the Imperial General Staff in 1915–16), argued that disarmament would be greatly assisted by all nations signing a general defensive pact, in which their commitments were limited to specific quarters of the globe. He also voiced the common Liberal view that preparation for war invariably leads to war.[45] A year later, Walter Layton showed how disarmament could fit into a broad financial plan, in a paper on 'A Budget for 1933'. Layton set out specific Liberal spending proposals, in which he wanted, over ten years, to reduce the spending on arms from the 1923–24 level of £130m, to the pre-war level of £80m. This assumed that there could be an agreement on limiting land forces.[46] Usually though, disarmament was linked to the League.

As regards imperial policy, the discussions at the LSS reveal Liberals to be firmly in favour of gradual progress towards self-government in the colonies. In 1922, Hamilton Grant (Indian foreign secretary, 1914–19), argued that Britain could not yet leave India as it had interests there, but made a general case for reform based on 'trusteeship' – the idea that Britain should help native peoples develop towards self-government. With regard to Egypt, J.A. Spender (editor of the *Westminster Gazette*, 1896–1922, and a member of the Special Mission to Egypt in 1919–20), argued that Britain must recognise that Egypt should be self-governing in many areas, and that Egypt should recognise Britain's interests in the area.[47] Both of these were based on traditional Liberal ideas of Britain as a benevolent imperial power, in which trusteeship loomed large as a justification for Britain's imperial presence. Two years later, some concern was shown over the Empire's role in foreign policy, with Edward Grigg MP speaking on the necessity of involving the Dominions in negotiations with foreign powers, through a system of special representatives. This was necessary, he argued, because Britain could not go to war without the consent of the Empire – a point which had been effectively accepted at the 1923 Imperial Conference, when it was agreed that defence was an issue for individual Dominion parliaments to legislate on. However, the main imperial concern was always self-government, with Lord Meston speaking in 1924 on the need to work for the full implementation of the Montagu–Chelmsford Reforms in India.[48] In 1928, there was strong consensus in favour of moves towards self-government in the Empire, revealed in papers by Sheldon Amos (a former adviser to the Egyptian government) and Philip Kerr on Egypt, India and East Africa.[49] The 1930 LSS saw further consideration of imperial issues, with speeches from leading Indian politicians, Srinivasta Sastri and Ameer Ali, on the situation in India. They were joined by Robert Hamilton (Liberal MP for the Orkneys, and a former East African judge), Herbert Samuel and Lord Lothian, who all emphasised the need for Britain to show native peoples that it was committed to them obtaining self-government. They emphasised that the Empire should be seen as a bridge to self-rule.[50]

There were then, four major concerns in LSS discussions on international relations in the 1921–30 period: finance, the League, disarmament and self-government. However, one speech at the 1929 session gave a clear sign of things to come. This was made by Herbert Samuel who, as the *Manchester Guardian* said, gave a theoretical speech that was more in the LSS style than was usual for a senior Liberal MP. The topic of Samuel's talk was how the traditional Liberal commitment to nationalism was complementary to internationalism – an international system must always be based on the national principle, but that it was also necessary to develop a framework of international law, recognising that 'The rules of right and wrong were not bounded by frontiers. Peace was to be sought as a good thing in itself. The duty of the State could not be narrower than the bounds of the human race.'[51] As peace became more uncertain in the 1930s, the LSS was to consistently return to the themes raised in Samuel's speech.

INTERDEPENDENCY, ECONOMIC DISARMAMENT AND APPEASEMENT:
1931–39

International relations took a dramatic turn for the worse in 1931 as the full effects of the 1929 Wall Street Crash were felt throughout Europe. In Britain, the consequence of this was the collapse of the Labour government, and its replacement with a National Government. At the 1931 LSS, whilst these events were taking place, Walter Layton spoke on 'The Present Crisis in Europe'. In this, Layton focused on the economic crisis in Europe. He said that a major result of this was 'that the world has had an object lesson on the interdependence of nations such as it has never had before'. This was the first occasion on which the idea of 'interdependency' was raised at a major political forum, and by the mid-1930s, it had become the foundation of the Liberal world-view.[52] It has already been discussed in Chapter 2 on Liberal Thinkers, and is further discussed in Chapter 4 on the National Liberal Federation, but it is important to note here that the Liberal Summer School was a key vehicle for promoting the idea. Not only were Liberal activists made more aware of the idea through Layton's paper, but it received considerable coverage in the Liberal press, thus reaching a wide audience throughout the country.

More relevant to the specific British government response to the crisis, were Liberal discussions on tariffs, which were a major concern at the LSS throughout the 1930s. As was seen earlier (see above, p. 2), Liberals were traditionally committed to free trade; this was at odds with the National Government's introduction of tariffs, first in March 1932, and then in the Ottawa Agreements of July and August of the same year. As a result of Liberal opposition to tariffs, the 1932 LSS actually saw Conservative speakers invited to speak against the Ottawa tariffs – Lord Astor and C.R.S. Harris (editor of *Nineteenth Century*).[53] But the strongest criticisms were left to Liberals. Walter Layton was again prominent, and he put a pragmatic view on tariffs: his belief was that it would be impractical to sweep away all tariffs immediately, but that there should be an attempt to work with other nations to define a 'standard of reasonableness'.[54] A year later, Layton argued that a new World Economic Conference must assemble to 'consider how we can create groups which would agree on monetary and tariff policies and restore the maximum movements of trade without creating friction with other nations not in the group'.[55] The context of this was partly a recent statement by Lloyd George, to the effect that following the recently failed World Economic Conference, nations were unlikely to surrender protection. The Liberals at the summer school did not take this view, and wanted to try again – Kingsley Griffith, the MP for Middlesbrough had opened the LSS on this theme.[56]

Similar points on tariffs were made in 1934, with Layton continuing to advocate a low tariff group,[57] and in 1935, Ramsay Muir developed many of the points previously made by Layton, in an address on 'The New Era in Human History'. In this he argued that the nations which had defied the League (Germany, Japan and Italy), had been driven to desperation by their lack of natural resources, and their overpopulation; their only safety-valve had been trade, but due to the imposition of tariff barriers, this was no longer open to them. A major problem here was that they had no colonies, and so he wanted to see not only the lowering and eventual abolition of tariffs, but the placing of all dependent colonies under a mandate system, with all countries having equal access to them.[58] The idea re-emerged in a debate at the 1937 Women's Liberal Federation, and became party policy in 1942 (see below, p. 148). In 1936, Karl von Abshagen, a propagandist for Germany, argued the German case for having colonies; he was vigorously attacked by Arthur Salter who argued that Germany would not need colonies if there was genuine global free trade, and Germans could have access to raw materials. Salter also put the view that giving Germany colonies now would only encourage it to make more demands.[59] By the 1937 LSS, the party leadership was pushing this line. Archibald Sinclair, in his inaugural address, spoke about 'economic disarmament', a phrase he used to encompass all that had been said previously about lowering tariffs, and ensuring that all nations had equal access to colonial resources. He argued that this was more preferable than a military alliance between the democracies, which would only make Germany more likely to strike, out of fear of encirclement. Sinclair argued, 'Economic disarmament and appeasement is the only road to military disarmament and political peace.'[60]

Aside from being relevant to problems of global security, the issue of economic disarmament was also applied to imperial matters, and so for many Liberals, imperial policy and foreign policy were very closely linked. This could be seen particularly in the 1939 LSS, when Muir developed the idea of economic disarmament, arguing that to ensure equal access to resources, colonies should be controlled through an international authority. This would not only provide all powers with access to raw materials, but it would help native peoples develop along the path to self-government.[61] LSS discussions on tariffs were thus clearly very wide-ranging, and it is important to note that they did not simply go over old ground, asserting Liberal platitudes about the moral force of free trade. At the LSS, Liberals sought to relate the historic commitment to free trade to the specific problems of the day, and they developed a distinctive view of the world in the 1930s, in which 'economic nationalism' was an evil, and 'economic disarmament' was a remedy.

Liberals were also thinking more about their overall world-view, which was sometimes expressed in a commitment to federalism. The 1932 LSS led to the publication of a book entitled *Whither Britain? A Radical Answer*. It was based on papers given at the LSS by a group of Liberals who were concerned over the divisions in the Liberal Party over the National Government. They were mainly former Liberal candidates, who had worked in business, and as lawyers, journalists and economists. They argued that the book updated some points of the *Yellow Book*, but it also included new areas, especially the 'International Framework'. The book argued that the authors'

> ultimate goal is a world federation of nations in a disarmed world with a central authority for imposing decisions where a dispute between nations has failed of settlement by mutual agreement. This goal will remain at an almost unattainable distance until statesmen and peoples alike in all countries are willing to accept as the basis for lasting peace a surrender of the full doctrine of national sovereignty, and a recognition that the good of the community of nations as a whole must transcend the interests of individual nations.

The book also outlined specific short-term proposals, including disarmament. On this issue, they argued that the United Kingdom should abolish all aggressive weapons (rather than defensive ones), and they highlighted large battleships, military aircraft, chemical weapons, heavy guns and tanks. They also put forward specific ideas on how the League should impose sanctions on aggressive powers. The first sanction they envisaged was a simple moral one of condemnation. If this was ineffective, economic sanctions could then be imposed, and ultimately, the League could take military action. This should be done, they said, through an international police force, which could be established

> by means of quotas from internal 'police' forces of the various nations, or it might be made a real international army or air force with bases at strategic points; or it might be a combination of the two systems, with a differentiation of weapons permitting the use of more strictly 'offensive' arms only to the international force.[62]

Whither Britain? was yet another contribution made by the LSS to the development of Liberal international thought, and it was closely linked to the idea of interdependency.

The idea of federalism was also developed by Lord Lothian in 1933, when he called for 'An economic League of Nations, the pooling of sovereignty and armaments and the creation of a Federation of Nations.' He said, 'I do not mean that world federation is in sight to-day, but the League of Nations, good as it is, is not enough. Progressive and democratic nations would have to move towards federation, pool their armaments, and create one economic system pledged to Free Trade among themselves.'[63] Federalism was again raised in 1939, when it was clear that there was far from being a consensus view. This was clear in a debate between Ramsay Muir and Lionel Curtis. Curtis put the view associated with the recently published book by the US journalist, Clarence Streit, *Union Now* (1939), arguing that the world was on the edge of a crisis, and only a world government could deal with it. Muir agreed that a world body was necessary, 'and that perhaps it was time they went back to the mediaeval conception that there is a moral order overriding national sovereignty'. However, setting up a world order of around 15 democracies might lead to the states not in it combining together in an alternative, perhaps led by the Soviet Union and Germany. Furthermore, Muir's 'conviction was that democracy got less effective as the size of the unit increased'.[64] No definite view emerged from the LSS on federalism, and the idea did not find its way into discussions in formal party bodies. However, the value of the LSS in being a forum for discussion can be seen clearly here: bold new ideas could be discussed by Liberals, without reference to formal motions, and without the danger that debate would be overshadowed by more short-term party political considerations.

One issue which often surfaced at the LSS in the 1930s was that of a Popular Front: cooperation of non-Conservative parties against the Conservatives. Effectively, this meant Lib–Lab cooperation, but Liberals were not completely averse to involvement from communists. It was raised twice at the LSS, first in 1934, when the LSS was largely hostile to the idea.[65] However, after the Conservative victory at the 1935 general election, the Popular Front was considered more seriously at the 1936 LSS. On that occasion, those attending were, on balance, in favour of some collaboration at the next election. One speaker, F.L. Josephy, summed up the reasons why when she said that Liberals must fight for Liberalism rather than the Liberal Party, and that Liberalism could be achieved through cooperation with other parties.[66] Similar views were repeated in 1939, and although the Popular Front was discussed largely in the context of domestic politics and political strategy, foreign policy also entered the debate. One of the reasons which Liberals gave for opposing the Conservatives, was the Tories' lack of commitment to 'collective security'. However, with the exception of three 'unity' candidates at post-Munich by-elections, and informal cooperation through organisations such as the Left Book Club,[67] little came of the idea of cross-party cooperation, largely due to opposition to it from Liberal and Labour leaders (see below, pp. 128–9).

More important than discussions about federalism or the Popular Front, were Liberal Summer School discussions on how to deal with the growing German threat. Underpinning the LSS approach to Germany was the idea of economic disarmament discussed earlier, and possible colonial concessions were a particularly important part of this. But military issues, first disarmament, then collective security, became equally important. In 1934, against the backdrop of discussion about Lib–Lab cooperation, the MP Geoffrey Mander argued that the first act of a 'progressive' government in Britain should be to summon a world disarmament conference, and to ban all weapons which had been forbidden to Germany in the Treaty of Versailles. Herbert Samuel, in his opening address, argued that whilst Liberals could not take part in wars of intervention to decide the form of government in any country, they should not hesitate to take action against another country which had already tried to intervene in the affairs of another. This was in the context of discussions over possible German intervention in Austria.[68] By 1935, speakers were regularly talking of resistance to the demands of dictators. Norman Angell argued that a major contribution to peace would be made by Britain making it clear that it would resist all aggression; he said that Italy had only dared to attack Abyssinia rather than Malta, as it was clear that Britain would defend the latter, but not the former.[69]

In 1936, the focus was on both resistance and remedying German grievances. Lady Layton argued that whilst it was necessary to make the sanctions clauses of the Covenant more definite, and to show Hitler that force was not productive, it was also vital to demonstrate that Britain was willing to work seriously on remedying unfair treaties.[70] In 1937, the LSS discussed similar issues. Themes on which all were agreed included the idea that strengthening the League's sanctions mechanism was vital, but also that it was important to appear willing to remedy grievances.[71]

A year later, in 1938, the issue of German grievances led to the most heated LSS debate on international policy: the row between Herbert (by then Lord) Samuel, and Ramsay Muir, on 31 July and 1 August. Samuel began the controversy by giving a speech on the European situation and collective security by saying that the League was now ineffective, and that any action Britain might take against German aggression with, for example, France and the Soviet Union, would lack the force of the League and be doomed to failure, as many nations stood by in a neutral position. He said that, therefore, Britain should make all efforts to meet Germany's legitimate grievances, and should not act against Germany simply because it disapproved of the German regime. This was based, he said, on the Liberal diplomatic tradition, of dealing with all nations in a Liberal spirit. Ramsay Muir was scheduled to speak on 'Property and Liberty' on the evening of 31 July, but instead took the opportunity to respond to Samuel. Muir said it simply was not possible to disregard the Nazi regime, because it kept on demanding more, whatever it gained. He claimed that, 'The dictators had declared war against liberty, they glorified racialism, they helped to spread the poison of economic self-sufficiency, and they repudiated treaties in the most cynical fashion.' To stop this, Muir said, 'Liberals believe the right way to avoid a universal war is quiet firmness in upholding the right, and on the other hand a generous readiness to proclaim to the world that we are ready to remove the evils which have contributed to the present situation.'

Samuel and Muir tackled the issue again the following evening, in a formal debate, chaired by Walter Layton. Samuel re-emphasised his point by saying that German grievances (which at this time related principally to the Sudetenland) must be met because it was right to do so – Liberals must treat all countries fairly. Muir's main emphasis was on saying that this involved 'a too purely theoretical insistence on the doctrine of non-intervention', without any consideration of the diffi-culties this could cause. Ultimately, Germany wanted power, and this would only be prevented by strong resistance from Britain and other democracies.[72] The overall response to the debate was mixed. The *New Statesman & Nation* said: 'The audience was clearly divided into two camps – those who believed that Nazi Germany might be made reason-able by concessions, and those who feared that the second (ideological) world war had already begun.' The *Manchester Guardian* commented that there was merit in both cases, but that in reality, a compromise would be necessary – standing firm against the dictators, but making it clear that redress of grievances would be considered. This was effectively Muir's argument, although the *Guardian* was at pains not to commit itself.[73] In the remaining year of peace though, more and more Liberals moved over to Muir's viewpoint, and the LSS debate was an important part of this process as it was the most public airing of different opinions amongst Liberals.

By 1939, it was clear to most that Germany would not be stopped without a fight, or at least the threat of war. Samuel made a provocative case against conscientious objectors, arguing that consciences could err. He said that simply because a conscience dictated an action, it was not necessarily the right action.[74] A major speech on foreign policy was made by Arthur Salter, who argued that the British government should propose a White Paper which could form the basis of a constructive peace policy for the world. He said that it should be announced after Britain had formed an alliance with the Soviet Union, and that it should involve the following elements: resistance of all aggression; settlement of grievances; cancellation of the war guilt clause of the Treaty of Versailles; expansion of free trade; support for France if it was attacked by Germany, but not if it initiated an attack on Germany.[75] Combined with Muir's views on the colonies, Salter's plan represented a clear strategy for action. Coming a month before the outbreak of war, however, it was far too late to offer an alternative to the Chamberlain policy.

CONCLUSION

The Liberal Summer School, then, had much to say on international relations in the 1920s and 1930s. It was obviously difficult for it to respond to every development in the period, meeting as it did only once a year; but it was able to deal with important long-term issues. In the 1920s, it helped to discuss why disarmament was important, and how it could be achieved. It tackled the important financial questions of reparations and inter-allied debts. The LSS also debated the League of Nations. An inability to define more clearly the role of the League was probably the LSS's major failing. Although some speakers recognised this, they did little about it. A case in point is the discussion around a League military force in 1929 and 1932. On both occasions, questions were asked, yet few answers were offered. Very little that was tangible emerged from the school on this issue and the lack of a clear policy dogged the Liberal Party's League position.

Throughout the 1920s, imperial questions were also considered. The LSS came up with little that was innovative on self-government, but it did confirm the idea as a foundation of Liberal beliefs on empire. In the 1930s, empire was considered as part of wider international issues, and the LSS was one of the Liberal bodies which promoted the idea of economic disarmament – lowering tariffs, and establishing international control of colonies – in order to remove some of the economic causes of instability.

The 1930s also saw some discussion of the doctrine of interdependency, although this was better developed by Liberal thinkers, and through the National Liberal Federation. More important, in the decade that led to war, was the debate between Samuel and Muir over when it would be necessary to resist German expansion, and the general thought given to how to deal with German grievances. It is clear from this issue that there were some divisions in the Liberal Party over appeasement. However, the debate also showed that many Liberals were involved in opposition to appeasement, and they had an alternative. In the first instance, from the rise of Hitler until 1938, that meant making it clear that the League was capable of, and willing to, remedy grievances through formal procedures which would lead to economic disarmament. That involved a use of the League that the government was not willing to consider, preferring as it did agreements between two or more countries on an *ad hoc* basis. But the Liberal alternative at this stage also involved a recognition that the League's sanctions procedures (including the use of military force) must be strengthened. That they did not specify more precisely how this might be done was a major weakness in the alternative policy.

However, by the time of the 1938 summer school, with the League all but dead, Liberals were coalescing on a more straightforward twin-track approach. One track involved making concessions on issues such as colonies to countries such as Germany: Liberals called it economic disarmament, and it had been a feature of their pre-1938 policy. But the second track, 'collective security', involved recognising that the League was finished and ensuring that all concessions were backed up by the threat of force from an alliance of powerful nations should those agreements be broken. Although that approach shared much with anti-appeasers in other parties, it was distinctive from the policy offered by the government. In the first instance, 'economic disarmament' involved making concessions outside Europe, on colonial issues and restoring free trade around the world. In the second instance, Liberals wanted to construct a military alliance to resist any aggressor, which was very different to Neville Chamberlain's policy, which did not involve any threat of military action until March 1939. This alternative is explored further in Chapters 4 and 5.

NOTES

1. Mary Stocks, *Ernest Simon of Manchester* (Manchester: Manchester University Press, 1963), p. 69.
2. Michael Hart, 'The Decline of the Liberal Party in Parliament and in the Constituencies' (Oxford, DPhil., 1982), p. 297.
3. Trevor Wilson, *The Downfall of the Liberal Party, 1914–35* (London: Collins, 1966), p. 343.
4. *The Times*, 20 May 1919, p. 10; 22 May 1919, p. 14; 26 May 1919, p. 9.
5. Ramsay Muir, *Liberalism and Industry: Towards a Better Social Order* (London: Constable, 1920); 'The New Manchesterism', *Nation*, XXVIII, 14 (1 Jan. 1921), pp. 470–2.
6. Simon, Scott and Guedalla were each accompanied by their wives, who were not recorded as being involved in the discussions.
7. National Liberal Federation, *Proceedings in Connection with the Thirty-Sixth Annual Meeting of the National Liberal Federation Held at Birmingham, November 27th and 28th, 1919* (London: LPD, 1919). Stocks, *Ernest Simon of Manchester*, pp. 69–70. R. Muir, 'The

Summer School Movement', *WW*, II, 14 (2 Aug. 1924), pp. 409–10. S. Hodgson, 'The Story of the Liberal Summer Schools', *DN*, 24 July 1926, p. 6. *MG*, 2 Sept. 1921, p. 9.

8. E.D. Simon, 'The Liberal Summer School', *CR*, 130, 729 (Sept. 1926), 298–303.

9. For tennis, see, *WG*, 4 Aug. 1924, p. 3. For a selection of reviews, see, *MG*, 9 Aug. 1922, p. 3; *DC*, 6 Aug. 1924, p. 5; *WG*, 6 Aug. 1924, p. 5.

10. *WW*, II, 3 (17 May 1924), p. 81; 'The Liberal Summer School', *FV*, I, 6 (June 1927), p. 92.

11. Quoted examples include: China, Japan, Sweden, Denmark, Holland, Poland, Germany and the United States in 1924; South Africa, Egypt, the USA, Greece, Poland, Finland, Sweden, Bulgaria and Denmark in 1935. See, *WG*, 31 July 1924, p. 5; *NC*, 2 Aug. 1935, p. 2.

12. *WWG*, 5 Aug. 1922, p. 2; *MG*, 7 Aug. 1922, p. 10; *DC*, 3 Aug. 1923, p. 3; *WG*, 31 July 1924, p. 5; 'Events of the Week', *Nation*, XXXVII, 18, 1 Aug. 1925, p. 533; *DN*, 6 Aug. 1925, p. 3; *MG*, 3 Aug. 1934, p. 6; Dingle Foot, 'The Liberal Summer School', *CR*, 140, 789 (Sept. 1931), pp. 324–30; *NC*, 2 Aug. 1935, p. 2; 'Dictators' Economy', *NC*, 5 Aug. 1939, p. 2. It has not been possible to verify the 1939 figure in any other source, and it may be inaccurate, as an increase from 400 in 1935 to 1,400, would have been very much at odds with the fortunes of the Liberal Party. However, the *News Chronicle* could have been referring to figures for years earlier in the 1930s, rather than the record attendances of the mid-1920s, in which case, the 1939 LSS was attended by well over 500 people.

13. See, Michael Freeden, *Liberalism Divided: A Study in British Political Thought, 1914–1939* (Oxford: Clarendon, 1986).

14. Ramsay Muir, 'The Summer School Movement', *WW*, II, 14 (2-8-1924), pp. 409–10. Adrian Smith, *The New Statesman: Portrait of a Political Weekly, 1913–1931* (Ilford: Frank Cass, 1996), p. 152.

15. See, for example, A.F. Pollard, 'The British League and the Other League of Nations', *WW*, I, 1 (3 Nov. 1923), pp. 5–6. F. Maurice, 'The Road to Disarmament', *WW*, I, 2 (10 Nov. 1923), p. 45. J.A. Spender, 'Peace and Military Liabilities', *WW*, II, 19 (6 Sept. 1924), pp. 541–2. J.A. Spender, 'The Tasks Ahead for the League', *WW*, II, 20 (13 Sept. 1924), p. 565. R. Muir, 'The League of the Commonwealth', *WW*, II, 23 (4 Oct. 1924), pp. 650–1. R. Muir, 'Consultation on Foreign Policy', *WW*, II, 24 (11 Oct. 1924), p. 678. R. Muir, 'The Dominion Parliaments and Empire Policy', *WW*, II, 25 (18 Oct. 1924), p. 718.

16. Liberal Summer School, *Essays in Liberalism: Being the Lectures and Papers which were delivered at the Liberal Summer School at Oxford, 1922* (London: Collins, 1922). Frederick Maurice, *Disarmament* (*Daily News*, 1924). Lord Meston, *India and the Empire* (*Daily News*, 1925).

17. *MG*, 10 Aug. 1922, p. 8.

18. *DC*, 3 Aug. 1923, p. 3. *MG*, 3 Aug. 1923, p. 16.

19. *MG*, 3 Aug. 1928, p. 10.

20. National Liberal Federation, *Proceedings in Connection with the Thirty-Eighth Annual Meeting of the National Liberal Federation Held at Newcastle-upon-Tyne, November 24th and 25th, 1921* (London: LPD, 1922), pp. 21–2. National Liberal Federation, *Proceedings in Connection with the Thirty-Seventh Annual Meeting of the National Liberal Federation Held at Bradford, November 25th and 26th, 1920* (London: LPD, 1921), p. 28. S. Hodgson, 'The Story of the Liberal Summer Schools', *DN*, 24 July 1926, p. 6. E.D. Simon, 'The Liberal Summer School', *CR*, 136, 765 (1929), 273–9.

21. Michael Hart, 'The Decline of the Liberal Party in Parliament and in the Constituencies' (Oxford, DPhil., 1982), pp. 290–341. *Britain's Industrial Future: Being the Report of the Liberal Industrial Inquiry of 1928* (London: Ernest Benn, 1928).

22. *Nation*, XXXVII, 18 (1 Aug. 1925) p. 533; 19, 8 Aug. 1925, p. 561. 'The Liberal Summer School', *LM*, XXXIII, 384 (Sept. 1925), pp. 540–6.

23. *DN*, 3 Aug. 1929, p. 8. *MG*, 3 Aug. 1929, p. 7. 'Anglo-American Relations', *FV*, III, 32 (Sept. 1929), pp. 117–20.

24. *NC*, 2 Aug. 1930, p. 2; 5 Aug. 1930, p. 2; 7 Aug. 1930, p. 2. 'Liberal Summer School', *LM*, XXXVIII, 444 (Sept. 1930), pp. 428–9
25. *MG*, 4 Aug. 1931, p. 6. *NC*, 6 Aug. 1931, p. 2.
26. *NC*, 3 Aug. 1932, p. 2.
27. *NC*, 3 Aug. 1936, p. 2.
28. *NC*, 30 July 1938, p. 13. *NC*, 2 Aug. 1938, p. 7. *MG*, 3 Aug. 1938, p. 5.
29. 'Comments', *New Statesman & Nation*, XVIII, 442 (new series) (12 Aug. 1939) p. 235.
30. R. Muir, 'The Liberal Summer School and the Problems of Industry', *CR*, 132, 741 (Sept. 1927), 282–9. 'Liberal Summer School', *LM*, XXXV, 408 (Sep. 1927), pp. 553–63.
31. 'The Political Summer School', *Nation*, XXXI, 20 (12 Aug. 1921), pp. 643–4. *MG*, 26 Sept. 1921, p. 10. 'The Fresh Air of Liberalism', *DN*, 26 Sept. 1921, p. 3.
32. *DN*, 28 Sept. 1921, p. 3. *MG*, 28 Sept. 1921, p. 14. 'A Lake School of Liberals', *Nation*, XXX, 2 (8 Oct. 1921), pp. 44–5.
33. 'Lord Grey's Concluding Address', *LM*, XXX, 348 (Sept. 1922), pp. 609–16.
34. 'Liberal Summer School', *DN*, 10 Aug. 1923, Special Supplement.
35. Hansard, *236 HC Deb. 5s.*, col. 2514: 20 Mar. 1930.
36. Public Record Office, Kew: FO 371/11246, C 10831/10417/62, Memorandum by Viscount Chilston on Proceedings of Pan-European Congress held in Vienna, 6 Oct. 1926.
37. *DN*, 30 July 1926, p. 8. *DC*, 30 July 1924, p. 4. The full liability of Britain's debt was £46m per year. Bonar Law had authorised Baldwin to offer no more than £25m, but Baldwin's deal involved paying £34m for ten years and £40m for the next 52.
38. Robert Cecil, 'The League of Nations and the Rehabilitation of Europe', in LSS, *Essays in Liberalism*, pp. 1–18. *MG*, 3 Aug. 1922, p. 10.
39. A.F. Pollard, 'The Balance of Power', LSS, in *Essays in Liberalism*, pp. 19–36.
40. 'Liberal Summer School', *DN*, 10 Aug. 1923, Special Supplement.
41. *DN*, 29 July 1926, p. 8. 'The Liberal Summer School', *LM*, XXXIV, 396 (Sept. 1926), pp. 520–2.
42. *DN*, 8 Aug. 1928, p. 8.
43. Geoffrey Le M. Mander, 'Military Disarmament', *FV*, III, 32 (Sept. 1929), p. 124. 'Liberal Summer School', *LM*, XXXVII, 432 (Sept. 1929), p. 600.
44. For reference in NLF, see below, pp. 79–91.
45. Frederick Maurice, 'International Disarmament', in LSS, *Essays in Liberalism*, pp. 37–50.
46. *DN*, 6 Aug. 1923, p. 3; *MG*, 6 Aug. 1923, p. 12; *WG*, 6 Aug. 1923.
47. Hamilton Grant, 'India', and J.A. Spender, 'Egypt', in LSS, *Essays in Liberalism*, pp. 92–110, 111–19.
48. *DN*, 1 Aug. 1924, p. 3. *MG*, 1 Aug. 1924, p. 5. *DC*, 1 Aug. 1924, p. 4. *MG*, 2 Aug 1924, p. 6. For details of the Montagu–Chelmsford Reforms, see above, p. 13.
49. *DN*, 4 Aug. 1928, p. 9. Sheldon Amos, 'Liberalism in Egypt' and Philip Kerr, 'Imperial Policy', *FV*, II, 21 (Sept. 1928), pp. 3–4, 4–8.
50. *NC*, 2 Aug. 1930, p. 2; 5 Aug. 1930, p. 2; 7 Aug. 1930, p. 2. 'Liberal Summer School', *LM*, XXXVIII, 444 (Sept. 1930), pp. 428–9
51. *MG*, 10 Aug. 1928, p. 10.
52. *MG*, 3 Aug. 1931, pp. 7–8.
53. *MG*, 30 July 1932, p. 6.
54. *NC*, 2 Aug. 1932, p. 2.
55. *NC*, 9 Aug. 1933, p. 2.
56. *MG*, 4 Aug. 1933, p. 6; 5 Aug. 1933, p. 12.
57. *MG*, 7 Aug. 1934, p. 5.
58. *MG*, 7 Aug. 1935, p. 6.
59. *NC*, 5 Aug. 1936, p. 11. *MG*, 5 Aug. 1936, p. 5.
60. *NC*, 30 July 1937, p. 11. 'Sir Archibald Sinclair at the Liberal Summer School', *LM*, XLV, 527 (Aug. 1937), pp. 375–6.
61. *NC*, 9 Aug. 1939, p. 11.

62. *MG*, 4 Aug. 1932, p. 10. Hubert Phillips, Arthur Holgate, R. Moelwyn Hughes, T. Elder Jones, Ifor Lloyd, Jules Menken and Alan Sainsbury, *Whither Britain? A Radical Answer* (London: Faber & Faber, 1932), pp. 7–8, 18–19, 21–4.
63. *NC*, 7 Aug. 1933, p. 2.
64. *NC*, 5 Aug. 1939, p. 2. *MG*, 5 Aug. 1939, p. 15.
65. 'Comments', *New Statesman & Nation*, VIII, 181 (new series) (11 Aug. 1934) p. 171. See also, Peter Joyce, *Realignment of the Left? A History of the Relationship between the Liberal Democrat and Labour Parties* (London: Macmillan, 1999), pp. 87–96.
66. *NC*, 1 Aug. 1936, p. 13. *NC*, 7 Aug. 1939, p. 2.
67. John Lewis, *The Left Book Club: An Historical Record* (London: Victor Gollancz, 1970), p. 12.
68. *NC*, 3 Aug. 1934, p. 2; 7 Aug. 1934, p. 2.
69. *NC*, 7 Aug. 1935, p. 11.
70. *NC*, 1 Aug. 1936, p. 13.
71. *MG*, 31 July 1937, p. 4. *NC*, 31 July 1937, p. 5.
72. *NC*, 1 Aug. 1938, p. 2; 2 Aug. 1938, p. 7. *MG*, 1 Aug. 1938, p. 5; 2 Aug. 1938, p. 12. 'Liberals and the Dictators', *LM*, XLVI, 540 (Sept. 1938), pp. 437–40. Herbert Samuel, 'The European Situation and Collective Security', *CR*, 154, 873 (Sept. 1938), pp. 257–67.
73. *MG*, 4 Aug. 1938, p. 8. 'Comments', *New Statesman & Nation*, XVI, 398 (new series) (6 Aug. 1938), p. 206.
74. Herbert Samuel, 'Freedom and Defence', *CR*, 156, 885 (Sept. 1939), pp. 257–67.
75. *NC*, 7 Aug. 1939, p. 2.

—4—

The Official Liberal Party: Conferences

DESPITE THE high profile of the Liberal Summer School, it was still only an unofficial think tank. Its policy discussions would mean nothing unless the official Liberal Party could be persuaded to adopt some of its ideas. This would involve two key areas: the formal policy-making structure of the party and the parliamentary party. This chapter addresses the first half of this equation, by focusing on discussions held at the National Liberal Federation (NLF), and then on its replacement from 1936, the Liberal Assembly. It also looks at two other important Liberal bodies: the Liberal Party Council (from its inception in 1936) and the Women's National Liberal Federation (WNLF).

It will be seen in this chapter that foreign policy debates in these bodies can be divided into three main stages: first, from the end of the First World War until 1932 the NLF tended to endorse general reso-lutions favouring the League of Nations and disarmament. Sometimes these resolutions contained specific proposals, but more often, they were phrased in fairly general terms.

The year 1932 marked a key change as it was the first occasion that the NLF had the chance to respond to the Japanese attack on Manchuria, and to the formation of the National Government the previous year. Later in the year, following the NLF meeting in April, the signature of the Ottawa Agreements, establishing preferential trade tariffs with the Empire, signalled a shift in the discourse of Britain's international policy. Meanwhile, it had also become increasingly apparent that Nazism was a major force in Germany, and, in future years, this was the backdrop to Liberal debates on international relations. This all meant that from 1932 the party started to focus more on the restoration of free trade as part of economic disarmament and the strengthening of collective security through the grievance and guarantee procedures of the League. A small number of Liberals, notably Lord Lothian and F.W. Hirst, did not endorse the focus on collective security, believing that this would lead to the re-establishment of the pre-1914 European alliance system, and inevitably result in war. Instead, they focused on satisfying Germany's grievances, believing that Hitler had a limited set of demands, and could be trusted to abide by international agreements. In this, they were committed appeasers, but they represented only a small section of Liberal thought. The bulk of the party was certainly prepared to negotiate with Hitler, but they would only do so from a position of strength. Thus, by the middle of the 1930s the party was advocating a policy based on collective security, which was distinctive to that put forward by the National Government. It was distinct in two ways: it sought to use the League to remedy grievances through formal procedures, with the aim of securing economic disarmament, and it recognised that the League's sanctions procedures (including the use of military force) would have to be strengthened.

The third phase of Liberal policy began with the 1938 Liberal Assembly. This responded to the fears provoked by German–Austrian *Anschluss*, the Anglo-Italian Agreement accepting Italian control of Abyssinia and a realisation that the League was now finished as a body which could credibly impose sanctions on an aggressor. So from the May 1938 Assembly Liberals continued to advocate economic disarmament but also sought a Great Power alliance to make it clear that force could be used to defend any agreements that were made.

Much of this chapter focuses on the National Liberal Federation and its successor, the Liberal Assembly. The NLF was the broad Liberal body encompassing the Council, the General Committee, the Executive, constituency associations, district federations (consisting of about sixty constituencies each), MPs and organisations such as Junior Liberal Clubs. However, in contemporary parlance, the term 'NLF' was more specifically used to describe what was officially the Council of the National Liberal Federation, and except for in this introduction, that it how the term is used in this book. This NLF Council was the main policymaking body of the Liberal Party, and would today be called a party conference. It met once a year, although the month varied, and it was held in many different parts of the country (see Appendix 3). At the close of the First World War, the representation at the NLF Council consisted mainly of representatives from each constituency association, who were joined by the NLF Executive, district representatives and all Liberal MPs. Before the First World War, constituency representation was determined on the basis of one delegate for every thousand voters in a constituency, but in 1918, anticipating an increase in the number of electors under the Franchise Act, this figure was raised to one for every two thousand. However, this meant that the NLF could, potentially, have 9,000 people attending, and the NLF remained somewhat unwieldy. This was worsened by the fact that there was another level of decision-making, as the Council of the NLF was accompanied by an elected General Committee, consisting of three representatives from each constituency, plus district representatives and MPs. This General Committee was charged with the responsibility of electing the Executive and liaising between it and the constituencies. Therefore, in 1923, in an attempt to streamline the organisation, there was a significant reorganisation of the NLF. The representation at the Council was reduced to one delegate for every six thousand electors; district federations would no longer be directly represented at the Council, but they would organise constituency representation; the number of elected members on the Executive was enlarged from 20 to 24, with a provision for six extra members to be created if necessary by the Executive; and this Executive was to be elected by district federations, rather than the General Committee, which was to be abolished. The overall result of this was to give more power to district federations in electing representatives to the Executive, but they lost their representation at the Council. The focus of Council representation was now almost entirely on constituency associations. The Executive was enlarged, but also gained more power from the abolished General Committee.[1]

Against a backdrop of continued electoral failure, the Liberal Party again reorganised itself in 1936, with the National Liberal Federation as a whole being replaced by the Liberal Party Organisation. This was defined as consisting of the Assembly, the Council, area federations, constituency associations and other recognised units such as the Young Liberals. The Assembly was the policymaking body; it consisted of Liberal MPs, candidates from the previous general election, agents, the executives of recognised units, and particularly, constituency delegates. These were elected according to the size of the local Liberal association, with four for each constituency, plus an extra representative for every 100 members, up to a maximum of 20 in all. The Council dealt with finances, and with short-term policy statements between Assembly meetings. Its representation consisted primarily of five MPs, five members of the House of Lords, 30 constituency representatives and 30 Assembly representatives.[2]

In practice, the NLF Council, and later the Assembly, were attended by far fewer delegates than were entitled to be there. After the 1923 reorganisation, around 3,000 was the potential maximum size, but this figure was never reached. However, the numbers attending were still significant. The lowest figure noted by newspapers was 800 in 1934, but numbers were more usually well over 1,000, and often nearly 2,000. This latter level was consistent throughout the 1920s, and despite the 1934 low figure, 1,800 attended in 1936.[3] Many of the discussions were not, of course, to do with international affairs. The NLF Council was often dominated by domestic policy and by questions of electoral strategy. Thus the 1920 NLF Council was marked by denunciations of the Lloyd George Coalition; industry was a prominent theme in 1926 and 1928; discussion of a possible Popular Front was a major issue in 1934 and 1937. Much of this discussion was connected with domestic politics, with some Liberals believing that groups opposed to the government could form a common agenda on social and economic questions. Although international policy could be part of a broad agreement, it was not the driving force behind the pressure in the mid-1930s.[4] As we shall see later, this changed after the Munich Crisis (below, pp. 128–9). However, in most years there were discussions on international policy, and these almost always attracted a great deal of attention in the Liberal press – which gave extensive coverage to the conferences as a whole, often making them their leading story. Especially in the 1930s, NLF (and later Assembly) international policy discussions were seen by journalists as equal in importance to domestic politics. Here it will be shown that there were three stages in official Liberal policy: the first, from 1918 to 1931, focused on general support for the League and disarmament, with disarmament being a particular concern from 1928. This responded to recent setbacks to the cause of disarmament (see above, p. 14). By 1930, Liberals were becoming more concerned about economics as an aspect of international policy, in response to the global economic crisis. These concerns informed Liberal policy throughout the 1930s. But the real shift in policy came in 1932, when Liberals reacted to the Japanese attack on Manchuria by advocating a policy of 'collective security' in which it would be possible to make concessions to dictators where their grievances were just, but only from a position of strength. Then, from 1938, after clear evidence of the League's failure, Liberals began to focus on the need for a Great Power alliance.

THE LEAGUE AND DISARMAMENT, 1918–31

The tone of much future Liberal Party international policy was set by the 1918 National Liberal Federation Council (hereafter referred to as the NLF) meeting, held in Manchester at the end of September, only a fortnight before the armistice that would end the First World War. Moving a short resolution on *The War and the Peace*, Herbert Samuel called for the establishment of a League of Nations, arguing that this must provide for the settlement of future disputes between nations, and must bring about disarmament. Samuel, and other speakers, also reflected the Liberal commitment to a 'Clean Peace', a phrase Asquith had used a year before (see below, p. 101) to describe his view that in any peace settlement the victors must be magnanimous. The only more specific debate that took place in 1918 was on a resolution dealing with *The Control of Treaties*, put by Arnold Rowntree MP. This proposed that no treaty should become operative until it had been ratified by parliament, but had originally stated that 'foreign affairs' generally often needed to be secret. In an amendment supported by the Executive, the

Manchester Liberal Federation altered this to refer only to 'diplomatic negotiations', rather than foreign affairs in general. One can clearly see here the influence of the view that 'secret diplomacy' led to the outbreak of the First World War (see above, p. 6). Other than this, there were no specific proposals made at the 1918 NLF about the structure of the League, the type of disarmament necessary or the content of the peace treaties.[5] However, the general commitment to the League of Nations and disarmament set the tone of Liberal foreign policy for about the next 15 years.

By the time of the next year's NLF meeting, in November 1919, events had moved on significantly. The League of Nations had been established, and peace made with Germany under the Treaty of Versailles. The main resolution on the League as proposed by Gilbert Murray was extremely general (see Appendix 4). It welcomed the formation of the League, and merely noted regret that its work had not yet begun. Murray called for all nations to be admitted to the League, but neither he, nor the seconder of the resolution, Violet Bonham Carter, discussed the need for revision of treaties. This was left to a more radical amendment (see Appendix 4) put by two MPs on the left of the Liberal Party, J.M. Kenworthy and A.E. Newbould. They called for 'Treaties which are obviously provisional in character' to be revised, otherwise these treaties would 'be a continuous source of friction and the certain cause of future wars'. They also called for an end to conscription, the limitation of armaments and the establishment of an 'international force' to enforce the will of the League. Kenworthy claimed that the existing resolution 'was one which might be moved and seconded at a Grand Council of the Primrose League'. His amendment, however, was too radical for the NLF, and the original Murray resolution was passed.[6] As we shall see in Chapter 5, Kenworthy was to be a thorn in the side of the Liberal leadership in the mid-1920s, as a member of the 'Radical Group' of MPs. This debate on international policy in 1918 was a clear indication of why some MPs felt that the party was too moderate, and why, ultimately, Kenworthy and others would join the Labour Party (see below, p. 107).

If a clear statement calling for a revision of Versailles had been rejected in 1919, the NLF endorsed the idea a year later, passing a resolution in November 1920 saying that Versailles should be revised under the auspices of the League of Nations.[7] Proposing the resolution, Donald Maclean MP did not mention specifically which parts of Versailles should be revised, largely because it was already widely accepted publicly that the issue of reparations was the key issue – as we saw earlier, J.M. Keynes' work *The Economic Consequences of the Peace* (1919) had been crucial in this (see above, p. 30). It is also the case that specific details of strategy in foreign policy seem to have been left to the Liberal leaders.

This is discussed further in Chapter 5, but Gilbert Murray admitted as much two years later, in May 1922, when he put forward another resolution urging the revision of Versailles. There was nothing new in what he said: he stated that Asquith and Keynes (as discussed in Chapters 2 and 5) had already articulated a clear vision – he went on to say that Versailles did not need to be scrapped, and that only 15 of its 410 chapters needed revision.[8] But this was only a public endorsement by the NLF of an already well-established Liberal position. The NLF had little new to say on policy here.

Other than this, all NLF resolutions in 1919–27 on international policy followed two themes: they either made general statements in favour of the League of Nations and disarmament, or they responded to more specific issues by condemning government policy, and restating the Liberal position. The reason for this is that for much of the 1920s, British foreign policy was conducted along lines with which most Liberals could agree – Versailles was already being revised by each and every British government that participated in discussions on reparations or troop numbers. Only when the government seriously violated a Liberal principle did the Liberal Party need to protest. It is also important to note that it was the stated practice of the NLF to restrict itself to resolutions on 'subjects that are most prominent or urgent at the time of the meeting' rather than 'the production of a large number of Resolutions in the nature of a programme embracing subjects upon which the Federation has already declared itself and upon which Liberal views remain unchanged'.[9] Thus, in 1920, the NLF passed a resolution condemning the government's failure to reach an agreement with Russia and its failure to give Mesopotamia (Iraq) self-government. In 1921, while supporting British involvement in the Washington Conference (on naval disarmament and Far Eastern issues) and the US proposals made there, the NLF condemned the high level of military spending by Britain, and urged the government 'to support all practical projects for a progressive disarmament of all Nations'.[10] The 1923 NLF saw a resolution condemning the Ruhr occupation and calling for the revision of reparations agreements. Proposing the resolution, Violet Bonham Carter asked, 'What is the good of turning Krupps into a factory for making sewing machines, if you are making an arsenal of every German heart?' As the *Manchester Guardian* said, in invoking the League as a solution, Violet Bonham Carter 'had no difficulty in commending these impeccable Liberals sentiments to the gathering'.[11] In 1924 there was a resolution in favour of an agreement with Russia: 'the restoration of Russia is essential to European prosperity and calls for the sincere and active cooperation of the British Government and of the British people'. In 1925, the Geneva Protocol (which sought more rigid definition of when nations would be obliged to act under the terms of the League

Covenant) was supported, while in 1926, the government was condemned for its actions at the March 1926 League Council meeting, when the League had failed to reach an agreement on German entry to the League.[12] The major issue in British foreign policy in 1927 was trade and tariffs in China, and the NLF responded by calling for China to be given full control of its own affairs, through the revision of all of its agreements with foreign powers.[13] By this point, Liberal foreign policy was no different to that put forward in its 1923 general election manifesto (see Appendix 4), where the party had called for the settlement of reparations, the involvement of the United States and the Soviet Union in international affairs, and above all else, support for the League.

This pattern of general statements was also followed at a special Liberal Convention, held in January 1925, at Kingsway Hall, a regular venue for Liberal meetings and rallies in London. Attended by 1,800 delegates, it was a reaction to the electoral disaster experienced by the Liberal Party in the 1924 general election. The status of this convention within the party was an official one, approved by the NLF, and including elected representatives from the same range of bodies as usually attended the NLF. It had two purposes: its main aim was an organisational one – to establish a fighting fund which would allow Liberals to stand in every constituency at the next election, and to allow the appointment of a national organiser. However, it also passed a *Declaration of Liberal Principles and Aims*, which included a general statement that Liberals were committed to the League of Nations, saying that it should be the 'pivot' of British foreign policy. The declaration also made a clear statement on the Empire, saying that the ultimate aim of Liberals was for 'self-government in all our Dependencies'. This was a long-established Liberal aim, and was based on the idea of 'trusteeship', in which Britain was seen to be acting as a trustee in its colonies until native peoples could rule themselves. In the meantime, support was given to regular consultation within the Empire on defence and foreign policy issues. Unity within the Empire could also be promoted by migration to 'new lands' and development of imperial resources, but not by any measure of imperial preference, which the party, unsurprisingly, remained vehemently opposed to, sticking to its free trade guns.[14]

Throughout this entire period, the NLF Executive was reasonably well in control of debates. There were, of course, occasions on which delegates were critical of the Parliamentary Liberal Party. For example, in 1926, a delegate from Tynemouth criticised the failure of some Liberal MPs to take a stronger line in parliament against Austen Chamberlain's involvement in delaying German entry to the League of Nations.[15] This kind of denunciation is part and parcel of party conferences, however, and had no significant influence on Liberal policy. More important might be defeat for the platform view on particular resolutions, but this only happened on one occasion in the inter-war period. In 1921, in the resolution on the Washington Conference, the York Liberal Federation put an amendment urging Britain to end the Anglo-Japanese Alliance. The reason for this was that it was said to be a source of international misunderstanding, and that it was believed that it would be better to have the Far East regulated by international law. In the words of the *Daily News*, the Executive opposed this view, on the grounds that it 'would not be nice to Japan to say so'. Facing this opposition, the amendment was withdrawn, but then the Birmingham Liberal Federation put a further amendment saying that all international agreements should be made public. This too was withdrawn, when the Executive pointed out that it was already provided for in the League of Nations Covenant. However, the Dewsbury Liberal Federation pushed the point, arguing that this provision was actually under threat, and that Liberal support for it should be emphasised. The Executive again opposed the amendment, and the *Daily News* commented, 'By this time the delegates were getting annoyed. They said little, but they voted – for the amendment by an overwhelming majority.' The result of this was that 'the executive's steam roller came out of the day's engagement rather badly damaged'. The newspaper added: 'Delegates dispersed wondering why the Federation leaders are always so sensitive about amendments from the body of the hall, and why delegates are expected so consistently to believe that all wisdom dwells on the platform.' This was quite a blow to the Executive, although it made no material difference to Liberal policy, and it should be noted that no other Liberal newspaper gave it the same coverage as the *Daily News*. The *Manchester Guardian* only covered the debate briefly (and it always gave extensive treatment to international debates), while the pro-Lloyd George *Daily Chronicle*, and the pro-Asquith *Westminster Gazette*, both described the amendment as 'slight'. Perhaps unsurprisingly, the record of the debate published by the NLF simply says that the amendment was 'accepted', without saying that it took a vote to force it upon an unhappy Executive.[16] As we shall see later, the delegates only defeated the Executive once again on an international issue in the inter-war period (in 1935 over the establishment of an international police force). The only other serious attempt to do so was in 1933 over the idea of a low tariff union (see below, p. 89).

From 1928, the NLF began to focus more on disarmament. This was probably due to the disasters that the cause experienced in 1927–28 – the failure of the Geneva Naval Conference, and the setbacks to international negotiations caused by the Anglo-French naval compromise (see above, p. 14). It is noticeable that the party produced a number of pamphlets on disarmament in 1928,[17] and in that year the main focus of the NLF's discussion on international policy was a disarmament resolution (see Appendix 4): it called on the British government to take a lead in world disarmament discussions. The floor of the NLF made its voice heard in amending the initial resolution which had called for disarmament to 'the lowest limit compatible with national safety'. This was replaced with an amendment from the Birkenhead and Huddersfield constituencies calling instead for 'an immediate and substantial reduction' in accordance with Britain's obligations under the Covenant, Locarno and the Kellogg–Briand Pact. Some delegates spoke against this, saying that it was too vague, or that it would threaten employment, but there was no opposition from the platform, and the amendment was carried with a large majority. In addition to the disarmament aspects of the resolution, the NLF called for Britain to sign the 'Optional Clause' (see above, p. 16), and the resolution included a section on the Empire, urging the development of self-government throughout the colonies in order to encourage good relations between the different parts of the Empire. The resolution also urged closer consultation within the Empire on foreign policy, and this policy can be seen as a response to the growing assertiveness of the Dominions throughout the 1920s.[18] For the moment, though, imperial policy had no wider place in Liberal thought on international relations. As we shall see later, it had a much greater role in the 1930s.

This policy held firm through 1929, when there was no international policy debate at the NLF. Policy was already settled by this time. The core points could be seen in a pamphlet published in November 1927, signed by the presidents of the NLF, the WNLF and the Young Liberals. This focused on the need for the League to codify international law; for Britain to sign the Optional Clause; for all-in arbitration treaties; and for disarmament.[19] These four points were developed in a pamphlet published prior to the 1929 general election (see Appendix 4), putting forward nine points of Liberal foreign policy. These were: to strengthen existing treaties to encourage discussion rather than war; to maintain humanitarian activities at Geneva; to promote disarmament; to sign the Optional Clause; to accept the principle of the peaceful settlement of all disputes; to concede naval parity with the United States; to establish clear procedures for the revision of treaties; to re-establish normal relations with the Soviet Union; and to promote the reduction of tariffs throughout the world. This was a mixture of a long-term internationalist vision, accompanied by positions on the more immediate issues of the day, such as Britain's relations with the Soviet Union and the United States.

However, this policy soon needed modifying due to the Wall Street Crash in October 1929, and by 1930 the NLF's main interest was the global economic crisis. This involved some consideration of international policy, always interconnected in the Liberal mind with economic issues. At the October 1930 NLF, a free trade resolution called for a general reduction of tariffs throughout the world. It particularly condemned plans to concentrate upon trade within the Empire – the policy known as Empire Free Trade, which was gaining significant support in the country, especially in the Conservative Party.[20] Proposing the resolution, F.W. Hirst put the view that the current global economic problems were due to the Wall Street Crash and the effects of the war (which through debts and reparations had caused high taxes and reduced purchasing power). This was passed, as was a resolution on imperial development, proposed by Dr E. Leslie Burgin, who urged the establishment of an Imperial Economic Council in order to develop the resources of the Empire.[21] By May 1931, the NLF was linking high arms expenditure to the economic crisis, passing a resolution (moved by Charles Hobhouse and Megan Lloyd George) saying that this and high tariffs were the cause of the crisis.[22] However, no specific details on how to give effect to any of this were passed until the following year, by which time the world had been shaken by the Japanese attack on Manchuria.

ECONOMIC DISARMAMENT AND COLLECTIVE SECURITY THROUGH THE LEAGUE, 1932–37

The year 1932 was a crucial one for the development of the Liberal Party's international policy. Following Japan's attack on Manchuria it had become clear that the League of Nations was in grave danger of falling apart. Liberals, however, believed that it could be saved, and they put forward two ways of doing so. First, they believed that all nations in the League must make clear statements that if protests against aggression failed to work, they would join together in 'such measures of collective constraint' as were necessary to uphold the will of the League. This idea was soon put forward by Liberals as 'collective security'. It was not clear from the speeches proposing this at the April 1932 NLF exactly how far down the road to collective armed resistance Liberals would go, but they were now at least talking about resistance to aggression. Second, for the first time in the inter-war period, Liberals put forward specific disarmament proposals. In a resolution moved by two delegates, Gerald Bailey and Captain Reginald Berkeley, this included, for example, the abolition of tanks, the abolition of naval and military aviation and the international control of civil aviation. Thus by 1932, the Liberal Party had a clearer policy on disarmament, and was beginning to focus on the need to boost the sanctions and restraint clauses of the League Covenant.[23]

The 1932 NLF was also significant for the way in which the word 'interdependent' first found its way into a Liberal policy document. The idea of 'interdependency' of all the world's peoples has subsequently been at the heart of the British Liberal approach to international relations, and even today, it features in the constitution of the Liberal Democrats. As we have seen already (see above, p. 68), this idea was discussed at the 1931 Liberal Summer School, and it featured strongly in the writings of Ramsay Muir and Walter Layton. At the 1932 NLF it was placed at the heart of the Liberal world-view, in a general policy declaration (moved by Muir himself, and Lady Acland). This said that, 'All the peoples of the earth have become politically and economically interdependent, so that it is no longer possible for any nation or empire, however great, to be self-sufficient or wholly self-determined.' This was said to be one of two 'outstanding features' of 'a new era of human history', the other being that science was now so advanced that there was no reason why poverty could not be eradicated.[24]

This theme of interdependency was the basis of the May 1933 NLF resolution calling for a world economic conference to be held, in order to restore free trade. This resolution, proposed by Francis Acland and George Paish, called for Britain to argue for the end of tariffs, quotas, subsidies and all other limits to free trade, and the establishment of a stable world monetary system. Failing this, the resolution urged that Britain should take the lead in forming a low tariff union, in order to gradually bring about the reduction of tariffs throughout the world. This latter part of the resolution provoked much hostility from the floor of the NLF, with a number of strident speeches being made against what was seen as an attack on the principle of free trade. F.L. Josephy, raising the spectre of the National Liberal leader, John Simon, who had supported tariffs within the National Government, said 'It's pure Simonism and nothing else.' An amendment to remove the reference to the low tariff union from the resolution was only defeated by 254 votes to 210. Free trade was thus the major international discussion at the 1933 NLF, although a resolution on disarmament was also passed, restating the need for international control of air forces (see Appendix 4).[25]

With the Liberal Party now clearer that resistance to aggression was a major issue, the May 1934 NLF focused on how to put this into practice. This took place as part of a wide-ranging policy debate, which aimed to frame a general declaration to be published under the title *The Liberal Way*. The full text of the relevant section is reproduced in Appendix 4, but it is important to note that this resulted from an amendment to the original resolution. The resolution as moved by Margery Corbett Ashby urged that parliament should pass an act giving the government authority to deny financial and trade facilities to any aggressor state. This was to come into effect at any time after a parliamentary resolution, if other nations were ready to cooperate. One amendment proposed that Britain should not wait for other countries, but this was opposed by the Executive, and was defeated.[26] However, another amendment was added, proposed by Geoffrey Mander MP, who had seconded the resolution. This might appear to mean that he was on the 'inside' in this discussion, but there were certainly some on the Executive who opposed his view. His amendment urged support for the creation of an International Aerial Police Force under the League, and it was accepted by the Executive with the proviso that instead of supporting such a force, the NLF would urge its 'consideration'. There was no public discussion of this important difference, but clearly some Liberals were not whole-heartedly behind the idea.[27]

The backdrop to the May 1935 NLF was the fact that the Parliamentary Liberal Party had recently voted for the government's rearmament policy in the House of Commons. Italian involvement in Abyssinia continued, and in addition, a few days before the NLF met, Adolf Hitler made a speech to the Reichstag in which he claimed that he wanted to negotiate with the other great powers.[28] The resolution on international policy (moved by Geoffrey Mander MP) was couched in very general terms, in support of collective security and disarmament. However, a series of amendments were put. The first amendment, moved by W.C. Chisnall (East Toxteth and Wavertree), wanted to specify the importance of ensuring that there was adequate provision for revision of treaties: it called for 'a territorial and political revision of those treaties which are unjust and unworkable'. This was passed, and a second amendment (moved by L.G. Bowman) called for disarmament as a major plank of international policy – originally the resolution only stated that current problems were due to a failure to disarm, and had not said that this was still an important policy. This too was passed, with the Executive accepting it on condition that it was not seen as a criticism of the parliamentary party's support for rearmament. A third amendment, opposed by the Executive, urged the creation of an International Equity Tribunal for the settlement of non-justiciable disputes and the establishment of an international police force – an even bolder move than the previous year's aerial force, which the NLF had voted to consider rather than support. Garner Evans, moving the amendment, argued that, 'If they wanted the reign of law they must have their court and they must have their policeman. Force must be put behind justice.' Despite the Executive opposition, on the basis that the moment was not 'opportune' for this proposal, the amendment was accepted. The Executive did support a fourth amendment which was carried unanimously – for international control of the arms industry and for an embargo on the export of arms to states violating the Covenant. The resolution as amended was then carried unanimously, with E.L. Mallalieu MP ending on an optimistic note, saying that, 'Hitler had said: "If you will disarm to any level you may think of I too will disarm, and I will accept any supervision that you may devise provided you disarm also."' Mallalieu added, 'What more can the man do? Even the casuistry of the Foreign Secretary and the fine words of Mr Baldwin can't make me lose hope that an energetic Government could do something useful in the present situation.'[29] All of these amendments made clear the role of grassroots involvement in policy, and their desire for definite proposals on both resistance and concession.

The amendments also shed light on the principles at the heart of the Liberal approach. On the one hand, the issue of treaty revision was one to which Liberals were fundamentally committed. In the Liberal view, nations would always have grievances, and there must be clear ways of meeting those grievances. That would mean international acceptance of the methods for raising problems and reaching decisions. Sometimes that would mean that problems could be solved by reference to inter-national law, but the limits of international law were recognised. In non-justiciable disputes, where law did not exist, an International Equity Tribunal would be necessary, illustrating the strength of universalist and institutionalist assumptions in Liberal thought: it was believed that to be effective, international law required the support of all-encompassing institutions. But these were also to be underpinned by agreement on two military issues. First, the Liberal commitment to disarmament came out of the belief that with such a grievance procedure in place, high levels of national armaments would not be necessary, because any country committed to the grievance procedure would have no need to use military force independently. However, the call for an international police force also recognised that there would have to be some form of military sanction as a threat of last resort if grievance procedures were to work. For Liberals, military force was not unnecessary – rather, the use of it should be internationalised.

There were two implicit assumptions underlying this approach. The first was that nations could be made to behave like individuals in the face of the law, but that this could only be done if international mechanisms similar to those of nation states were in place. As Garner Evans had said when moving the amendment on the equity tribunal and the police force, the enforcement of law needs a court and a police-man. The second assumption was simply that of optimism. The Liberal approach was based on the view that many disputes previously settled by war or conquest would be solved peacefully, without ever having to use force. That marked out the Liberal approach from the more 'realist' Conservative approach to international affairs.

If 1935 was an important year for Liberal Party policy, 1936 was even more so. At the Liberal Assembly (meeting for the first time in place of the NLF) in June, there was only a brief discussion on international policy, with an emergency resolution passed condemning the government's abandonment of sanctions against Italy over Abyssinia.[30] However, with the Spanish Civil War beginning a month later, the importance of the Liberal Party Council in policymaking between assemblies was seen. Meeting in September, it held an extensive debate on Spain, and passed legislation favouring the policy of non-intervention pursued by the British government, believing a civil war to be no business of Britain. More specifically, an amendment to the resolution, from A.S. Comyns Carr and F.W. Hirst, called on Britain to mediate in the dispute. There was some unease over this, with Lady Horsley concerned that it would involve British recognition of Franco's rebels, while J.A. Spender and Harcourt Johnstone did not want Britain to mediate alone. However, the amendment was carried, along with one removing a proposal to extend the arms embargo to Portugal – instead, the Council simply called on Portugal to implement the existing Spanish embargo effectively. This non-intervention resolution thus became Liberal policy, and was formally endorsed by the Assembly in 1937. The Liberal Party never came to see events in Spain as an opportunity for making a stand against the dictators, as the party's main aim was to ensure that the war remained an internal dispute. By the time it became apparent that that would never happen, it was too late. The work of Wilfrid Roberts, the Liberal MP for North Cumberland, as a political and humanitarian campaigner for the Republic was the only significant Liberal contribution to the struggle.[31]

A much more divisive debate took place in the Liberal Party Council in December 1936, over the publication of a policy statement entitled *Peace or War?* Issued by the Council's executive early in December to coincide with a pro-collective security meeting held at the Albert Hall, this received extensive coverage in the Liberal press. It put forward three policies: the restoration of confidence in the League as a means of providing security and redressing grievances; the revival of trade through the removal of tariff barriers; and the reduction of armaments. It was explicitly stated that the League must consider using armed force if sanctions did not work, and this led to Lord Lothian's protest against the document at the Liberal Party Council meeting on 16 December. He believed that the party should support the League and only the League, and claimed that the alternative on offer would lead to a revival of the kind of alliance system that the League was meant to replace. There was a fierce dispute in the Council, with Lothian being supported most prominently by F.W. Hirst. The document as published was supported by Margery Corbett Ashby, Ramsay Muir and Harcourt Johnstone among others. Muir said that Lothian's arguments amounted to criticisms of the basis of the League, and the pamphlet was supported overwhelmingly by the Council.[32]

Economics was an increasingly important part of Liberal international policy, and at the 1937 Assembly this expressed itself in a resolution putting forward specific economic issues which needed to be settled (see Appendix 4). These were highlighted as 'the control of colonial territories, the distribution of raw materials, the stabilisation of exchanges and the accessibility of markets'. Ramsay Muir proposed this resolution, and it represented the fruition of some of the ideas put forward at the summer school, and in the work of Layton and Muir. In addition to this, Leonard Behrens of Manchester Withington put forward an amendment saying that the possession of armaments 'adequate for collective defence against aggression' was essential. The amendment recognised, though, that all League members must make it clear that they would only be used in support of the Covenant. This amendment, accepted by Muir, re-emphasised the Liberal commitment to collective security as a major plank of international policy.[33]

COLLECTIVE SECURITY THROUGH ALLIANCES, 1938–39

By the time the Assembly met again in June 1938, Hitler had brought about a German *Anschluss* with Austria. Also, the British government had made (in April 1938, operating from November following some Italian withdrawals from Spain) an agreement with Italy recognising Italian control of Abyssinia. Following these events, Liberals now recognised that the League had no credible way of imposing sanctions on aggressors. So the Assembly toughened the military side of its collective security policy, when Muir again proposed the foreign policy resolution (see Appendix 4). This openly stated that 'our security and the defence of freedom' required 'an expansion of British armaments'. This was coupled, however, with a statement that Britain should declare itself willing to join 'an open discussion' with other countries aimed at removing grievances that might lead to war. The resolution also focused on Spain, saying that the policy of non-intervention in the civil war had failed, and so the Spanish government should be allowed to purchase arms with which to defend itself. As with the previous year, this part of the resolution resulted from an amendment by Leonard Behrens, which was accepted by Muir. The only major opponent to the resolution was F.W. Hirst. He argued that the resolution as a whole favoured a preventive war. This was effectively the view he had put forward with Lothian at the December 1936 Liberal Party Council meeting, and it shows a clear division within Liberal ranks, between those who saw the military aspect of collective security as being as important as the negotiatory side. Though a clear division, it did not signify a split within the Liberal Party, which was overwhelmingly in favour of the view put by Muir.[34]

In the summer of 1938, events moved so quickly that there was obviously little that the Assembly could do in terms of formulating policy. Instead the task fell to the Executive of the Liberal Party Organisation, which rubber-stamped the view put by Archibald Sinclair in the House of Commons (see below, p. 127). This condemned government policy, arguing that Czechoslovakia had been betrayed, and that Germany now had the dominant position in central Europe. Instead of continuing appeasement, the Executive called for the formation of a new government, in which the Liberal Party would cooperate with other parties. This government would remedy grievances through an international conference, and bring about economic disarmament through the removal of tariff barriers.[35]

The Assembly held its last peacetime meeting in May 1939 at Scarborough, and when it met the situation was ominous. Hitler had invaded Czechoslovakia, and war looked almost inevitable. As a result, although the Assembly reaffirmed its policy of collective security, and called for an agreement with the Soviet Union, the main focus was on preparations for war. As one might expect, given the Liberal experience in the First World War, the key issue was conscription. Would the Liberal Party this time support compulsion? A resolution on compulsory 'National Service' was proposed by Archibald Sinclair, the Liberal leader. Sinclair's involvement was in itself a sign of the importance of the issue. This resolution proposed to support the government's decision to introduce conscription; it was phrased to suggest that Liberals were doing this so as to preserve 'national unity', and to show that Britain was resolved to resist aggression. An amendment from the floor against conscription was discussed: this was proposed by E.F. Allison and Willoughby Dewar, who argued that it violated individual liberty, and that, in any case, volunteer armies were always more effective that conscripted ones. The anti-conscription amendment was defeated by an overwhelming majority, and two smaller amendments were adopted: one from Frank Byers, to insert the word 'reluctantly' into the section accepting conscription, and another from Leonard Behrens, calling for effective provisions for conscientious objectors.[36] Thus ended a potentially damaging debate for the Liberal Party, which entered the Second World War far more united than it had left the First World War.

WOMEN IN THE LIBERAL PARTY

Although there were many prominent women speakers at the NLF and Assembly meetings, women in the Liberal Party also had their own separate forum, in which they could discuss issues and make policy: the Women's National Liberal Federation (WNLF, or WLF from 1936, when the word 'National' was dropped). Perhaps rather strangely, men sometimes also spoke, not just as guest speakers, but in debates: for example, Gilbert Murray moved a resolution on disarmament in 1924, on behalf of the Oxford Women's Liberal Association. However, the vast majority of speakers were women, and the meetings were attended by a large number of delegates: the *Manchester Guardian* noted that there were more than 700 attending in 1923. This was then the largest number ever, with the figure rising to 1,000 in 1924. Attendance was still at 800 in 1935.[37] On many occasions, the WNLF discussed topics in which women were said to have a particular interest. These included divorce law, housing and domestic service. However, the WNLF also discussed more general political issues, and international policy was high on the agenda of most meetings.

On some occasions, as at the NLF, these international policy resolutions were of the 'this conference condemns' or 'this conference welcomes' variety. So, for example, at the May 1923 WNLF, there was a condemnation of the Ruhr occupation; in March 1929, the WNLF deplored the government's failure to sign the Optional Clause; and in June 1936, the WLF said that all countries should refuse to recognise Italy's annexation of Abyssinia.[38] However, the WNLF did discuss many issues in detail, often paying closer attention to specific points of international policy than the wider party. Examples of this were seen in May 1938 and May 1939, when the WLF called for the government to pay more attention to civil defence, believing that with the threat of war, existing measures were inadequate.[39]

Often the WNLF passed resolutions similar to those passed by the NLF as a whole. For example, in May 1933, the WNLF proposed a limit to the number and weight of tanks, a limit to the weight of aircraft, the abolition of military and naval aviation, and the international control of civil aviation.[40] Much of this had been passed by the NLF a year earlier. But aside from repeating resolutions, the WNLF was often more ahead of the game than the party as a whole. In May 1934, the WNLF went considerably further than the NLF when it voted to support the creation of an international air force, while the NLF only agreed to consider the idea. In the same year, the WNLF voted to prohibit the private manufacture of arms, which the NLF did not adopt until a year later, although the parliamentary party had already taken initiatives on the issue.[41] The WLF similarly pre-empted the Assembly in October 1937, when it passed a resolution saying that non-intervention in Spain had failed, and so the Spanish government should be allowed to buy weapons with which to defend itself. The Assembly did not take this view until 1938, though admittedly this was partly because the Assembly did not next meet until then.[42]

The leading figures in these debates were: Margery Corbett Ashby (a substitute delegate for the United Kingdom at the disarmament conference in 1932–35, and a Liberal candidate at eight elections); Violet Bonham Carter (daughter of Asquith and a leading Liberal politician in the inter-war years, who was the first woman to be president of the Liberal Party Organisation in 1943–47); Megan Lloyd George (daughter of Lloyd George and Liberal MP for Anglesey in 1929–51, and subsequently a Labour MP in 1957–66); and Aline Mackinnon (a Liberal candidate in Holderness throughout the 1930s). Another prominent figure was F.L. Josephy (a leading Young Liberal and a candidate at various elections from 1929 to 1951), who in October 1937 put forward the most radical international resolution the WLF considered in this period, favouring international control of colonies. A major reason for doing this, Josephy argued, was that even if this did not satisfy Hitler, it would show the German people that they had true equality with the imperial powers, who would no longer have any colonies. However, Megan Lloyd George felt Hitler's position to be crucial, and wanted the resolution referred back, while a number of other delegates saw grave problems with the proposal. They asked who would defend colonies if they were attacked, and they were also concerned about the wishes of native peoples, which was not addressed in the resolution. In the face of this hostility, the resolution was rejected, but it was still an important debate. As the *Manchester Guardian* commented, it was 'the first time a nationally representative Liberal body or, indeed, a nationally representative body of any party was asked to endorse the principle of international administration of non-self-governing colonies'.[43] The idea was not discussed again by the WLF, but it was to be adopted by the Liberal Party as a whole in 1942. The fact that the WLF had already discussed the idea meant that Liberals were well aware of the idea for some time before this, and it shows that the WLF had a clear role within the Liberal Party as a source of radical ideas.

CONCLUSION

Neither the Assembly nor the WLF held an annual meeting in 1940. The Assembly next met in July 1941. Even by this stage of the war, with the United States still outside the conflict, and the Soviet Union having only recently entered, the Assembly was talking about what would happen after the war was over. Vague resolutions calling for the restoration of international free trade were passed, but in September 1942 a more detailed resolution was adopted. The war seemed to have had a radicalising effect on the party's international policy, for the policy went much further on key issues than the Assembly had ever done before. The party remained committed to an international body to keep the peace; it was firmly in favour of there being an international police force; and of international control of aviation – though in both cases it offered few specific suggestions. The party also continued to support establishing stable rates of exchange. However, it added a provision for state control of armaments, and also said that employment rates should be maintained at a high level through the adjustment of investment rates by the same body that was to maintain currency stability. Most importantly, Liberals had firmly broken with empire, and advocated international supervision of all colonies, accompanied by preparation for self-government.[44]

The NLF had similarly taken definite positions on international policy throughout the inter-war period. In the first phase of policy, the 1918–31 period, Liberal policy had been marked by an unequivocal commitment to the League and disarmament. Disarmament became a particular concern from 1928, following the Geneva Naval Conference and the Anglo-French naval compromise. From 1930, the NLF also began to see economics as an important aspect of international policy, and consistently hoisted the flag of free trade in the face of creeping protectionism. However, the real change in Liberal international policy came in 1932, after the Japanese attack on Manchuria, when Liberals began to see 'collective security' as the way forward – this represented a second phase of policy. Collective security was coupled with a policy of encouraging free trade throughout the world, and meant strengthening the grievances procedures of the League, to make it clear that all just complaints would be settled fairly. But it also meant making it clear to all potential aggressors that aggression would not be tolerated, however just a nation's grievances might be. From 1938, that meant pursuing cooperation with nations outside the failed League. This was opposed by some Liberals, such as Lothian and Hirst, who feared that it would revive a system of European alliances, though the bulk of the party accepted it. This idea of collective security through alliances represented a clear alternative to appeasement. With the NLF and Assembly having provided a clear policy, it was now down to the Liberal leaders to articulate this view in parliament, and to try to impress the validity of the policy on the country as a whole.

NOTES

1. In 1922, a limit of ten delegates from each constituency had been unsuccessfully proposed by the NLF Executive. *NLF, 1922*, pp. 45–6. *NLF, 1923*, pp. 6–9, 16–17, 30–3.
2. *Constitution of the Liberal Party* (London: LPD, 1936).
3. *DN*, 15 May 1925, p. 8. *NC*, 28 Apr. 1932, p. 2. *NC*, 3 May 1934, p. 2. *MG*, 19 June 1936, p. 6. *NC*, 20 May 1938, p. 13. Numbers fell to 1,000 again in 1938.
4. *DN*, 26 Nov. 1920, p. 1. *NLF, 1926*, pp. 41–3. *NLF, 1928*, pp. 49–53. *NC*, 4 May 1934,

p. 9. *NC*, 27 May 1937, p. 19.
5. *NLF, 1918*, pp. 18–31. *DN*, 27 Sept. 1918, p. 5. *MG*, 27 Sept. 1918, p. 6.
6. *NLF, 1919*, pp. 50–9. *MG*, 28 Nov. 1919, p. 6.
7. *NLF, 1920*, pp. 61–2.
8. *NLF, 1922*, pp. 39–45.
9. *NLF, 1923*, pp. 17–18.
10. *NLF, 1920*, pp. 61–2. *MG*, 27 Nov. 1920, p. 12. *NLF, 1921*, pp. 39–40.
11. *NLF, 1923*, pp. 46–7. *DN*, 1 June 1923, p. 3. *MG*, 1 June 1923, p. 12.
12. *NLF, 1924*, pp. 60–1. *NLF, 1925*, pp. 37–8. *NLF, 1926*, pp. 48–9.
13. *NLF, 1927*, pp. 34–6.
14. 'Liberal Principles and Aims' (London: LPD, 1925), in LPD, *Pamphlets & Leaflets, 1925* (London: LPD, 1926). *LM*, XXXII, 375 (Dec. 1924), pp. 726–7. *DN*, 30 & 31 Jan. 1925, pp. 1, 3.
15. *MG*, 19 June 1926, p. 9. *DC*, 19 June 1926, p. 3. Richard S. Grayson, *Austen Chamberlain and the Commitment to Europe: British Foreign Policy, 1924–29* (London: Frank Cass, 1997), pp. 86–94.
16. *NLF, 1921*, pp. 39–40. *DN*, 25 Nov. 1921, p. 3. *MG*, 25 Nov. 1921, p. 11. *DC*, 25 Nov. 1921, p. 9. *WG*, 25 Nov. 1921, p. 1.
17. 'When Armaments Decrease Wars Will Cease', 'Peace in Our Time', and C.J.L. Brock, 'Peace and Disarmament', in, LPD, *Pamphlets & Leaflets, 1928* (London: LPD, 1929).
18. *NLF, 1928*, pp. 18–23. *MG*, 12 Oct. 1928, p. 10.
19. *Forward View*, I, 11 (Nov. 1927), pp. 168–9. Leonard F. Behrens, 'Liberal Foreign Policy: The Four Points', *Forward View*, I, 12 (Dec. 1927), pp. 187–8.
20. Stuart Ball, *Baldwin and the Conservative Party: The Crisis of 1929–1931* (New Haven, CT: Yale University Press, 1988), pp. 46–63.
21. *NLF, 1930*, pp. 19–31. *MG*, 17 Oct. 1930, p. 14.
22. *NLF, 1931*, pp. 17–21.
23. *NLF, 1932*, pp. 78–82.
24. *Liberal Magazine*, XL, 464 (May 1932), pp. 233–6.
25. *NLF, 1933*, pp. 32–3. *MG*, 19 May 1933, p. 6. *NC*, 19 May 1933, p. 2.
26. No justification of the executive's opposition to the amendment is given in any of the accounts, but it is clear that it would have violated the principle of collective security, and this is likely to have been the reason.
27. *NLF, 1934*, pp. 56–60.
28. *MG*, 22 May 1935, p. 12. *NC*, 22 May 1935, pp. 1, 5, 15.
29. *NLF, 1935*, pp. 41–7.
30. *LM*, XLIV, 514 (July 1936), pp. 193–200. *MG*, 20 June 1936, p. 18.
31. *MG*, 17 Sept. 1936, p. 11. *LM*, XLV, 525 (June 1937), pp. 254–61. Tom Buchanan, *Britain and the Spanish Civil War* (Cambridge: Cambridge University Press, 1997), p. 85.
32. 'Peace or War?', *LM*, XLIV, 519 (Dec. 1936), pp. 362–6. *MG*, 3 Dec. 1936, p. 5. *NC*, 3 Dec. 1936, p. 15. *MG*, 4 Dec. 1936, p. 10. *MG*, 17 Dec. 1936, p. 12. *NC*, 17 Dec. 1936, p. 13.
33. *LM*, XLV, 525 (June 1937), pp. 254–61. *MG*, 29 May 1937, p. 15.
34. *LM*, XLVI, 537 (June 1938), pp. 266–7. *NC*, 20 May 1938, pp. 5, 13.
35. *MG*, 19 Oct. 1938, p. 9; *NC*, 19 Oct. 1938, p. 2.
36. *LM*, XLVII, 549 (June 1939), pp. 257–64. *NC*, 13 May 1939, p. 15. *MG*, 13 May 1939, p. 16.
37. *MG*, 9 May 1923, p. 10. *DN*, 28 May 1924, p. 3. *MG*, 22 May 1935, p. 18.
38. *LM*, XXXI, 357 (June 1923), p. 327. *LM*, XXXVII, 427 (Apr. 1929), pp. 249–51. *LM*, XLIV, 514 (July 1936), pp. 210–11.
39. *LM*, XLVI, 537 (June 1938), pp. 283–5. *NC*, 18 May 1938, p. 17. *LM*, XLVII, 549 (June 1939), pp. 273–7. *NC*, 10 May 1939, p. 14.
40. *LM*, XLI, 477 (June 1933), pp. 283–5.
41. *LM*, XLII, 488 (May 1934), p. 213. *MG*, 2 May 1934, p. 17. *LM*, XLIII, 501 (June 1935),

pp. 307–9. *MG*, 22 May 1935, p. 18.
42. *MG*, 13 Oct. 1937, p. 13. *NC*, 13 Oct. 1937, p. 13.
43. *MG*, 13 Oct. 1937, p. 13. *NC*, 13 Oct. 1937, p. 13.
44. *LM*, XLVIII, 558 (May–June 1940), p. 234. *LM*, XLIX, 565 (July–Aug. 1941), p. 231. *LM*, L, 571 (July–Sept. 1942), p. 196.

The Official Liberal Party: Liberals in Parliament

W E HAVE SEEN thus far that the Liberal Party was thriving in the 1920s and 1930s in terms of discussions on international policy. In order to make a real impact on British foreign policy though, and to achieve wider publicity in the country, these ideas would have to be articulated by Liberals in parliament. This chapter looks at how the nation's leading Liberal politicians dealt with international policy. It begins by looking at Asquith's leadership of the party, and then others who might have provided an alternative to him – Grey, Cecil and the Radical Group. It moves on to give close consideration to the importance of Lloyd George in the 1920s and the 1930s, and then examines the problems faced by the party under the leadership of first Herbert Samuel, and then Archibald Sinclair, in the 1930s. It will be argued that all of these leaders had problems defining a Liberal international policy, until Archibald Sinclair, and that even then, Sinclair's hostility to cooperation with other parties, meant that the party's potential for influence was greatly reduced.

H.H. ASQUITH AND THE 'CLEAN PEACE'

At the start of this period, the Liberal leader was formally and spiritually Herbert Henry Asquith, who had led the party since April 1908. However, he was not Liberal leader in practice because he lost his seat at the 1918 general election, and did not return to parliament until his success in the Paisley by-election of February 1920, during which time some in the parliamentary party had wanted him to step aside as leader.[1] He did not do so, retaining the support of the party in the country as a whole, but for nearly a year and a half the Liberals were led in the House of Commons by Donald Maclean. Maclean was particularly vocal in urging that Britain should discontinue its intervention in the Russian civil war.[2] However, Maclean's influence on Liberal international policy, and policy more generally, was minimal, and the Liberals in the Commons who did not support Lloyd George's Coalition saw themselves as Asquithian Liberals, not Maclean Liberals. It was still Asquith they looked to for a lead. As we shall see, aside from the idea of a 'Clean Peace', the lead he provided amounted to little else.

International policy, of course, had been the major reason for Asquith's downfall as prime minister in 1916. Though he had been part of the 'Liberal Imperialist' grouping during the Boer War, he was essentially one of the more radical Liberals, and had been a leading social reformer as Campbell Bannerman's chancellor of the exchequer in 1905–08. As prime minister, in 1908–16, he continued to lead an extremely progressive government, which laid the foundations of the modern welfare state. However, Asquith had a bad war. In May 1915, in the face of munitions shortages, he constructed a coalition with the Conservatives in order to pursue the war more vigorously. This coalition lasted until the end of 1916, when Asquith resigned in the face of demands from colleagues that he should establish a war committee to coordinate Britain's war effort, but that he should have no role in running it. Having left office, Asquith adopted a position towards the Lloyd George government which has been described by one biographer as 'benevolent neutrality'.[3] Finding himself out of parliament in 1918–20, and again after 1924, Asquith was not in an ideal position to direct Liberal criticisms of government international policy; often, as we shall see in the next section, this task fell to others. His influence was felt, however, in his advocacy of a 'Clean Peace', and one cannot understand Liberal international policy in the early 1920s without some sense of the importance of this idea.

Asquith's Clean Peace speech was delivered at a meeting of the cross-party War Aims Committee in Birmingham, on 11 December 1917. Asquith was keen to point out that Britain did not intend to destroy Germany, and did not have any ambition to dismember the country. However, this could only remain the case if the German people showed that they 'are as ready as we are to set up the rule of Common and Equal Right, as not only technically sovereign, but as, in fact, by means of appropriate and effective sanctions, the controlling authority in the world'. If this was done, then there should be a 'Clean Peace'. By this he meant that it would not be acceptable merely if arms were laid down, with a 'veiled war' continuing 'by other methods'.[4] He did not specify what this meant, but it was clear that this could include excessive reparations, a harsh territorial settlement which undermined German sovereignty, or the failure to establish a League of Nations as a way of solving future grievances. This 'Clean Peace' message was widely reported, not only in the Liberal press, and it lay at the heart of Asquith's message in future years. It also bore some similarities to the peace terms put forward by the Union of Democratic Control, although it used far more bellicose language than the UDC would ever have done. In talking of the need to destroy 'Prussian militarism', Asquith continued an important theme of his approach while prime minister and was also at one with the 'knock-out blow' that underpinned Lloyd George's policy.[5] He soon expanded on the message, less than two weeks later, in the House of Commons, when he said that the UK needed to counteract German propaganda which had suggested that the allies were fighting for 'Plutocracy and Imperialism'. Instead, Britain needed to show that it stood for 'real security for liberty and justice in the world as a whole, through a free confederation of both great and small States'. For Asquith, this meant a League of Nations.[6] He again developed the 'Clean Peace' theme a year later at the National Liberal Federation, defining it as

> a peace which attains for the world the objects for which we have been fighting, which is clean in the sense that it cleans the slate, and clean also in another and higher sense, that … it does not offend the conscience either of the victor or of mankind.[7]

The second half of what Winston Churchill called the 'Moral of the Work' in his *The Second World War, Vol. 1* (1948), springs to mind as a later example of this attitude: 'In Victory: Magnanimity. In Peace: Goodwill.'

None of Asquith's fine words, though, meant that the Parliamentary Liberal Party opposed the Treaty of Versailles. As we saw earlier, Asquith had not held his seat in 1918, but he still exerted influence over the party as its leader, and did not disagree with the support given by Maclean to Lloyd George in the July 1919 debate on Versailles. In this, Maclean praised Lloyd George, supported reparations and supported a trial of the Kaiser. His only adverse comment was to say that he wished the exact level of reparations had already been fixed.[8] It was in this attitude that the impact of the 'Clean Peace' theme was seen: as the logic of *The Economic Consequences of the Peace* was about to imply (see Chapter 2), high levels of reparations effectively represented a continuation of war against Germany. Asquith and the Liberals argued that these should be fixed at a definite level, and lowered, as soon as possible. After his success at Paisley, Asquith made this the theme of his foreign policy in a number of speeches in parliament and elsewhere.[9] In particular, on 19 May 1922 at the National Liberal Federation, and in the Commons on 25 May, he spoke of the need for the UK to make concessions on the amount of money it was to receive, a view which was soon to be endorsed by Keynes.[10]

This much was clear – reparations must be reduced, and Britain might have to make concessions to help bring about a settlement. This was a definite Liberal policy, and it was well known that the party stood for it. However, two questions need to be asked about this policy: first, was it really very different to the policy that was already being pursued by the Lloyd George Coalition? Lloyd George, of course, has been blamed for the harshness of the Versailles settlement, but it is also now accepted that he set about revising it almost as soon as he arrived home from signing the treaty. This meant, as the *Manchester Guardian* commented in response to one of Asquith's May 1922 speeches, that the Liberal Party was saying very little that was new:

> WE like very well MR. ASQUITH's proposals for dealing with the outstanding questions between Germany and France. MR. LLOYD GEORGE also will like them. They represent the very objects he has in view and for which he has been labouring.[11]

The *Manchester Guardian* was far from being a friend to Lloyd George, and its comments on Asquith are damning.

The second question that needs to be answered about Asquith's international policy was how far he had thought beyond reparations? In the first instance, up until early 1923 he spoke of little else, other than regarding a general commitment to the League. However, from this time (especially after the Ruhr occupation) he started to link reparations to French security and disarmament, saying that all 'three interlocked problems' needed to be settled by the League.[12] To tackle these problems, Asquith called for the League 'to devise a pact of defence between its constituent members which will secure France'.[13] However, he never went beyond anything more specific than this, and it would be an exaggeration to say that Asquith had developed a definite plan for a security pact.[14]

In addition to having no plan for a pact, Asquith was also quiet on the Empire, despite his origins as a Liberal Imperialist. Few of his speeches tackled imperial issues, probably because there were few issues on which the Liberal Party could take a distinctive position. As we saw earlier (see above, p. 13), Liberals supported moves towards self-government within the Empire in India under the Montagu–Chelmsford Reforms of 1918, and there was little else that was pressing in the early 1920s. This quiescence on empire was accompanied by a lack of speech-making on foreign policy outside parliament. Most of his speeches reported in the *Annual Register* show that Asquith was primarily concerned with two old Liberal rallying cries – free trade, and economy in expenditure: in June 1919, he gave a major speech on free trade, and in October of that year, he focused on the economies necessary in Britain as a result of war debts. He repeated this at the Paisley by-election, at the start of the campaign in late January 1920, and he also spoke regularly on Ireland, as Home Rule once again became a burning issue in 1920.[15]

Aside from his strong interest in domestic issues, Asquith was also unable to take a lead on foreign affairs because, in the November 1924 election, he again lost his seat. Though he formally led the party until October 1926 (from early 1925 from the House of Lords as the Earl of

Oxford and Asquith), leadership in the Commons passed to Lloyd George, who led the Liberal response to, for example, the Treaty of Locarno in 1925.[16] Asquith was probably more occupied with trying (unsuccessfully) to secure his election as chancellor of Oxford University.[17] He died in 1928.

ALTERNATIVE LEADERS: GREY, CECIL AND THE RADICAL GROUP

Asquith's position as a formulator or leader of Liberal international policy was not helped by the fact that many Liberals saw two other figures as being more authoritative on foreign policy: Viscount Grey of Falloden, and Lord Robert Cecil – who was not even a Liberal.

Grey had unrivalled experience as foreign secretary in 1905–16. Despite some criticisms from Radicals over his alleged 'secret diplomacy' (p. 6), he retained the respect of the mainstream in British politics, and Liberals often looked to him more than to Asquith for a Liberal view on foreign policy. A key example of this was seen during the Chanak Crisis of September 1922, when Grey wrote to *The Times* saying that Lloyd George was wrong to have pursued a policy separate from France. Great authority was attached to Grey's statement by Conservative and Liberal papers alike, and he was supported by *The Morning Post*, *Daily News*, *Westminster Gazette* and *Manchester Guardian*, as well as *The Times*.[18] This marked a significant moment for Grey – he had been largely inactive in politics since 1916, other than as an advocate of the League of Nations.

Along with Gilbert Murray, Grey was the leading Liberal supporter of the League. He was the figurehead of the first booklet to appear arguing the case for the League, and produced a chapter in it himself. In it, he argued that the League could work if two conditions were met. The first was that all nations must join and place the League at the heart of their foreign policy. The second was that all must accept some limitations on their actions, and some obligations. A crucial limitation was that nations would give up aggressive action as a way of imposing one's will on peaceful nations, in the sure knowledge that if they did not, 'the other nations must one and all use their combined force against it'. That force might be economic, but he recognised that 'those States that have power must be ready to use all the force, economic, military, or naval, that they possess'.[19]

A number of attempts had been made to persuade Grey to re-enter politics in 1920–21, especially by Asquith, but Grey's failing eyesight meant that he was not attracted to the idea.[20] Later, he was president of the Liberal Council, an Asquithian faction within the Liberal Party, formed when Lloyd George became leader in 1926, and which aimed to persuade Liberals that 'true Liberalism' remained alive in the party, despite Lloyd George's leadership. The Council focused on traditional Liberal concerns such as free trade and economy, rather than taking distinctive positions on international policy.[21] Though he was persuaded to lead the Liberal Party in the Lords in 1923–24, he took no other formal party role. Unlike Asquith, he was successfully elected as chancellor of Oxford University, an office he held from 1928 until his death in 1933. Grey's publication of a book on *The Charm of Birds* in 1927, also reflected his desire to explore life outside politics in the 1920s.

A more unlikely source of Liberal leadership was Lord Robert Cecil. Cecil, though a Conservative, was a maverick. He had resigned from the Cabinet in November 1918 protesting against the disestablishment of the Welsh Church (a long-standing Liberal aim), but was almost immediately given a role within the League of Nations section of the Foreign Office, and played a leading part in the establishment of the League. That was a difficult task, made more complicated by the fact that the Foreign Office was fighting a turf war against a separate League Secretariat based in the Cabinet Office, over the control of League policy, which was eventually resolved in the Foreign Office's favour only in 1922. Meanwhile, as chairman of the League of Nations Union's Executive, Cecil endeared himself to many Liberals, and as we saw earlier (see above, p. 60), was a prominent speaker at the Liberal Summer School. Though he refused to become a Liberal formally, he did hold discussions in 1921 with Asquith, Grey, Maclean and other senior Liberals, over the possibility of participating in a centrist coalition. Cecil wanted Grey to lead this, partly because, according to Walter Runciman, Cecil 'apparently does not think highly of Asquith'. However, this foundered when Grey refused to lead such a new coalition, and Cecil drifted away from the Liberals.[22] By May 1923, he was sufficiently back in favour with Conservatives for Baldwin to appoint him as lord privy seal with a special responsibility for the League, and he served under Baldwin again in 1924–27. Nevertheless, Cecil was significant for the Liberals, because he enthusiastically promoted the League of Nations in Britain, making it the foundation of his view of international affairs. This he did far more effectively than Asquith.

While Grey and Cecil undermined Asquith simply by being more prominent than him in debates on international policies, some Liberal MPs expressed their frustration over the Liberal leadership by forming a 'Radical Group' in the House of Commons in 1924. This, however, was not a challenge to Asquith – far from it. The Radical Group existed because Asquith was not in parliament, and Lloyd George became chair of the Parliamentary Liberal Party in his absence. The Radical Group believed Lloyd George to be unreliable, and unlikely to pursue 'radical' policies.

The group was formed in December 1924, partly out of radical discontent over Lloyd George becoming chairman of the Parliamentary Liberal Party. However, the final catalyst was a meeting of the parliamentary party, in which Radical MPs tried to persuade the party to declare that it was definitely in opposition to Baldwin's government. They urged a statement that while prepared to 'support any proposals conducive to social reform and international peace', the Liberal Party 'declares itself definitely to be in Parliamentary opposition'. This was rejected in favour of a motion simply saying that the party would act as a 'Liberal Opposition, opposing 'every motion or measure against Liberal principles'. This was not enough for the Radicals, and 11 Liberal MPs publicly announced the formation of a Radical Group: Walter Runciman, William Wedgwood Benn, Frank Briant, Percy Harris, J.M. Kenworthy, MacKenzie Livingstone, Trevelyan Thomson, George Thorne, H.E. Crawfurd, T.D. Fenby and Hopkin Morris.[23] Godfrey Collins also later worked with the group.[24] Recalling their aims, Wedgwood Benn said that,

> The parliamentary Radical group was formed for two reasons:
>   First, and chiefly, to present and pursue unfettered a Radical policy in the House of Commons;
>   Secondly, to secure freedom to act, when necessary, independently of Mr Lloyd George, whose leadership we mistrusted.[25]

According to the *Manchester Guardian*, the group said that if the official Liberal Party did not adopt radical proposals in parliament, it would adopt an independent stance without leaving the party.[26]

The group produced regular private reports on its activities, which largely related to the organisation of a Radical presence in parliament for major debates and votes.[27] On international policy this meant taking distinctive positions on a number of key issues, in particular, pressing the government to bring forward disarmament proposals.[28] The Radical Group was also active outside parliament, especially through giving speeches to groups of other Liberals. Perhaps unsurprisingly, a particular Radical line in these speeches was to urge support for the League of Nations. In a speech in Manchester in December 1924, Runciman said that Britain's problems in the Sudan (which it was running as a joint Anglo-Egyptian 'condominium' as part of its strategy of defending Egypt's border) could be solved by trying to obtain a League mandate for the country. That would also demonstrate the UK's commitment to the League. A month later, Kenworthy told a meeting at the National Liberal Club that Liberals must, above all, be internationalists, to remove the threat of nationalism from the world, and to uphold the principle of public law in international affairs.[29]

In its early stages, the group had been looked upon favourably by the pro-Asquith *Daily News*, which commented that its members 'combine a great deal of Parliamentary talent, and it is probable that they will prove to be lively pace-makers for the rest of the party in the House'.[30] But by the middle of 1925, the newspaper was more comfortable with Lloyd George's role in the Liberal Party, and had ceased to cover Radical Group activities. Meanwhile, although the *Manchester Guardian* gave substantial coverage to the group in its early stages, it too took little notice of it within a few months of its formation. By the end of 1925, many of the Radicals were drifting towards Labour. As early as December 1925, Benn made note in his diary of 'the growing friendliness' towards the Radical Group from the Labour Party.[31] When Asquith was elevated to the Lords in late 1926, and Lloyd George replaced him as Liberal leader, there was little to keep the Radicals in the Liberal Party. In January 1927, Benn resigned from the party to support Labour instead, formally joining the Labour Party in March of that year. The *Daily News* commented that Benn could not preserve Liberalism in the Labour Party, as his 'new allies ... are as deadly enemies of real liberty as the most hardened Tory reactionaries'.[32] Benn was probably not particularly concerned about this, as he told his constituency party president that he had left partly because Lloyd George was now formally leader of the party, but also because 'for some time I have questioned the truth of an economic outlook based upon a theory of private enterprise and free competition'.[33] Earlier, in October 1926, Kenworthy had joined Labour. Three of the group's members lost their seats in 1929 (Briant, Crawfurd and Fenby). Thomson died in 1928. Thorne and Livingstone retired in 1929, though the latter joined Labour a year later. Morris retired in 1932, on becoming a Metropolitan Police Magistrate, though he was again a Liberal MP in 1945–56. In the face of national crisis, Runciman and Collins became National Liberals in 1931. Only Percy Harris, who was the Liberal chief whip in 1935–45, remained a Liberal MP throughout the 1930s. But the Radical Group had ground to a halt by 1927, deprived of Benn and Kenworthy, two of its most important members. It did little to preserve Radical Liberalism, though it had done much to ease the passage of Liberals into the Labour Party. Ironically, though the Radicals despised Lloyd George for going in with the Conservatives in 1916–22, his *Yellow Book* probably did more for the Radical cause than they did.

DAVID LLOYD GEORGE

The most prominent Liberal during the inter-war years was David Lloyd George. Certainly, no other Liberal wielded more power than Lloyd George in this period, even if his term of office as prime minister in 1916–22 was as the head of a Tory-dominated coalition. He was also leader of the Liberal Party in the House of Commons in 1926–31; and in 1924–25, with Asquith out of parliament, Lloyd George effectively led the party in those years too. In the 1930s, though, he drifted away from the Liberal Party, standing as an Independent Liberal in 1935 and supporting Labour candidates in many constituencies when no Liberal stood. However, with his undoubted experience in foreign affairs as prime minister, the voice of Lloyd George was still one to be listened to by Liberals and non-Liberals alike. As we shall see, however, Lloyd George did not manage (or even particularly try) to develop a Liberal Party alternative to government policies in the 1930s.

Liberals, justifiably, might have had high hopes of Lloyd George in 1918, as he prepared to attend the Paris Peace Conference. At first, it seemed as if he might be a Liberal voice at the conference. Lloyd George put his views forward at a meeting of Liberals MPs in 10 Downing Street on 12 November 1918. He pledged that there would be no revenge peace, using the harsh settlement that Germany had imposed on France in 1871 as a warning.[34] However, only a few weeks later, such sentiments were swept aside in the fervour of the 1918 general election campaign. Lloyd George's coalition allies, the Conservatives, had sensed what people wanted, calling for a settlement which would punish Germany in general, and the kaiser personally. Lloyd George's slogans soon included 'Punish the Kaiser', and 'Make Germany Pay'.[35] He later complained that he had never used the popular slogan 'Hang the Kaiser',[36] but he had come very close. At the Paris Peace Conference (the results of which were embodied in the Treaty of Versailles), Britain and France enforced harsh penalties on Germany – penalties which many, most notably Keynes in his *The Economic Consequences of the Peace*, had warned could not be afforded by Germany, and would eventually lead to another conflict. To be fair to Lloyd George, he had supported plans to postpone the fixing of Germany's exact reparations liabilities, in the belief that in more settled times more generous terms could be given to the Germans. He was also less harsh on territorial issues, in particular, opposing permanent detachment of the Rhineland from Germany.[37] However, when he returned to Britain to justify Versailles, he was still using the language of punishment. Despite telling the House of Commons in April 1919: 'We want a peace which will be just, but not vindictive', he added, 'We want a stern peace, because the occasion demands it. The crime demands it.' Later, in July, he commented, 'The terms are in many respects terrible terms to impose upon a country. Terrible were the deeds which it requites.'[38] Understandably then, Lloyd George's pandering to domestic political pressures demanding revenge has been severely criticised by some historians.[39]

On the surface, it appears that Lloyd George maintained an illiberal position in aspects of his foreign policy for the rest of his term of office.

Intervention in Russia was one particular issue, but in fact, Lloyd George was held hostage on that issue by hotter heads in his Cabinet, such as Winston Churchill. In 1918, British and other allied troops had intervened in Russia to assist the White Russians against the Bolsheviks, in order to keep Russia in the war; by 1919, with the war over, British troops were still there, scattered throughout Russia, but now seen by some as fighting the battle of democracy against Bolshevism. Churchill's view of this, as he described it in March 1920, was 'Peace with the German people, war on the Bolshevik tyranny.'[40] Others in Cabinet took the same view, and it was difficult for Lloyd George to withdraw troops. That he wanted to is certain. His own view was that 'Russia must save herself.' Though he was far from being a supporter of Bolshevism, he believed that if Russia was 'saved by outside intervention she is not really saved. That kind of parasitic liberty is a sham.'[41] By the end of 1919, Lloyd George had persuaded the Cabinet that this view was correct, and British troops had withdrawn. In March 1921, real progress in Anglo-Soviet relations was marked by the signature of a trade treaty.

It was this policy towards Russia that represented his post-war position more than that of the Paris Peace Conference. Even on Germany, as soon as he had returned home from Paris, he set about trying to lessen the effects of the peace settlement on the German people, particularly by aiming to set a lower level of reparations for Germany, often linked to unresolved questions of French security. His first attempt to do this was at the San Remo Conference in April 1920, and at a series of conferences in 1920 (Boulogne in June, Spa in July and Brussels in December), 1921 (London in March) and 1922 (Cannes in January, and Genoa in April), he tried, with some success, to modify French demands.[42] These essentially remained a problem until the Dawes Plan of 1924 made significant progress, but Lloyd George was certainly pursuing a more Liberal policy than his contemporaries credited him for. This is certainly the position taken by K.O. Morgan in his masterly study of the Lloyd George Coalition. Morgan says that the government was having a bad press: it was, after all, criticised from all sides. But Morgan claims that 'the Coalition, above all through Lloyd George himself, offered some kind of vision of social harmony and international conciliation which many young men and women entering politics in 1919 found neither ignoble nor undeserving of support'.[43] Morgan argues that through attempting the revision of Versailles, and through signing the trade treaty with Russia, Lloyd George essentially appeased Germany and Russia, in an attempt to make them satisfied members of the international order. He even goes so far as to say that Lloyd George was effectively pursuing the aims of the Union of Democratic Control, though, 'He sought peace and disarmament, however, through summit conclave rather than through the mirage of open diplomacy.'[44] Morgan also cites the government's concession of self-government on domestic matters to Egypt, the Montagu–Chelmsford Reforms in India and the reduction of government defence expenditure from £604 million in 1919 to £111 million in 1922, as further evidence of the coalition's Liberal credentials.[45] This may be more true of the government as a whole than of Lloyd George in particular – as Martin Pugh argues, Lloyd George himself showed little enthusiasm for Egyptian nationalism, and self-government was pushed through at the insistence of Lord Milner, the colonial secretary.[46]

Ironically, it was a rash Liberal-inspired adventure that made Lloyd George appear warlike, and ultimately brought down his coalition. This episode was the Chanak Crisis of August–October 1922. It arose from the Greek retreat of 1921–22, in the face of Turkish advances. As Pugh says, 'Lloyd George had enough Gladstonianism still in him to sympathise with the Greeks',[47] and he authorised British troops at Chanak to reinforce them. However, this seemed to bring Britain dangerously close to war with Turkey, which alarmed many of Lloyd George's colleagues. The former Conservative leader, Bonar Law, now briefly out of politics, wrote to *The Times* that Britain 'cannot act alone as the policemen of the world'.[48] That attitude was shared by most Conservatives, and within weeks, their party had met at the Carlton Club and voted to end the coalition. Thus Britain lost its last Liberal prime minister.

Out of office, in speeches and in print, Lloyd George continued to advocate the need to reduce reparations, promote disarmament and revise Versailles.[49] In particular, in a 1923 book, *Is It Peace?*, he was highly critical of French policy, saying that Germany simply could not pay all that the French were trying to extract from it.[50] By 1932, he was calling for the complete cancellation of reparations.[51] Lloyd George was strangely quiet, though, on one Liberal sacred cow – the League of Nations. As prime minister, of course, he was widely criticised for neglecting the League, in favour of conference diplomacy. This did not endear him to Liberals, nor indeed to League enthusiasts such as Robert Cecil, yet Lloyd George believed it reflected the realities of the world situation, where the main forces in diplomacy were individual powers, rather than an international body with few powers.[52] This view continued to inform his attitude to the League when out of office: he was for example, far from enthusiastic about the Geneva Protocol, which he described as 'a booby trap for Britain baited with arbitration'.[53] This attitude may be partly explained by him seeing US participation in the League as vital for its success, believing that the League could not 'hope to dominate [the] international affairs of Europe and be a real security for peace until you have got all the great nations there'.[54] However, it is also explained by his belief that disarmament was the major issue that needed to be settled. Writing in the *Sunday News* on 5 September 1926, he said: 'A multiplication of covenants, protocols and pacts carries the world no further towards Peace … Disarmament is the best guarantee of security; it is the only test of sincerity.'[55] This was a position that he had already taken in responding to the Locarno agreements, when he argued that the next step in the pacification of Europe must be disarmament – 'Until we have disarmament in Europe, no treaties will avail to prevent war.'[56]

Aside from urging disarmament, Lloyd George was not more active in promoting a Liberal lead on foreign policy, for two reasons. First, he was distrusted by many in the Liberal Party. From the end of the coalition in 1922, it took four years for him to be accepted as Liberal leader – and even this was only due to Asquith's elevation to the House of Lords. Prior to 1926, as we saw earlier, a Radical Group within the parliamentary party was deeply opposed to him; and his accession to the leadership in 1926 initiated a series of defections to the Labour Party. Second, when he did become Liberal leader, he was far more interested in developing the party's domestic policy, through his industrial enquiry and the development of the *Yellow Book* (see above, p. 7). Though this was a remarkable document, it did nothing to develop Liberal international policy.

As we have seen, the Liberal Party was divided on a number of issues relating to the National Government in the summer and autumn of 1931. Lloyd George, in particular, did not wish the government to fight an election as a coalition, and when the bulk of the party decided to do so, Lloyd George (who was ill at the time, and unable to stamp his authority on the party), severed his links with the other Liberal MPs, except for three in his 'family group'. Samuel had effectively been leading the party through Lloyd George's illness, and was formally elected as party leader in November. Like they were for Churchill, the 1930s were to be Lloyd George's wilderness years.

In the early 1930s, Lloyd George, like all Liberals, remained firmly committed to disarmament, and he had an opportunity to shape government policy in March to July 1931, as a member of the government's CID Sub-Committee on the Disarmament Conference (Three Party Committee). This consisted of seven Labour ministers (including MacDonald, Henderson and the service ministers), five Conservatives (Chamberlain, Samuel Hoare, Anthony Eden, Robert Cecil and Thomas Inskip) and three Liberals – Lloyd George, plus Herbert Samuel and Lothian. This committee held ten meetings, with the aim of framing an agreed policy for the British delegation at the Geneva conference. It was an excellent opportunity for Lloyd George and his colleagues, who now had access to the service chiefs and military experts, in a way that none of them had enjoyed since 1922. This had two advantages. First, where 'expert' opinion coincided with the Liberal view, Liberals could use this evidence to back up their case. For example, at the third meeting of the committee, the chief of the Imperial General Staff, Field Marshal George Milne, made it clear that in his view, French armaments made France 'heavily over-insured' – this coincided with the Liberal view that many German grievances were just. Backed up with this expert advice, Liberals were able to put this case forcefully within the committee.[57] Access to experts also helped the Liberals, because if the expert view did not coincide with Liberal views, clear arguments against the experts could be made. This was done by Herbert Samuel in particular. The Admiralty had argued that Britain's naval requirements could never go below certain levels, but Samuel put the case, with some success, that all requirements must be relative, and that if the rest of the world was disarmed, the Royal Navy would have no threats with which to concern itself. The presence of Liberals on the committee meant that views put by the services which were against the Liberal position could be challenged.[58]

Aside from having access to experts, the committee also gave Lloyd George and his colleagues a chance to have a real influence on policy. This was the case, in particular, on the Liberal view that any British proposals at the disarmament conference must tackle the fact that Germany had been made to feel inferior and insecure. There was some Conservative resistance to this, but although the initial Liberal draft was altered by agreement within the committee, it was the Liberal case that underpinned the committee's stated view 'that Germany should be given security against invasion by her neighbours, who, collectively, are at present in a position to overwhelm her'. This was a fundamental aspect of Liberal foreign policy in the 1920s and early 1930s, and involvement in this Three Party Committee ensured that it had an influence on policymaking.[59]

However, Lloyd George still believed there were severe problems preventing agreement, and he did not make it a major issue in the campaign. Though people such as Gilbert Murray believed it was possible to make real progress by limiting military aviation and controlling submarine warfare, Lloyd George saw the French military as the major barrier to agreement. Writing to Murray in January 1932, he said that Germany's major grievance was that while it was restricted to a small, poorly equipped army,

> France has an army which is infinitely more powerful than that with which the Germans invaded France and Russia in 1914. As long as this state of things continues even approximately, it is idle to talk about the disarmament promises of the Peace Treaty being carried out.

Murray had asked Lloyd George to lobby the government on the opportunities available at the forthcoming Geneva disarmament conference;

but because of his scepticism, he refused, saying that Arthur Henderson, as president of the conference, could be just as authoritative as him.[60]

From 1935, Lloyd George was one of many people advocating a new world settlement. He did this through his 'Council of Action for Peace and Reconstruction', a predominantly Liberal organisation, which also attracted support from people of other parties and of none – such as the former Labour chancellor, Philip Snowden, the Independent MP Eleanor Rathbone and the future Conservative prime minister, Harold Macmillan, then a renegade MP on the left of the Conservative Party. The Council also represented the last rally of political nonconformity, as it included several leading Free Church figures, such as the Rev. F.W. Norwood from the National Council of Evangelical Free Churches, and F. Luke Wiseman of the Methodist Union. This movement arose out of Lloyd George's proposed 'New Deal' of measures to end unemployment in Britain, which had been put to the government in 1935 and rejected. The Council of Action promoted centrist ideas on economic recovery through all parties; on international affairs, it supported revision of unjust treaties, combined with a strengthening of the collective security provisions of the League. More specifically, it called for a five-year truce, during which no military agreements would be made, and there would be no expansion of armaments; the Council also wanted to review the existing colonial mandates system, with the aim of pacifying Germany through the return of some colonies. There were some problems with this approach from the point of view of creating a Liberal international policy. The only specific concession to Germany that was envisaged was the return of selected colonies. But Lloyd George himself was well aware that the return of colonies was unlikely to satisfy the German leadership.[61] In April 1935, Beaverbrook asked Lloyd George if he could say in an article, in the *Evening Standard*, that Lloyd George was in favour of the return of colonies. Lloyd George responded,

> On the whole I think it would be a mistake for me to make any declaration about the German colonies at the present moment. If there is a chance of a general appeasement, then the colonies might play a part in the transaction. But by themselves I do not believe that they would offer sufficient inducement to the Germans. There are other things they care far more for. The time has not therefore arrived to make any pronouncements of that kind.[62]

Nevertheless, Lloyd George's views on colonies show that like many other Liberals the foreign and imperial aspects of international policy were closely linked in the important area of establishing a workable collective security system.

Aside from the problems of the Council of Action's specific proposals, Lloyd George also created problems for the Liberal Party by so obviously working outside it. Though he rejoined the parliamentary party 11 days after the 1935 general election, and nominated Archibald Sinclair as party leader, he had little to do with the party's international policy except for occasional consultations with Sinclair.[63] It would have been a source of strength to the party if Lloyd George had in the first instance promoted his ideas through the party, and then looked outside it for support, to create a form of 'Popular Front'. But it could only be a source of weakness for such a prominent Liberal effectively to admit that the party was inadequate for his purposes, and to set up an entirely new idea. Lloyd George's own lack of interest in the Liberal Party did not help to suggest to the rest of the country that the party was worth bothering with.

Another reason for Lloyd George failing to create a Liberal lead in international policy from the mid-1930s was that he, like most other British politicians, was duped by Hitler. He came to believe that the Führer posed no particular threat – partly out of a strong fear of communism as a greater danger. As early as February 1934, Frances Stevenson recorded in her diary, 'D. [Lloyd George] regards Hitler as a very great man.'[64] This opinion was only confirmed by his visit to Hitler at Berchtesgaden in 1936, when he was impressed by the dictator's personality. Moreover, he admired the way in which Hitler had revived Germany through expenditure on public works – a policy which Lloyd George himself had already argued for in Britain.[65] However, he did not have the same admiration for Mussolini, going so far as to blame him for Hitler's involvement in the Spanish Civil War. Writing in December 1937, he said that it was not Hitler's fault that the British government had not acted on his offers to discuss Spain.

> He made us two or three offers which I urged the Government to act upon promptly. The present muddle is entirely due to the hesitancy and the nervelessness of the Baldwin Administration. They never saw an opportunity until it was too late to act upon it. Things are much more difficult now. It looks as if the Führer had committed himself to Mussolini – that adds enormously to the obstacles in the path of a friendly accommodation to the troubles of Europe. Mussolini is temperamentally an aggressor. I have never thought that Herr Hitler was and I do not believe it now.[66]

Such an attitude meant that Lloyd George consistently attacked the government over its Italian policy. This was especially the case on 18 June 1936 in the House of Commons, when he accused ministers of undermining the League by abandoning the sanctions which had been imposed on Italy after its occupation of Abyssinia a year earlier. Lloyd George said:

there is an end to the authority of the League of Nations. It is like a Government that is confronted with gunmen, with organisations to defy the law; they make every effort to re-establish law, order and authority, and they say, 'We are very sorry, we have got to give it up.'

Ending his speech facing ministers, he stated emphatically, 'To-night we have had the cowardly surrender, and there are the cowards.'[67] On Spain too, Lloyd George was hostile to Mussolini, urging the British government to end the policy of non-intervention, and allow British and other companies to supply the Spanish government with arms. All that the existing policy meant, Lloyd George claimed, was that the Spanish fascists had all the arms they needed, whilst the Spanish government was handicapped by the lack of supplies.[68]

Lloyd George's attitude to Hitler became more complicated after Munich. He vigorously denounced the agreement (although through the columns of the *Sunday Express* rather than in the House of Commons),[69] saying that Germany should have been told that Britain and France would defend Czechoslovakia against aggression.[70] He maintained this tough line on Germany after Prague was occupied in March 1939, by joining Winston Churchill in calling for an Anglo-Soviet Alliance, which he believed was particularly important if the guarantee to Poland was to be effective.[71] The high-point in this was on 19 May, when he opened the debate in the House of Commons on the idea of a Russian alliance, and vigorously denounced the government's unwillingness to make an agreement with the Soviet Union.[72]

However, when the war broke out, Lloyd George took a new position. At first, he pledged his loyalty to the British cause, in the House of Commons on 3 September 1939.[73] But a month later, he was arguing that the government should not reject all offers for peace from its enemies. In the House of Commons, he said on 3 October that it seemed that Hitler might offer peace terms to Britain, and that if he did so, these should be considered, rather than being ruled out immediately.[74] Then, on 12 October, at a meeting of the Council of Action, he proposed that Hitler should be invited to state his terms – if these were unacceptable, Britain would have the moral high ground in continuing with the fight. He again made this point in his constituency on 21 October, when he argued that Hitler could be brought into a conference with Stalin.[75] This of course, came to nothing.[76] Lloyd George had been the man to win the war in 1916, but in 1940 this mantle passed to Churchill, who pursued a policy of victory at all costs. Churchill did offer Lloyd George a place in his Cabinet in May 1940, but he refused – piqued that Churchill had made Chamberlain's approval of his appointment a condition.[77] Lloyd George had nothing else that was distinctive to contribute to the war effort. By September 1940, he was firmly behind fighting on. He told the Duke of Bedford (an advocate of negotiations) that it would have been possible to negotiate from a position of strength in October 1939, with the Maginot Line intact, 'and a very formidable French Army behind it'. But in the changed circumstances of late 1940 he believed that 'Were we to make peace overtures now whilst the threat of invasion was impending over our heads, it would be stigmatised as a Petain[78] move inspired by fear of utter defeat.'[79]

There is no doubt that Lloyd George was the most remarkable Liberal politician of the inter-war years; he was, after all, the only Liberal to lead the country in this period. However, he was essentially out of step with the rest of the party for most of the period. As prime minister, he committed the sin of working with Conservatives. In the mid to late 1920s, he was not trusted, even though his commitment to disarmament was indisputably Liberal. Even at the time of Munich, his calls to resist Hitler were undoubtedly marred by his previous admiration for the dictator. He was again out of step with his party in 1940 in his advocacy of an early peace.

HERBERT SAMUEL

Lloyd George's illness in the summer of 1931 meant that Herbert Samuel led the Liberal Party through the crisis of that time. He formally took over from Lloyd George as party leader in November 1931. Samuel first entered parliament as MP for Cleveland in 1902, and served in the Cabinet from 1909 to 1916, as chancellor of the Duchy of Lancaster, postmaster general, president of the Local Government Board and home secretary. As a loyal Asquithian, he refused to serve under Lloyd George, and lost his seat in 1918. Samuel remained prominent in the 1920s, though, first as high commissioner of Palestine in 1920–25, and then as the head of the Royal Commission on the Coal Industry in 1925–26. He returned to the Commons in 1929 as MP for Darwen, and on leading the Liberals into the National Government, became home secretary.

Following the 1931 election, Samuel was not the only Liberal in the Cabinet of the National Government. He was also joined by Archibald Sinclair (Scottish secretary), and Donald Maclean (president of the Board of Education). Neither of these had close dealings with international policy; but one other 'Liberal' did – John Simon, the foreign secretary, and leader of the Liberal Nationals. This group was deeply divided from the rest of the Liberal Party because over 1929–30 they had drifted away from Liberalism, and towards the Conservative Party, out of discontent over the record of the Labour government. Simon had tacitly accepted protection, thus ditching the traditional Liberal commitment to free trade, and by 1932, as his biographer argues, there was little to distinguish the Liberal Nationals from the Conservatives.[80] However, as foreign secretary, even if he would receive little credit for it from his former Liberal colleagues, he did show some remnants of Liberalism. In particular, in 1932, he tried harder than a Conservative foreign secretary might have done to develop a disarmament policy,[81] although as we shall see, Samuel was responsible for some of this. However, Simon was very much outside the Liberal Party, and his policies are beyond the remit of this study.

One might imagine that as home secretary in the National Government, Herbert Samuel would have had no role in international policy, but this was far from true. His reputation as a financial expert meant that he was in demand to assist the British delegation at two important international conferences taking place in the summer of 1932.[82] His role at the Lausanne Conference, where the prime minister, Ramsay MacDonald, headed the British delegation and where reparations were being discussed, was not a high profile one, nor did he have any great influence on British policy. However, he was far more active at the Geneva disarmament conference as an assistant to John Simon, the British foreign secretary.[83] Samuel, like all Liberals, was strongly committed to disarmament, and had already gained some experience on the issue as a Liberal representative on the government's Three Party CID Sub-Committee on Disarmament in mid-1931. Hugh Dalton, who attended three meetings in Arthur Henderson's absence, described one meeting as 'wretchedly inconsequent', noting 'They all say whatever comes into their heads, and no one except Samuel wants to disarm.'[84] The line that Samuel took in these meetings was to back up the case made by Lloyd George for Britain to make specific and ambitious proposals at the forthcoming Geneva disarmament conference.[85] Thus, on becoming home secretary, Samuel was already a recognised expert on disarmament, and though he did not formally join the Cabinet's 'Ministerial Committee on the Disarmament Conference' June 1932,[86] he attended its meetings from its inception in March. His involvement in these meetings revealed him to be someone who had considerable sympathy for the view that Britain's broad imperial interests meant that the country required considerable flexibility on, for example, the use of bombing for 'police' purposes in India. But he did not want this to lead to Britain rejecting out of hand all proposals for the restriction of bombing. This was because, as he told the committee, he had seen an alarming official report on the dangers of aerial bombing, which suggested that in a war with France, 50 tons of bombs dropped every 24 hours, could kill 2,500 people. This meant, that statesmen ought not to be deterred by technical difficulties in connection with civil aviation or be put off by questions of police control in the north-west frontier of India or other places, but rather they should set to work with a view to overcoming these difficulties.[87]

This involvement meant that in late June and July 1932, Samuel headed the British delegation in Geneva, when Simon moved on to Lausanne.[88] Samuel wrote to his wife that at the conference, 'There is a real desire to reach the maximum measure of disarmament.' He was thus able to make some provisional agreements with the French and the Americans, in favour of abolishing bombing of civilians, and restricting bombers to the size of 3 tons.[89] However, these were overtaken by a number of proposals made by President Hoover, which included the abolition of tanks, large guns and most military aircraft; the reduction by one-quarter of aircraft-carriers and cruisers and a one-third reduction of battleships. Samuel also wanted Britain to propose that national armaments could be limited by budget size, that is, each nation should be restricted in the amount of money it could spend on arms. He had originally been persuaded of this in March 1932,[90] but the Cabinet eventually rejected the idea, with Hoover's proposals, after they were strongly opposed by the service chiefs. Hoover's proposals were said not to allow Britain significant flexibility on imperial defence, especially where the navy was concerned. The budgetary limitation plan was opposed mainly because, it was argued, Britain had been reducing its arms expenditure steadily since the war, whilst other countries had maintained high levels of spending – any settlement reached on current estimates, therefore, would be disadvantageous to Britain.[91] Samuel thus had nothing to propose to the conference, which, in any case, effectively collapsed after Germany withdrew in September 1932.

Aside from being impressed by Simon's work on disarmament, Samuel also had another reason for supporting the National Government on international policy – India. It was a well-established Liberal position that the 'native peoples' of the Empire should be encouraged towards self-government within the Empire, and in the Government of India Bill (1935), the government supported such developments. Samuel spoke favourably in the Commons of India's desire for Dominion status (i.e. self-government within the Empire) and described the India Bill 'as the one sure means of maintaining the connection between Britain and India on conditions which may be acceptable to both'.[92] Between the second and third readings of the bill, the Liberal Party did put a motion (moved by Isaac Foot, who played a prominent role in the India debates) urging direct election to the Indian Federal Assembly, as opposed to election by state assemblies, but this was heavily defeated.[93] Otherwise, the party was fully behind the government on India.

However, the stumbling block for Liberals in the National Government was the tariff question. Samuel resolutely opposed the government's creeping imposition of food tariffs throughout the latter part of 1931, but because of collective responsibility within the Cabinet, he was not able to voice his objections publicly until January 1932, when the Cabinet agreed that ministers who were unable to accept the planned general tariff, could 'agree to differ'. This meant that Samuel was able to speak out against tariffs publicly, while remaining loyal to the government on other issues. Even this position became untenable, however, when the government agreed to longer-term measures of imperial preference on tariffs in the Ottawa Agreements of October 1932. Samuel and his Liberal colleagues resigned their ministerial positions (giving as another reason the failure to adopt budgetary limitations on arms), although they did not formally take up a position on the opposition benches for another year. By that point there was very little on which they could support the Conservative-dominated 'National' Government.[94]

Following this, until he lost his seat in November 1935, Samuel's main stance on international policy was to urge disarmament. In 1934, he was deeply opposed to Churchill's support for rearmament. On 14 March, he spoke of his 'very grave concern that it should appear that the race of armaments is again beginning'. Samuel criticised Churchill's 'delusion that two neighbouring Powers can both obtain security by each of them being stronger than the other'. Instead, he said that disarmament and control of arms (particularly air forces) by agreement was necessary. Four months later, on 13 July, he again criticised Churchill, saying that calls for dramatic increases in the size of the RAF were 'rather the language of a Malay running amok than of a responsible British statesman'. On 30 July, Samuel spoke in the House of Commons against the government's plans to increase expenditure on the RAF.[95] On 11 March 1935 (five days before Hitler's announcement of German rearmament), the Liberal Party (Samuel included) voted against the government's rearmament plans contained in the defence White Paper. Geoffrey Mander, who was increasingly prominent in the Liberal Party on foreign policy issues, led the Liberal attack in the Commons.[96]

Mander, and other Liberals, were also active in a further area of disarmament policy: the private manufacture of armaments. Within the League of Nations, several moves had been made to limit the manufacture of arms for profit by private companies, on the grounds that this encouraged a warlike attitude. It was a policy of concern to both Labour and the Liberals, with MPs from both traditions taking the lead. The first initiative in parliament came from the Labour MP, Rhys Davies, in February 1934, who called for an end to private manufacture. But others soon followed suit, including Geoffrey Mander and Robert Bernays (who was still formally a Liberal, but effectively worked as a Liberal National, prior to formally becoming one in 1936). Liberals did have some difficulties with the issue. As Archibald Sinclair pointed out in a debate on 8 November 1934, they did not believe that either a state monopoly on arms production or unilateral action by Britain alone would solve the problem of excessive armaments. Liberals sought instead to secure international agreements.[97] Nevertheless, the Liberal Party was a significant voice in the broad movement against the private manufacture of arms.

By May 1935, however, Samuel and the Liberal Party had changed their tune, in the face of the publicly announced German rearmament. Though still urging a disarmament agreement, he was able to support increases in British air expenditure, on the basis that it was necessary for national defence in the short term. This marked a split between the opposition parties, as Labour continued to oppose rearmament.[98] Meanwhile, with Italy threatening to attack Abyssinia in the summer of 1935, Samuel suggested that as a gesture towards Italy, Britain could guarantee Italian colonies against attack. This plan was pursued by the government for a brief time, but ultimately came to nothing when Italy invaded Abyssinia in October that year. Samuel was quick to pledge support for economic sanctions against Italy, which was hardly surprising given the established Liberal commitment to collective action through the League.[99] The time for a more vigorous Liberal response was later in the year, when the government had abandoned sanctions. By this time, Samuel had left the scene, having lost his seat at the general election, and the leadership passed to Sinclair.

For the rest of the 1930s, Samuel (who was elevated to the Lords in 1937) drifted away from his Liberal colleagues. In part, this was because he himself turned more to his activities as a writer and speaker on philosophy.[100] He was also active outside the party as the chairman of the Council for German Jewry, an organisation which helped German–Jewish refugees.[101] His experience as high commissioner for Palestine also meant that he was closely involved in that country in the late 1930s. Despite his close links with the Zionist movement, he earned some hostility from Zionists in Palestine when he argued that conciliation with Arab nationalism was necessary. He also tried, unsuccessfully, to persuade the British government to lift its restrictions on Jewish immigration into Palestine.[102] However, it was not just Samuel's interests in other areas that led him away from the Liberal Party. As we saw earlier in relation to his important speech at the 1938 LSS (see above, p. 72), and as his biographer argues, Samuel essentially believed that Hitler was an ordinary German statesman, who would respond to British concessions in a conciliatory fashion.[103] In particular, he urged the return of some (unspecified) Germany colonies as part of an all round settlement of international grievances,[104] and he supported the Munich Agreement, unlike the bulk of his party. On Munich, he said in the Lords that he saw it as a basis for the League to settle further problems, such as colonial issues, so 'that Europe and the world may at last emerge out of these troublous times into an era of tranquillity and ordered progress'.[105] Neville Chamberlain even offered Samuel a seat in the Cabinet in October 1938, as lord privy seal, but Samuel did not feel able to accept responsibility for government policy as a whole.[106] The task of organising Liberal opposition to appeasement was left to Samuel's successor as leader, Archibald Sinclair.

ARCHIBALD SINCLAIR

Archibald Sinclair was born in 1890, and was educated at Eton. Having then attended Sandhurst, he became a regular soldier in 1910, and served with distinction in the First World War, before entering parliament in 1922 as Liberal MP for Caithness and Sutherland. With Herbert Samuel, he was a member of the National Government, serving as secretary of state for Scotland in 1931–32, prior to the resignation of the Liberals over the Ottawa Agreements. Over 1932–35, he emerged as the successor to Samuel, and took over the leadership when Samuel lost his seat at the 1935 general election. From then, until 1939, Sinclair was an opponent of the government's international policy, and maintained a high profile in parliament and the country. However, as we shall see, his message was at odds with what most British people, even some within his own party, wanted to hear. He was also prevented from being more influential by his belief that working with people in other parties might lead to the dismemberment of the Liberal Party. That is not to say that he refused all cross-party cooperation. He was in fact a close ally of Churchill, having served with him in the First World War, and was willing to join MPs of all parties on anti-appeasement platforms. But what he would not do was lead his party into any formal alliance.

Sinclair's international policy can be stated in simple terms as a policy of collective security: this involved strong defences and the resistance of aggression through collective agreements, accompanied by the revision of grievances through international conferences – rather than the kind of agreement eventually pursued by Neville Chamberlain at Munich. All of this was underpinned by a belief that obedience to international law should be the basis of international relations. Initially though, Sinclair, like Samuel, was highly critical of rearmament. In November 1934, he said in the Commons that 'to concentrate on armaments will not lead to security but to insecurity and disaster'.[107] However, by May 1935, in the face of German rearmament, Sinclair (again like

Samuel) was supporting the government's plans to increase air defences, arguing that this should be seen as 'not a permanent addition to our national armaments but an emergency contribution to the collective system of peace under the League of Nations'.[108] This marked the beginning of Sinclair's commitment to 'collective security', in which strong defences would play a key part, and from then on, whenever rearmament was discussed, he welcomed the expenditure, but said that it was only part of what was necessary; and it was clear to Sinclair that the government felt very little commitment to the League. This was particularly clear after the Hoare–Laval Pact had shown that all of the government's warm words about the League of Nations meant nothing in terms of real action: Britain would do nothing to remove Italy from Abyssinia, despite having earlier agreed to a policy of sanctions. In a Commons speech on 19 December, Sinclair vigorously attacked the government, saying,

> The British Empire is neuter now in the counsels of the League. The British Empire, on which rests the capacity and responsibility for giving a lead to the League of Nations, is going to the League and saying 'These are our proposals. We do not press them. They are not definitive or sacrosanct. We make no complaint even if you reject them.' That is the pass to which the Prime Minister and the Foreign Secretary have sunk after holding the leadership of the League – they even deny responsibility for their own proposals.[109]

Instead, Sinclair wanted the government to hold firm to its earlier sanctions strategy, in order to remove Italy from Abyssinia. Anything else would serve only to reward aggression, and undermine the League.

Sinclair was able to elaborate further on these ideas in March 1936, when Hitler reoccupied the Rhineland. Though there was no question that Britain should intervene militarily – almost everybody in Britain accepted that German claims in the area were justified – Sinclair was not entirely happy with the line that the government had taken. In the Commons he said that the reoccupation was exactly the kind of event that would take place if German grievances were not satisfied, because in his eyes, Hitler was an aggressor who would go as far as he was allowed to go (short of war) to achieve what he wanted. To prevent Hitler behaving in this manner again, Sinclair believed that Hitler must be shown that Germany could only achieve its aims through the processes of international law in a world conference. Sinclair wanted this to discuss all German grievances, and, in particular, to reach a new settlement on colonial and economic issues, through abolishing tariffs and ensuring an 'open door' for all traders in colonial territories. Such an open door policy, Sinclair believed, must be insisted upon if Western powers were to keep their colonies, as must a policy of 'trusteeship for the natives'. In addition to such concessions, Hitler must recognise that disarmament was fundamental to world peace. This represented a summary of the many ideas which had been discussed in Liberal circles since the early 1930s, as we have seen in the previous chapters on the LSS and Liberal conferences. Sinclair summed it up as, 'a policy of military and economic disarmament, of collective security in which all countries, and not merely groups of allies, must participate, and of justice and equality for all nations'.[110] This was the line he would argue until the Munich Crisis, when more drastic measures, such as an alliance with the Soviet Union, moved on to the agenda.

Many people in other parties thought similarly to Sinclair, and there was some pressure within the Liberal Party for involvement in a Popular Front. As we saw earlier (p. 71), this idea largely related to domestic policy, and although international policy could be part of a broad agreement, it was not the driving force behind the pressure in the mid-1930s. Furthermore, as Sinclair's biographer argues, Sinclair always believed in the imminence of a Liberal revival, and felt that involvement in a Popular Front would dilute the Liberal message. It would also have divided the Liberal Party, because local parties adopted markedly different attitudes to 'popular' non-party candidates in the 1930s.[111] Sinclair made his views clear in a letter to A.W. Wood in November 1936. Wood was a Liberal activist at Oxford University (and was later president of the Union), and in 1936 he was involved in the *Oxford Guardian*. One of this newspaper's journalists, Marguerite Black, had talked with Sinclair prior to a meeting at the Union. Sinclair had spoken openly about the fact that he thought that a broad Popular Front was a good idea, but that at present, there were too many small groups who potentially could be involved (he included left-wing Conservatives amongst these), so it would need some crisis like that of August 1931 to weld them together. When Wood wrote to Sinclair to have an article reporting this approved, Sinclair said that this had been a private conversation, which was not intended for public broadcast. Although, Sinclair said, he supported the idea of a Popular Front, he did not want to say so publicly because:

> The position is that at the present moment I am leader of the Parliamentary Liberal Party and that my job is to work with my fellow Liberals in strengthening the Liberal Party. ... the stronger we can make the Liberal Party the greater the contribution it will be able to make to the political life of the nation either independently or in cooperation with other political groups. At the present moment opinion inside the Party is much divided about the Popular Front. My job must be to talk about the things which unite and strengthen the Party rather than those which arouse suspicions and dis-unity.[112]

Sinclair made similar points 18 months later, when he told Wood that if the Liberal Party 'is merely going to grovel under the Labour umbrella it will lose in the process its rank and file support and will bring no substantial reinforcement to your Popular Front'.[113] Fortunately for Sinclair, Wood withdrew the article, but it was an interesting insight into the Liberal leader's views on the role of his party in politics, and it showed that until there was a national crisis Sinclair would continue to bang the party drum. That crisis came in late 1938 after Munich, and as we shall see, Sinclair was then quick to endorse 'unity' candidates.

If Sinclair objected to formal cooperation between the Liberal Party Organisation and other parties, he was not averse to working with non-Liberals himself. Of course, this kind of elite cooperation was much easier to control, and, in moderation, would not result in a dilution of the Liberal message. Thus Sinclair became involved in 'Focus', the short name of the 'Anti-Nazi Council', a group set up by a German *émigré*, Eugen Spier, consisting of leading political 'dissidents' such as Winston Churchill, Liberals such as Violet Bonham Carter, and some Labour figures such as Margaret Bondfield, Walter Citrine and Hugh Dalton.[114] This did not seem to Sinclair to be a dilution of Liberalism because it did not consist of any formal cross-party cooperation. It was, more or less, a collection of individuals. Originally established in May 1936, Sinclair joined the group a few months later, and its main activity was to work towards launching its 'Arms and the Covenant' campaign at a meeting at the Albert Hall in December. This campaign, as its name suggests, sought to promote collective security through the League of Nations – this would involve rearmament, and making it clear that the League would resist all acts of aggression.[115] However, when the meeting took place on 3 December, it was also the day that King Edward VIII's affair with Mrs Simpson was announced to the press. Despite an impressive range of politicians being on the platform, and the campaign receiving messages of support from leading politicians such as Austen Chamberlain and J.R. Clynes, the Albert Hall meeting received less attention at the time than it tends to in history books and the memoirs and biographies of anti-appeasers.

The Abdication Crisis did not only overshadow the Albert Hall meeting. It also darkened the name of one of the leading lights in the Focus movement – Winston Churchill, who emerged as a staunch defender of the King, and was seen to be generally out of touch with sentiments in the House of Commons. This view of Churchill applied not only to the Abdication, but to politics more generally. As Harold Macmillan recorded in his memoirs, 'All the effect of the Albert Hall meeting was destroyed – first by the Abdication and secondly by the catastrophic fall in Churchill's prestige.'[116] A further reason why the 'Arms and the Covenant' movement failed to make a greater impact on public opinion was that the public did not want to hear what Sinclair and his allies had to say. Within the Liberal Party, Churchill was regarded as an extremist. F.W. Hirst, a prominent Cobdenite Liberal free trader did not want Sinclair associated with the likes of Churchill; he told Sinclair in March 1937, 'I want you to be leader of the peace party.' Any association with Churchill, Hirst said, 'will alienate Liberal pacifists & pacifists who w[ou]ld become Liberal again if they thought you were less jingo than the Labour Opposition'. Then later, in September, Hirst emphasised the need for the traditional Liberal commitment to reducing public expenditure through cutting armaments, to which Sinclair replied, 'in view of the world situation at the present time I could not honestly advocate putting economy first'.[117] Nevertheless, through being associated with Churchill, and through supporting rearmament, Sinclair appeared to many (including some Liberals) as a warmonger. The fact that he was just as commonly called a pacifist by a small number of people who believed that no concessions should ever be made to Germany,[118] showed the difficult position he was in.

Striking such a balance between warmonger and pacifist was inevitable as long as Sinclair continued to advocate both strength and concession, and this he did at every available opportunity. Writing in the *Contemporary Review* in April 1937, Sinclair justified rearmament on the basis 'that it will serve to buttress the rule of law against force, that it will contribute to the creation of a system of collective security under the League of Nations'. But he added that the world must be told that Britain would stop its rearmament if others did so too, and,

> We must make it clear to Germany and other nations who are still outside the League that, if they will return to the League, accept third-party judgment in all international disputes, and as the acid test of the sincerity of all members of the League, join in a measure of general disarmament, no grievance, whether political, economic, or colonial, will be regarded as undiscussable, but, on the contrary, that it will be regarded as the main objective of the League to promote the revival of international trade and the economic prosperity of all its members.[119]

This was a clear statement of the Liberal view of collective security, and it represented a definite alternative to appeasement: negotiations would take place, but only from a position of strength. Crucially, they would take place through the League, which was something that the government had not placed anywhere near the heart of its policy. As we have seen (p. 69), a key part of this policy was the idea of 'economic disarmament', a phrase which Sinclair himself used in speeches throughout the country and in the Commons [120] where, throughout 1937, he put the views he had outlined in his *Contemporary Review* article.[121] It is important to note, however, that this did not involve supporting intervention in Spain, as Sinclair had no desire to support the socialist and communist Republicans – instead he simply wanted to make the policy of non-intervention a reality, by persuading Germany and Italy to withdraw their support for Franco.[122] Nor did it involve an alliance with the Soviet Union, which Sinclair believed would undermine the idea of collective security, and make Germany feel encircled – although his view on this was to change after the Munich Crisis.[123] Rather, Sinclair's policy involved standing firm whenever the dictators made demands over treaty revision, in order to show that force would yield nothing, in the belief that this would ensure peace.[124]

Despite Sinclair's opposition to appeasement, he did meet Chamberlain and Attlee, the Labour leader, to see if any joint policy could be framed in response to the *Anschluss* between Germany and Austria in March 1938. Nothing was possible, and Sinclair thus remained an opponent of government policy.[125] Following the *Anschluss*, Sinclair developed his ideas on collective security to include more specific short-term measures, including support for France if it was forced to make good its guarantee of Czechoslovakia, and consulting more actively with the United States and the Soviet Union on the international situation. He also denounced the British government for not taking the lead in the type of international conference he had been suggesting since becoming Liberal leader.[126] Matters reached a head in the summer of 1938, when Hitler was encouraging dissent amongst Sudeten Germans in Czechoslovakia. War seemed a possibility, and Chamberlain dispatched Lord Runciman (once a Radical Liberal, but by that time a Simonite) to Prague to try to reach a settlement. In parliament, Sinclair welcomed the Runciman mission, arguing that the Czechoslovaks might have to make some concessions to the Sudeten Germans. As Sinclair's biographer says, this seemed to undermine his previous position of resisting threats of aggression.[127] However, by September, when it became clear that some kind of territorial concession to Germany was likely, Sinclair vigorously opposed the government. Speaking at the Liberal Party Council on 21 September, he defined the basis of Liberal policy as,

> firm loyalty to the Covenant of the League of Nations, that great effort to substitute for the existing anarchy between nations the rule of law – involving collective resistance to violent aggression – and, equally vital, machinery for peaceful change and the collective enforcement of justice.

This effectively meant that a general European settlement was necessary, but he emphasised the need for Britain to prove to Germany that aggression would be resisted, and that the democratic powers would not retreat each time a demand was made. On the more immediate issue of the Sudetenland, he argued that the dispute should be settled by a 'fair plebiscite', supervised internationally, and accompanied by a demobilisation of German forces.[128]

Following this, Sinclair met twice with his 'Focus' allies as Chamberlain negotiated with Hitler, where they discussed sending a telegram to Chamberlain (in Harold Nicolson's words) 'begging him not to betray the Czechs'.[129] This was not sent as there was not enough time. Chamberlain met Hitler at Munich, and did indeed 'betray' the Czechs through the Munich Agreement. It was not until the major Commons debate on 3 October that Sinclair was able to speak out publicly against Munich. In this debate he condemned 'the forfeiture of liberty for hundreds and thousands of Czechs' as part of a 'policy of successive retreats in the face of aggressive dictatorships ... which so nearly brought us into war last week'. He made clear his belief that Munich was a surrender to force, and that Hitler now had the upper hand in European diplomacy. He urged Chamberlain to read *Mein Kampf* as a statement of Hitler's true and extensive intentions.[130] A day later, Geoffrey Mander also spoke for the Liberal Party, arguing that 'The danger is greater than it was before and it may be that we are in a position, if a conflict takes place, of having very little chance of winning.' On 5 October, Richard Acland spoke of the need to defend the remnants of Czechoslovakia against further German expansion, and, in the final day of debate, H. Graham White put familiar arguments in favour of an international conference to settle all grievances. In particular, he believed that,

> statesmen to-day in all countries should make it their duty to consider how the raw materials of the world, the resources of the world and the open spaces of the world can be made available on equal terms to the common people of the world. That is the only basis on which the great longing of mankind for peace can be realised at this moment.[131]

In the two votes (one on an alternative policy put forward by Arthur Greenwood for Labour, involving an international conference and collective security through the League, another being a simple resolution in favour of the government's policy) held on 6 October, Sinclair voted against the government, supported by 13 Liberal colleagues, and opposed by four, none of whom had spoken in the debate. Two Liberal MPs did not vote. Full details of the voting are contained in Appendix 5.

This anti-Munich position was strongly endorsed by the two main Liberal newspapers, the *News Chronicle* and the *Manchester Guardian*. Both argued that Munich was a betrayal of the Czechs, with the *News Chronicle* condemning 'the sacrifice of a small and noble people'.[132]

During October 1938, these newspapers, like Sinclair and the rest of the Liberal Party, called for two steps to be taken. First, there were calls for there to be a new foreign policy to be adopted by the government – this would show that aggression would be resisted, but also that just grievances would be settled through international conference, rather than secret diplomacy. That further grievances needed to be settled was not doubted by Liberals; as the *News Chronicle* argued, if Hitler really had been satisfied at Munich, why was Neville Chamberlain saying that rearmament must continue?[133] Second, it was argued that there must be a reconstruction of the government along broad lines. The *Manchester Guardian* called for 'the combination of those who have an alternative to the present policy of weakness and drift'. The Conservatives who were of most interest to the Liberal press were Churchill (especially in the *News Chronicle*[134]) and Eden, but the papers also called for Liberals to cooperate with Labour. The Executive of the Liberal Party Organisation endorsed cross-party cooperation on 18 October,[135] but it remained a problem until Labour made its position on cooperation clear; when it did so favourably in late October, the door was open.

Sinclair responded favourably to this development, by supporting joint action at two by-elections. Munich was obviously the national 'crisis' that he had thought to be lacking in 1936 when he wrote to A.W. Wood against a Popular Front. This allowed joint action at two by-elections. One of these was in Oxford in October, where Sinclair[136] was happy to support the master of Balliol, A.D. Lindsay, who stood as an Independent with Liberal, Labour and much unofficial Conservative support, but lost to the government candidate, Quintin Hogg. In part, this may have been because Labour support was grudging – the local members were divided, and the National Party had not formally decided to support cooperation until it was too late to campaign vigorously for Lindsay.[137] However, in November, Vernon Bartlett, a former Liberal standing as an Independent Progressive with Sinclair's support,[138] beat the Conservatives in Bridgwater, and in the next month, the Duchess of Atholl was supported by Liberals as an (unsuccessful) anti-appeasement candidate in Kinross and West Perthshire. This all came to nothing, though, in terms of creating an alternative to the government, in part because there were simply not enough by-elections to remove the government.

The Labour Party national executive also had its say on the issue. Somewhat to Violet Bonham Carter's surprise, she was approached by Stafford Cripps in late 1938 regarding the possibility of organising a United Front to argue for resistance to Hitler, and to agree a common candidate for each by-election. This was unexpected, coming as it did from a pacifist who had shown no previous inclination for a military policy against Nazism. But Cripps told Violet Bonham Carter, 'I have changed. There is only one thing that can be done now – to save Europe from Hitler – by any means one can, including force.' Violet Bonham Carter pledged her support, and believed that she could persuade Archibald Sinclair to support the move, but Cripps failed to deliver.[139] In January 1939, the plan was decisively rejected by Labour's executive, which expelled Cripps from the party, and normal party competition remained the order of the day. In particular, at the Holderness by-election of February 1939, there was a bitterly fought battle between the two parties. This was despite the offer of Aline Mackinnon, the Liberal candidate who was second to the Conservative in 1931 and 1935, to stand down for a Popular Front candidate if Labour would do likewise.[140]

It is not fair, however, to blame the failure of the Popular Front entirely on the Labour Party. Sinclair's enthusiasm had some limits: even if he had come to favour cross-party cooperation, he did not want parties to submerge their identity in non-party organisations. One such organisation was 'The New Commonwealth', which described itself as 'A Society for the promotion of International Law and Order through the creation of a Tribunal in Equity and an International Police Force'. Its chairman was Lord Davies of Llandinam (David Davies), and Churchill's name appeared on its letterhead as 'President of the British Section'. Brian Goddard, one of the New Commonwealth's organisers wrote to Sinclair in November 1938, asking if he could speak at a meeting. Sinclair wrote back that he was sympathetic to the organisation's policies, but that he was too busy with Liberal Party engagements. Moreover, he added,

> those who believe in the causes for which the N.C. stands ought to give their full help and support to the Liberal Party which is fighting for the League. In critical times like these it is the activities of organised political parties, rather than those of non-political organisations, that have the best chance of influencing the Government.[141]

In December, Sinclair took a similar line to the anti-appeasement Conservative Leo Amery, who had written suggesting that a joint parliamentary committee could be established in order to work out a joint position between anti-appeasers. Even though this would take place at a relatively elite level, and would have involved little threat to the distinctiveness of the Liberal Party, Sinclair rejected the idea. Instead, he told Amery, he wanted each party to decide its own policy, followed by 'personal consultations' between leading members of the parties.[142]

More than all of these tactical problems though, the campaign against Munich did not gain more support because Munich itself enjoyed enormous support throughout the country. The bulk of the British people were jubilant to have avoided another war, and Sinclair's message was not one that people wanted to hear. This was even the case for a small section within the Liberal Party, from which Sinclair faced some dissent over his criticisms of Neville Chamberlain and which reached a peak in the spring and early summer. These prompted J.A. Spender, a writer and devout Asquithian Liberal, to write to *The Times* on 10 July, that although he could only speak for himself, he believed that many Liberals were firm in their support for Chamberlain. As we saw earlier, this was certainly the case for Herbert Samuel (although he told Spender that he wished he had not written such a letter),[143] and Asquith's widow, Margot, endorsed Spender's views. Though a number of prominent Liberals (including Walter Layton, Violet Bonham Carter, Dorothy Gladstone, A. G. Gardiner and Lord Meston) wrote in support of Sinclair, and though his views received prominent coverage in the *Manchester Guardian* and the *News Chronicle*, this controversy showed that he did have problems dragging some members of his party with him.[144] None of this prevented Sinclair from continuing to argue 'that appeasement has proved to be a miserable failure',[145] but he had difficulty in presenting his party as united behind an alternative.

The European situation worsened in March 1939, when Hitler occupied the rest of Czechoslovakia. Sinclair responded by developing new positions on conscription and an alliance with the Soviet Union. On the first of these issues, throughout late 1938 and early 1939, he had opposed the introduction of compulsory service under the Military Training Bill. Sinclair believed that conscription would divide the country, and instead, he wanted to see the vigorous pursuit of recruiting volunteers.[146] However, this position did not find favour with the Conservative majority in the Commons, and the bill was passed in May 1939. As we saw earlier, Sinclair believed that having lost the debate, it was the duty of all in Britain to support the government, and he successfully proposed a motion at the Liberal Assembly in favour of cooperating with conscription. The party as a whole endorsed this position 'reluctantly' (see above, p. 94). Meanwhile, in May 1939 Sinclair supported an alliance with the Soviet Union as a way of bolstering Europe against further German expansion. As early as December of the previous year, Sinclair had argued that Britain should consult with the Soviet Union on how to maintain peace;[147] but on 19 May, in the major Commons debate on a Russian alliance, he said that he was now 'certain ... that we cannot preserve peace without Russia'. He said that Britain should make an agreement with the Soviet Union to guarantee the security of the Baltic states and Poland. Without such an alliance, he believed that Britain's guarantee of Poland was meaningless; with an alliance in place, other countries such as Turkey would be encouraged to rally against Hitler, which would show both Germany and Italy 'that aggression would inevitably mean disaster for them'. All of this fell on deaf ears in the government. A similar case was made in the same debate by Eden,

Churchill, Attlee and Lloyd George. But the government was so uninterested in these arguments that when Eden spoke, it did not even extend the established courtesy of having a member of the Cabinet in the chamber to hear the former foreign secretary's speech.[148] Chamberlain's own personal hostility to an agreement with the Soviet Union was telling here. Though he (perhaps rightly) believed that the Poles and the Romanians would oppose any agreement between Britain and the Soviet Union, his hostility was also based on a view that the Soviet Union could not be trusted, and that it would be able to contribute little to a defence of Poland.[149] In the summer of 1939, Chamberlain instead preferred to trust a guarantee of Poland backed by the implausible idea of Britain intervening militarily in eastern Europe.

Sinclair continued to argue for a Soviet alliance through to July.[150] With the world in crisis, collective security through the League was clearly only a dream, but an old-fashioned alliance might yet save the day. However, by the end of August, war was imminent, and with the agreement of the Nazi–Soviet Non-Aggression Treaty, an alliance with the Soviet Union was out of the question (even though there was doubt in the House of Commons even into October over exactly what the treaty would mean[151]). Sinclair told the Commons on 24 August that he withdrew none of his past criticisms of the government's foreign policy, but 'now that we are in a crisis, criticism must be set aside'.[152] When war broke out in September, Chamberlain offered Sinclair a seat in the Cabinet. Sinclair refused, as the offer did not include a place in the War Cabinet, and he told the prime minister that he could not commit the Liberal Party to the government unless it was to be at the heart of decision-making.[153] Thus, until the reorganisation of the government under Churchill in May 1940, Sinclair and the Liberals remained in opposition. Then, Sinclair accepted the post of air minister, and served in this post for the rest of the war.[154] Although not formally part of the War Cabinet, he became a *de facto* member – a move in which Churchill was instrumental – and soon became a regular attendee. In 1945, Sinclair lost his seat in the Commons, and Clement Davies became Liberal leader. Sinclair went to the Lords as Viscount Thurso in 1952, and died in 1970.

CONCLUSION

This chapter has argued that the Parliamentary Liberal Party was in disarray for much of the 1920s and 1930s, though this was particularly so in the 1920s. In that decade, the former Radical hero, Lloyd George, was leading a Tory-dominated coalition until 1922, whilst the Leader of the party, Asquith, was not even in parliament for much of the time. From 1924, Lloyd George was effectively the party leader in parliament, but he was despised by many Liberal MPs, especially those in the Radical Group. Despite these difficulties, Liberals in parliament did manage to sustain a distinctive Liberal position on disarmament, which they rightly believed was not a priority for the Conservative government of 1924–29. However, other Liberal desiderata on the revision of the Treaty of Versailles were a matter of consensus in British politics in the 1920s. Even one of the makers of Versailles, Lloyd George, wanted to revise the treaty, and there was little distinctive in anything that the Liberals said on this matter.

But by the end of the 1930s, even by the time of the Munich Crisis, the Liberal leadership had a much clearer policy position. The party had developed an alternative to appeasement, based partly on the many ideas that had come from different roots within the party – Liberal thinkers, the Liberal Summer School and official conferences of party organisation. It is also fair to point out that from mid-1938, with its advocacy of an alliance policy, the Liberal Party shared much common ground with appeasers in other parties, particularly Winston Churchill. This view was based on the belief that it was right to negotiate with the dictators where they had just grievances, but that this could only be done from a position of strength and that strength could be secured through alliances with other nations. This approach assumed that, essentially, the dictators could not be trusted to abide by treaties unless an adequate security system was in place. It was accompanied by a commitment to make concessions to the dictators on territorial issues, especially colonial matters. Unlike Conservative anti-appeasers such as Churchill, who had been highly critical of the League through the 1930s, Liberals consistently looked forward to a day when the League would be able to settle disputes. Even at the time of the Munich Crisis, when Liberals recognised that an alliance was the best way of resisting Hitler, their motion tabled in the House of Commons called for a world conference linked to the League to settle all disputes.[155]

We can never know, of course, whether this strategy would have worked. There are certainly grave doubts over whether colonial questions actually meant that much to Hitler, and this issue is discussed in the conclusion. For the moment, it is enough to note that much of appeasement was based on the view that there was no other possible policy which could be followed. As work by R.A.C. Parker has suggested,[156] and as this chapter has maintained, there were clear alternatives, which Neville Chamberlain consciously decided not to follow. Appeasement was not set in stone as the *only* possible policy for Britain in the 1930s.

None of this is to say, however, that the Liberal Party emerges from the late 1930s as a beacon of truth which only fools ignored. In the same way that Churchill undermined his stance on appeasement with his reactionary views on India and his support for Edward VIII during the Abdication Crisis, Liberal leaders too helped to make their own policy unattractive. Party divisions between Simonites and Samuelites in the early 1930s left in the public mind a legacy of disunity, and made the Liberal Party appear not to be a realistic alternative government. The failure to put forward clear proposals on the idea of an international police force also prevented a serious debate on how to strengthen the League. Later, Archibald Sinclair showed a marked unwillingness to cooperate with members of other parties, fearing a dilution of Liberalism. Though this was an understandable and defensible position to take, it was a course of action chosen by Sinclair, from a range of other options. Meanwhile, on the fringes of the party, Lloyd George's equivocal stance on Hitler was a misjudgement; if Sinclair was too unwilling to look outside the Liberal Party, Lloyd George made it more difficult to put a Liberal view by being too unwilling to look inside the party. He was much more concerned with his own family group and his Council of Action. However, as much as one can point to strategic and intellectual misjudgements on the part of Liberal leaders in the late 1930s, one fact remains: they were right that appeasement was a dangerous policy which encouraged Hitler to take more and more, until war was the only way of stopping him. Unfortunately, the general public did not want to hear the Liberal message that the only alternative was to arm and threaten, thus making war a more immediate possibility. Sinclair and the Liberal Party, like Winston Churchill, were thoroughly out of tune with the mood of the times, and there was little they could do about this without compromising their message. Analysing Liberal Party foreign policy adds strength to the view that there were alternatives to appeasement; but it also shows why so many people supported Neville Chamberlain.

NOTES

1. Bodleian Library, Maclean Papers, Dep. a. 49, f. 25: Cutting from *Edinburgh Evening News*, 25 Jan. 1919. J.M. Hogge (Radical Liberal MP for Edinburgh East), 'Asquith Must Go'.
2. Hansard, *116 HC Deb. 5s*, cols. 2445–2450, 6 June 1919. Maclean Papers, Dep. c. 465, ff. 206–7: Maclean memorandum of conversation with Lloyd George, 17 Nov. 1919.
3. Stephen Koss, *Asquith* (London: Allen Lane, 1976), p. 227.
4. 'A Clean Peace and National Reconstruction: A Speech by H.H. Asquith, Birmingham, 11 December 1917' (London: LPD, 1918), pp. 9, 11.
5. See, for example, *The Times*, 12 Dec. 1917, p. 9. Marvin Swartz, *The Union of Democratic Control in British Politics During the First World War* (Oxford: Clarendon, 1971), pp. 80–1.
6. Hansard, *100 HC Deb. 5s*, cols. 2228–30, 20 Dec. 1917.
7. *DN*, 28 Sept. 1918, p. 5. *NLF, 1918*, p. 116.
8. Hansard, *118 HC Deb. 5s*, cols. 952–5, 21 July 1919.

9. Hansard, *139 HC Deb. 5s*, cols. 1113–17, 14 Mar. 1921. *141*, cols. 1301–04, 5 May 1921.
10. *MG*, 20 May 1922, p. 11. Hansard, *154 HC Deb. 5s*, 1473–75, 25 May 1922.
11. *MG*, 20 May 1922, p. 10.
12. Hansard, *160 HC Deb. 5s*, cols. 29–36, 13 Feb. 1923.
13. Hansard, *161 HC Deb. 5s*, col. 1389, 13 Mar. 1923.
14. Hansard, *167 HC Deb. 5s*, col. 105, 23 July 1923. *176*, col. 69, 14 July 1924.
15. *Annual Register, 1919* (London: Longmans Green, 1920), pp. 77, 125; *Annual Register, 1920* (London: Longmans Green, 1921), pp. 6–7, 118–19.
16. Hansard, *188 HC Deb. 5s*, cols. 447–59, 18 Nov. 1925.
17. Koss, *Asquith*, pp. 274–5.
18. Bodleian Library, Maclean Papers, Dep. c. 466, ff. 192–202: Near East Crisis – Press Comments on Lord Grey's Letter, 21 Sept. 1922.
19. Edward Grey *et al.*, *The League of Nations* (Oxford: Oxford University Press, 1918), p. 25.
20. Bodleian Library, Asquith MS 34, ff. 1–10, 19–31: Grey to Asquith, 20 Oct. 1920; Cecil memorandum (n.d. June or July 1921); Asquith memoranda, 24 June, 5 & 19 July, and 4 & 10 Aug. 1921. Bodleian Library, Maclean Papers, Dep. c. 466, f. 68: Lord Cowdray to Maclean, 19 July 1921.
21. John Campbell, *Lloyd George: The Goat in the Wilderness, 1922–31* (London: Jonathan Cape, 1977), pp. 158–61. University of Bristol, NLC Archives, DM668: Liberal Council Executive Minutes, 1927–37, 1938–39.
22. Bodleian Library, Asquith MS 34, ff. 1–10, 19–31: Grey to Asquith, 20 Oct. 1920; Cecil memorandum (n.d. June or July 1921); Asquith memoranda, 24 June, 5 & 19 July, and 4 & 10 Aug. 1921. Bodleian Library, Maclean Papers, Dep. c. 465, ff. 218–20: Walter Runciman to Maclean, 30 Dec. 1919.
23. *MG*, 4 Dec. 1924, p. 9. House of Lords Records Office, Stansgate Papers, ST/66, 1922–26: 2 and 3 Dec. 1924.
24. *The Times*, 24 June 1926, p. 11.
25. House of Lords Records Office, Stansgate Papers, ST/80/2/75-76: William Wedgwood Benn memorandum, n.d. (1926?). See also, ST/80/1/28: Benn to Thorne, 21 Nov. 1924.
26. *MG*, 5 Dec. 1924, p. 14.
27. House of Lords Records Office, Stansgate Papers, ST/80/7/167-172: Report of the Activities of the Parliamentary Radical Group, Easter to August 1926.
28. For the main debate see, Hansard, *171 HC Deb. 5s*, cols. 360–69 (Benn), 373–9 (Sinclair), 382–4 (Muir) and 384–97 (Simon): 18 Mar. 1924. See also, Kenworthy and Harvey in Hansard, *170 HC Deb. 5s*, cols. 444, 723: 27, 28 Feb. 1924. The pressure was continued under the Conservatives: Hansard, *182 HC Deb. 5s*, col. 2204: 8 Apr. 1925.
29. *MG*, 15 Dec. 1924, p. 11. *The Times*, 15 Dec. 1924, p. 24; 16 Jan. 1925, p. 16.
30. *DN*, 4 Dec. 1924, p. 1. See also, *DN*, 5 Dec. 1924, p. 6; 9 Jan. 1925, p. 1.
31. House of Lords Records Office, Stansgate Papers, ST/66, Diary 1922–26: 6 Dec. 1925.
32. *DN*, 7 Feb. 1927, p. 7.
33. House of Lords Records Office, Stansgate Papers, ST/85/1/189: W. Wedgwood Benn to A. Munro, Jan. 1927.
34. This included the forcible annexation by Germany of Alsace-Lorraine.
35. Trevor Wilson, *The Downfall of the Liberal Party, 1914–35* (London: Collins, 1966), pp. 144–6.
36. David Lloyd George, *The Truth About the Peace Treaties, Vol. I* (London: Gollancz, 1938), p. 177.
37. Michael L. Dockrill and J. Douglas Goold, *Peace without Promise: Britain and the Peace Conferences, 1919–23* (London: Batsford, 1981), pp. 52–3. Lloyd George, *Truth About the Peace Treaties, Vol. I*, pp. 511–13. Martin Pugh, *Lloyd George* (London: Longman, 1988), p. 135.
38. Hansard, *114 HC Deb. 5s*, col. 2950: 16 Apr. 1919; Hansard, *117 HC Deb. 5s*, col. 1213: 3 July 1919.

39. Most notably in, A. Lentin, *Guilt at Versailles: Lloyd George and the Pre-history of Appeasement* (London: Methuen, 1985).
40. Martin Gilbert, *Winston S. Churchill, Vol. IV: World in Torment, 1917–1922* (London: Heinemann, 1975), p. 384.
41. House of Lords Records Office, Lloyd George Papers, F/89/2/25: Lloyd George to Philip Kerr, 19 Feb. 1919.
42. Pugh, *Lloyd George*, p. 138.
43. K.O. Morgan, *Consensus and Disunity: The Lloyd George Coalition Government, 1918–22* (Oxford: Clarendon, 1979), p. 375.
44. Ibid., pp. 145–6.
45. Morgan, *Consensus and Disunity*, pp. 119–22, 146.
46. Pugh, *Lloyd George*, pp. 145–6.
47. Ibid., p. 156.
48. A.J.P. Taylor, *English History 1914–1945* (Oxford: Clarendon, 1965; 1976 edn), p. 192.
49. Campbell, *Lloyd George*, pp. 65–6, 93–4, 103–4, 113, 169, 171.
50. David Lloyd George, *Is It Peace?* (London: Hodder and Stoughton, 1923), pp. 31–2, 40–1.
51. David Lloyd George, *The Truth about Reparations and War Debts* (London: Heinemann, 1932), pp. 140–1.
52. Morgan, *Consensus and Disunity*, pp. 110–11, 145–6, 304.
53. Hansard, *182 HC Deb. 5s*, col. 333: 24 Mar. 1925.
54. Campbell, *Lloyd George*, p. 66. Hansard, *188 HC Deb. 5s*, col. 449: 18 Nov. 1925.
55. Quoted in Campbell, *Lloyd George*, p. 170.
56. Hansard, *188 HC Deb. 5s*, col. 458: 18 Nov. 1925.
57. CAB 16/102, D.C. (P.): 3rd Mtg. 7 May 1931.
58. CAB 16/102, D.C. (P.): 5th Mtg. 21 May 1931.
59. CAB 16/102, D.C. (P.): 8th–10th Mtgs. 2, 13 & 15 July 1931. CAB 24/222, C.P. 195(31): The Disarmament Conference, The Three Party Resolutions, 27 July 1931.
60. House of Lords Records Office, Lloyd George Papers, G/33/2/7, 8: Lloyd George and Gilbert Murray correspondence, 8 & 18 Jan. 1932.
61. House of Lords Records Office, Lloyd George Papers, G/159, 162: Council of Action Policy Documents. Stephen Koss, *Nonconformity in Modern British Politics* (London: Batsford, 1975), pp. 195–219.
62. House of Lords Records Office, Lloyd George Papers, G/3/6/30, 31: Beaverbrook and Lloyd George correspondence, 2 & 3 Apr. 1935.
63. Churchill College Cambridge, Thurso Papers, THRS II, 38/4: Sinclair to Geoffrey Mander, 17 Sept. 1938.
64. A.J.P. Taylor, ed., *Lloyd George: A Diary by Frances Stevenson* (London: Hutchinson, 1971), p. 254: 18 Feb. 1934.
65. Chris Wrigley, *Lloyd George* (Oxford: Blackwell, 1992), p. 138.
66. House of Lords Records Office, Lloyd George Papers, G/6/14/3: LG to T.P. Conwell Evans, 17 Dec. 1937.
67. Hansard, *313 HC Deb. 5s*, cols. 1221–22, 1232: 18 June 1936.
68. Hansard, *328 HC Deb. 5s*, cols. 307–16: 28 Oct. 1937. See also, Tom Buchanan, *Britain and the Spanish Civil War* (Cambridge, Cambridge University Press, 1997), p. 84.
69. House of Lords Records Office, Lloyd George Papers, G/42/ 1, 2: Munich Crisis Letters, Sept. & Oct. 1938.
70. David Lloyd George, 'Democracy and the Dictators', *Sunday Express*, 9 Oct. 1938, p. 16.
71. Wrigley, *Lloyd George*, pp. 139–40. Sidney Aster, 'Ivan Maisky and Parliamentary Anti-Appeasement, 1938–39', in A.J.P. Taylor, *Lloyd George: Twelve Essays* (London: Hamish Hamilton, 1971), pp. 317–60. Hansard, *347 HC Deb. 5s*, col. 1817–1818: 19 May 1939.
72. Hansard, *347 HC Deb. 5s*, cols. 1809–1820: 19 May 1939.
73. Hansard, *351 HC Deb. 5s*, cols. 299–300: 3 Sept. 1939.

74. Hansard, *351 HC Deb. 5s*, cols. 1870–1874, 1879–80: 3 Oct. 1939.
75. Frank Owen, *Tempestuous Journey: Lloyd George, his Life and Times* (London: Hutchinson, 1954), pp. 745–6.
76. For further coverage of this issue, see Antony Lentin, '"A Conference *Now*": Lloyd George and Peacemaking, 1929: Sidelights from the Unpublished Letters of A.J. Sylvester', *Diplomacy and Statecraft*, 7, 3 (Nov. 1996), pp. 563–88; Paul Addison, 'Lloyd George and Compromise Peace in the Second World War', in Taylor, (ed.), *Lloyd George*, pp. 361–84.
77. House of Lords Records Office, Lloyd George Papers, G/4/5/47: LG to WSC, 29 May 1940.
78. Marshal Pétain, the leader of Vichy France, who had negotiated with Germany.
79. House of Lords Records Office, Lloyd George Papers, G/3/4/8, 9: Duke of Bedford and Lloyd George correspondence, 2 & 14 Sept. 1940.
80. David Dutton, *Simon: A Political Biography of Sir John Simon* (London: Aurum, 1992), p. 121.
81. Ibid., pp. 157–60.
82. Bernard Wasserstein, *Herbert Samuel: A Political Life* (Oxford: Clarendon, 1992), p. 349.
83. Ibid., pp. 349–50.
84. Ben Pimlott (ed.), *The Political Diary of Hugh Dalton, 1918–40, 1945–60* (Jonathan Cape, 1986), p. 145: 14 May 1931.
85. CAB 16/102, CID Sub-Committee on the Disarmament Conference (Three Party Committee): 4th Mtg. 14 May 1931.
86. House of Lords Records Office, Samuel Papers, A/155(VIII)/53: R. MacDonald to Samuel, 24 June 1932.
87. CAB 27/505, Ministerial Committee on Disarmament Conference, 1932. Samuel attended the meetings, from 21 Mar.–15 Sept. 1932. The quotation is from the fourth meeting, on 6 June.
88. Wasserstein, *Samuel*, pp. 352–4.
89. House of Lords Records Office, Samuel Papers, A/157/1219, 1220: Samuel to Beatrice Samuel, 22, 25 June 1932. CAB 24/231, CP 222 (32), Annex I: Samuel memorandum, 21 June 1932.
90. FO 800/286/465–67: Herbert Samuel to John Simon, 29 Mar. 1932.
91. CAB 23/71, CC 38 & 39 (32): 24 & 27 June 1932. CAB 24/231, CP 226 (32): Draft Declaration of British Disarmament Policy in Relation to the Hoover Proposals, 26 June 1932.
92. Hansard, *297 HC Deb. 5s*, cols. 1175–89: 6 Feb. 1935.
93. Hansard, *298 HC Deb. 5s*, cols. 1985–2002, 2066–67: 6 Mar. 1935.
94. Wasserstein, *Samuel*, pp. 337–43, 355–60, 365–6.
95. Hansard, *287 HC Deb. 5s*, cols. 419–28: 14 Mar. 1934; *292 HC Deb. 5s*, cols. 675, 2351–63: 13, 30 July 1934.
96. Hansard, *299 HC Deb. 5s*, cols. 127–34: 11 Mar. 1935.
97. Hansard, *285 HC Deb. 5s*, cols. 1935–2006: 14 Feb. 1934; Hansard *290 HC Deb. 5s*, col. 329: 31 May 1934; Hansard, *292 HC Deb. 5s*, col. 168: 10 July 1934; Hansard, *293 HC Deb. 5s*, cols. 1293–416: 8 Nov. 1934.
98. Hansard, *301 HC Deb. 5s*, cols. 583–93: 2 May 1935. Viscount Samuel, *Memoirs* (London: Cresset Press, 1945), pp. 270–1.
99. Hansard, *304 HC Deb. 5s*, col. 2905: 1 Aug. 1935. House of Lords Records Office, Samuel Papers, A/155(IX)/27: Samuel Hoare to Herbert Samuel, 6 Aug. 1935. Hansard, *305 HC Deb. 5s*, cols. 47–58: 22 Oct. 1935.
100. Wasserstein, *Samuel*, pp. 372–5.
101. Ibid., pp. 375–9.
102. Ibid., pp. 387–9.
103. Ibid., p. 390.
104. Hansard, *107 HL Deb. 5s*, cols. 139–51: 17 Nov. 1937.

105. Hansard, *110 HL Deb. 5s*, cols. 1389–90: 4 Oct. 1938.
106. House of Lords Records Office, Samuel Papers, A/111/1-5: Samuel memorandum of conversation with Neville Chamberlain, 26 Oct. 1938; correspondence between Samuel and Crewe, 26, 27 Oct. 1938.
107. Hansard, *295 HC Deb. 5s*, col. 900: 28 Nov. 1934.
108. Hansard, *302 HC Deb. 5s*, col. 394: 22 May 1935.
109. Hansard, *307 HC Deb. 5s*, cols. 2049–50: 19 Dec. 1935.
110. Hansard, *310 HC Deb. 5s*, cols. 1461–68: 26 Mar. 1936.
111. Gerard J. De Groot, *Liberal Crusader: The Life of Sir Archibald Sinclair* (London: Hurst, 1993), pp. 119–20, 130–1, 145.
112. Churchill College, Cambridge, Thurso Papers, THRS II, 31/1: Sinclair and A. W. Wood correspondence, 20, 23 Nov. 1936.
113. Churchill College, Cambridge, Thurso Papers, THRS II, 39/3: Sinclair to A.W. Wood, 4 May 1938.
114. Martin Gilbert, *Prophet of Truth: Winston S. Churchill, 1922–1939* (London: Heinemann, 1976), p. 739. De Groot, *Liberal Crusader*, pp. 119–20.
115. Eugen Spier, *Focus: A Footnote to the History of the Thirties* (Oswald Wolff, 1963), especially pp. 58–77 for the Albert Hall meeting.
116. Harold Macmillan, *Winds of Change, 1914–1939* (London: Macmillan, 1966), p. 479.
117. Churchill College, Cambridge, Thurso Papers, THRS II, 34/5: Hirst and Sinclair correspondence, 15 Mar., and 7, 9 Sept. 1937.
118. De Groot, *Liberal Crusader*, pp. 128, 132–3.
119. Archibald Sinclair, 'Rearmament', *CR*, CLI, 856 (Apr. 1937), pp. 385–92.
120. Archibald Sinclair, 'Freedom and Peace': Speech delivered at LPO dinner, 30 June 1937, Park Lane Hotel, and reproduced as a pamphlet (National Liberal Club Pamphlets, University of Bristol, Store 400123). Hansard, *317 HC Deb. 5s*, col. 43: 3 Nov. 1936.
121. See for example, Hansard, *325 HC Deb. 5s*, cols. 1537–45: 25 June 1937; *326 HC Deb. 5s*, cols. 1837–45: 19 July 1937.
122. De Groot, *Liberal Crusader*, p. 128.
123. *MG*, 30 July 1937, p. 12: Sinclair speech at LSS.
124. Churchill College, Cambridge, Thurso Papers, THRS II, 34/5: Sinclair to Hirst, 18 Mar. 1937.
125. De Groot, *Liberal Crusader*, p. 135. Nigel Nicolson (ed.), *Harold Nicolson: Diaries and Letters, 1930–1939* (London: Collins, 1966), p. 332: 16 Mar. 1938.
126. Hansard, *333 H.C. Deb. 5s*, cols. 56–62: 14 Mar. 1938.
127. De Groot, *Liberal Crusader*, p. 137.
128. *MG*, 22 Sept. 1938, p. 4.
129. Nicolson (ed.), *Nicolson Diaries*, pp. 366–7, 371–2: 26, 29 Sept. 1938.
130. Hansard, *339 HC Deb. 5s*, cols. 66–77: 3 Oct. 1938.
131. Hansard, *339 HC Deb. 5s*, cols. 224–32, 383–93, 514–20: 4, 5, 6 Oct. 1938.
132. *MG*, 1 Oct. 1938, p. 12; *NC*, 1 Oct. 1938, p. 6.
133. *NC*, 2 Oct. 1938, p. 10; 13 Oct. 1938, p. 13; 19 Oct. 1938, p. 2. *MG*, 19 Oct. 1938, p. 9.
134. At first, the *News Chronicle* simply gave Churchill's views a high profile. By mid-1939, it was openly calling for his inclusion in the Cabinet. *NC*, 31 Oct. 1938, p. 2; 11 Oct. 1938, p. 10; 10 July 1939, p. 10.
135. *MG*, 19 Oct. 1938, p. 9; *NC*, 19 Oct. 1938, p. 2.
136. MS Gilbert Murray, 85, ff. 193–94: Sinclair to Murray, 26 Oct. 1938.
137. *MG*, 29 Oct. 1938, p. 12.
138. Churchill College, Cambridge, Thurso Papers, THRS II, 37/3: Sinclair to Miss Cooke (Bartlett's secretary), 16 Nov. 1938.
139. Autobiographical note, Violet Bonham Carter MSS, quoted in Mark Pottle (ed.), *Champion Redoubtable: The Diaries and Letters of Violet Bonham Carter, 1914–45* (London: Weidenfeld & Nicolson, 1998), p. 145. See also, Peter Joyce, *Realignment of the Left?* (London: Macmillan, 1999), pp. 93–5.

140. Churchill College, Cambridge, Thurso Papers, THRS II, 66/6: File on Holderness by-election. De Groot, *Liberal Crusader*, pp. 146–7.
141. Churchill College, Cambridge, Thurso Papers, THRS II, 39/2: Sinclair's secretary to Brian Goddard, 7 Nov. 1938.
142. Churchill College, Cambridge, Thurso Papers, THRS II, 37/2: Amery and Sinclair correspondence, 9 and 13 Dec. 1938.
143. House of Lords Records Office, Samuel Papers, A/155(X)/56 & 56(a): correspondence between Spender and Samuel, 9 and 12 July 1939.
144. *The Times*, 10 July 1939, p. 13; 12 July 1939, p. 10; 13 July 1939, p. 17. *MG*, 12 July 1939, p. 11. *NC*, 12 July 1939, pp. 1–2. See also, MS Gilbert Murray, 119, ff. 72–6: Murray and Margot Asquith correspondence, 4 and 7 Mar. 1939.
145. *MG*, 12 July 1939, p. 11: Speech in Folkestone on 11 July 1939.
146. Hansard, *346 HC Deb. 5s*, cols. 1361–70: 27 Apr. 1939.
147. Hansard, *342 HC Deb. 5s*, cols. 2537–8: 19 Dec. 1938.
148. Hansard, *347 HC Deb. 5s*, cols. 1809–76: 19 May 1939.
149. Parker, *Chamberlain and Appeasement*, p. 223.
150. Hansard, *350 HC Deb. 5s*, cols. 1994–97: 31 July 1939.
151. Doubts came from both Sinclair and Attlee: Hansard, *351 HC Deb. 5s*, cols. 15, 1862: 24 Aug. and 3 Oct. 1939.
152. Hansard, *351 HC Deb. 5s*, col. 16: 24 Aug. 1939.
153. University of Bristol, National Liberal Club Archives, DM 668, Sir Archibald Sinclair: Notes of Sinclair's interviews with Neville Chamberlain and leading Liberals, 2, 3 Sept. 1939.
154. De Groot, *Liberal Crusader*, pp. 151–5.
155. See below, Appendix 5.
156. Parker, *Chamberlain and Appeasement*, p. 347.

—6—

Liberal Activists

POLITICAL PARTIES can be unruly beasts. Despite the efforts of Liberal leaders in parliament, and those passing policy at party conferences, party activists can seek to take the party in an altogether different direction to the wishes of those engaged in 'high' politics. The most graphic example of that in twentieth-century British politics is the Labour Party in the early 1980s, when the far left, operating at grassroots level, aided and abetted by a small number of parliamentarians, gradually seized control of much of the party machine.

In the Liberal Party, differences between leaders and activists manifested themselves much earlier in the century, both in local differences over the implementation of the electoral agreement with the Labour Party prior to the 1906 landslide, and in reactions to the Lloyd George Coalition. So in seeking to establish the extent to which the views expressed by Liberal thinkers and leaders represented those of the wider party, it is necessary to examine the 'low' politics of the Liberal Party. In part, that can be done through analysing Liberal gatherings such as meetings of the NLF or the LSS, both of which brought together significant numbers of party activists from across the country. However, it is also important to look at how activists behaved in their constituencies, and in other local or less formal Liberal bodies.

This chapter argues that such analysis reveals the discussion and formulation of international policy to have been more important to the ordinary Liberal activist than has traditionally been acknowledged. If one had been an 'average voter' in the 1920s or 1930s, international issues would certainly have been important, but less so, perhaps, than jobs, housing or trade unionism. However, if a Liberal knocked on your front door to campaign or canvass, there was a fairly high probability that when asked what the Liberal Party stood for, this earnest man or woman would talk about 'Peace' and the League of Nations prior to anything else. Of course, in individual areas, and at certain times, plans for conquering unemployment loomed large; but as the cause of choice, many Liberals were motivated by a strong concern about international issues.

REGIONAL LIBERAL FEDERATIONS

Evidence for local Liberal activism can be hard to find: low politics often involved much lower forms of record-keeping than high politics. If records existed in the first place, they relied on the diligence and efficiency of one or two individuals in a constituency to maintain and preserve them. However, we can conclude from the records of the NLF and the LSS, and from Liberal newspapers, that international policy was a major issue for Liberals well beyond parliamentary circles.

We also know from newspaper reports that international policy was extremely important in the regional Liberal Federations; for example, in 1919, the Manchester Liberal Federation (MLF) produced a detailed policy programme (which, as we saw earlier, was influential in industrial policy), in which the League of Nations loomed large. The MLF proposed that 'The League's most vital functions should be to enforce the compulsory limitation of armaments and the abolition of conscript armies by all constituent nations.' A more specific proposal, aimed at ensuring some degree of democratic control on policy, was for a country's delegates to at least one of the League's organs of government (i.e. Council or Assembly) to be elected by their own country's parliament.[1]

Other regional Liberal Federations also discussed foreign policy in considerable detail. In *The London Liberal Programme* of 1920, the London Liberal Federation put forward a series of radical proposals on international relations as part of a wider package of reforms. On the Empire, the LLF proposed that complete self-government should be the aim for India and Egypt. It argued that 'Foreign Policy should be democratically controlled and Secret Treaties abandoned.' The LLF also wanted the prohibition of military alliances between League members, and the possibility that League mandates could be extended to all colonies. Foreign policy was certainly an important part of politics for the LLF, the policies of which did not merely reproduce the party line. By the end of the 1930s, around half of the resolutions passed by its Council and Executive (a total of about ten each year) related to international policy.[2]

The Executive of the Western Counties Liberal Federation (attended by 20-50 constituency representatives) was another noted forum for discussions of international policy. On 8 October 1932, it stated its 'deep disappointment at the slowness of the progress being made at the Geneva Conference on international disarmament'. It discussed the Rhineland remilitarisation on 13 March 1936, although no resolution was passed. A resolution was passed on 19 September 1936, on the Spanish Civil War, deploring intervention by Germany and Italy, and urging the government to reconsider its policy of non-intervention if it could not be made effective. Whereas resolutions in the 1920s and early

1930s had concentrated on domestic issues such as proportional representation, international policy was now a major interest. On 18 October 1937, the WCLF called for the strengthening of the League as a body able both to resist aggression and to redress grievances. In a lively debate on 4 April 1938, it was agreed to call on the government to arm the Spanish Republicans, and to guarantee the security of Czechoslovakia. Though much of this was in sympathy with national policy, a resolution passed on 5 June 1939 was not. This dealt with conscription, and emphasised the unease that Liberals felt over the Liberal Assembly agreeing to support conscription – the resolution said that this should not be taken 'as the official and static opinion of the Liberal Party as a whole'. Over 30 executive members supported this view, as against 14 who wished to support the Assembly wholeheartedly.[3] Some of these resolutions were passed on to constituency associations for further discussion, in part with the aim of passing statements that could then be used to lobby the government.

It is important to note though, that interest in international policy varied in different regions. In the 1920s, the Home Counties Liberal Federation was preoccupied with passing resolutions on industrial policy and (perhaps because the Liberals had performed badly in the region's elections) proportional representation. Its annual reports survive for 1908 and 1924–46, and it was not until 1939 that international policy was discussed in any detail at official meetings, and then only to support (unanimously) the line taken by Sinclair on conscription, prior to his addressing the annual meeting. However, the HCLF did hold a 'Week-end Conference' in November 1937, to discuss issues rather than make policy, and three of the six sessions dealt with international policy: 'Ottawa and its Implications', 'The Colonial Question and Raw Materials' and 'World Politics and British Foreign Policy'.[4]

ELECTIONEERING

Beyond internal party bodies, Liberals gave international policy a high priority in their campaigns. One tactic used to emphasise Liberal policy was to target groups of voters such as members of the League of Nations Union by sending them specially produced leaflets.[5] More generally, though, further sources for 'low politics' are the general election addresses of candidates. For the 1929 election, an extensive study was completed in 1959, although it was never published.[6] This included a survey of 1,259 addresses, using a sample of one in four of the addresses for each main party. Though election addresses were admittedly vague, the study concluded that a general commitment to 'Peace' was given a much greater emphasis by Liberal candidates than by other parties. This, combined with unemployment (because of the *Yellow Book*), was the major Liberal election issue in 1929. Table 1 contains figures on how the issues were put forward by candidates.

Table 1: Issues in Election Addresses, 1929 General Election

Candidates	Unemployment mentioned in address (%)	Unemployment given special emphasis in address (%)	'Peace' mentioned in address (%)	'Peace' given special mention in address (%)
Conservative	87	30	77	20
Liberal	100	79	94	72
Labour	100	47	97	48

Source: E.A. Rowe, 'The British General Election of 1929' (Oxford B.Litt. thesis, 1959), pp. 198–200.

There could have been several reasons for Liberals giving inter-national policy such a high priority. They might have made a political calculation that their message in this area was likely to win votes. They might have decided that because other parties were focusing on the subject, the Liberal Party had to make its position clear. They might have believed that the issue was so important to the electorate that they had a duty to place their views before the country. Or they might have believed that the issue was not getting enough coverage in other ways and that they should therefore raise its profile. There is no way to be sure. However, we can be certain that, for whatever reason, international policy was a high priority issue for Liberals, and that it was a key part of inter-war Liberal politics and campaigning in the country as a whole.

YOUNG LIBERALS AND THE 8.30 CLUB

An illuminating source, recently discovered,[7] adds weight to the view that when Liberals gathered together, international policy loomed large in their thoughts: the Minute Book of the '8.30 Club', a debating society of young Liberals (as distinct from the formal, capital 'Y', Young Liberals organisation), which met at 8.30 on the last Tuesday of six months of the year – usually January, February, March, May, October and November. The 8.30 Club was formed in 1936, and by 1938, its membership was over 150; by mid-1939, it had held 21 debates, regularly attended by over 50 people. The Minute Book ends in May 1939: there is a membership list dated January 1947, but the Club never regained its pre-war activism (some members died in the war, and others had moved on to other things), and soon ground to a halt. Prominent speakers and members included the future Liberal leader, Jo Grimond, then in his mid-20s; the future MP, and Liberal leader in the Lords, Frank Byers; and persistent candidates such as Roger Fulford, well-known for his *The Liberal Case* (1959). The Club also included a host of people who in post-war years kept the Liberal Party alive, and held office within the party, such as Nelia Muspratt (later Penman), a general election candidate in the post-war years and president of the Women's Liberal Federation in 1978–79. Although members were overwhelmingly Liberal, they represented a range of opinions within the party,[8] and speakers did include people from other parties.[9] The Club met at 14 Wilton Crescent, SW1, the home of the Borthwicks, a well-known Liberal family, who were central to founding the Club.[10]

The importance of international issues in these debates can be seen in the range of topics discussed at the 8.30 Club. Of the 21 debates held between February 1936 and March 1939, 11 were on international politics, ranging from the manufacture of armaments, to the Munich Crisis. Two further debates were on issues related to international policy (the idea of a Popular Front, and the suppression of communist and fascist parties); two were on light-hearted topics; and six were on domestic issues. A full list of the debates and speakers is given in Appendix 6, but six debates were particularly interesting. Two of these showed that at low levels within the party new ideas on foreign policy were being discussed, prior to their being raised on a wider national platform. The first of these debates was on 31 March 1936 when, by a large (unspecified) majority, the Club voted for a motion saying that the League should develop an international police force. In the debate, it was argued that without such a force the League was ineffective, and we have seen earlier that this idea was discussed widely in the party. A second debate on new ideas took place a year later, in March 1937, when by 22 votes to 16, the Club decided 'that the present distribution of colonies among World powers is inequitable'. In opposition to this, a view put by (amongst others) Jo Grimond was that Britain managed its colonies better than other colonial powers, and that colonies were strategically necessary for Britain. However, the decisive point, put by W. Fordham and Betty Arne, was that colonies gave prestige to their owners, and that unless prestige was spread more equally, there could never be peace – this meant that all colonies should be placed under the mandate of the League. This proposal was soon to be discussed in the WLF, and during the Second World War, it became Liberal Party policy.[11]

Aside from being a forum for discussing new ideas, the 8.30 Club also highlighted divisions within the Liberal Party. One of these was the tension between the need to revise Versailles, and the need to maintain collective security. This was seen in a May 1936 debate, on the motion

'That this House prefers to support France rather than Germany';[12] 25 voted for France and 13 for Germany, which revealed the difficulty in reaching a unified view of how to proceed in European policy. Most accepted that Germany had justifiable grievances, but many did not trust Hitler, and wanted the focus of policy to be on preventing aggressive expansion through an Anglo-French collective security system. Over the next two years, this would be a contentious issue within the Liberal Party. As we saw earlier, by the end of 1936, the Liberal Council had taken a clearer position, while by the 1938 LSS, the revisionists had dwindled in numbers, and the party was more settled on collective security. Two opportunities that the 8.30 Club had for debating specific responses to aggression showed similar divisions. In October 1936, the Club actually rejected a motion condemning the government's non-intervention policy in Spain, accepting the view that the civil war was an internal matter, and that, even though other countries had intervened, British intervention would only cause a wider war.[13] In January 1937, the Club also decisively rejected conscription,[14] as the party as a whole consistently did until it became a *fait accompli* in 1939. Perhaps the most important debate, though, was that on the Munich Crisis – on 8 November 1938 the Club condemned the government's policy by 26 to 15.[15] Though decisive, this vote represented a significant division, which shadowed that of the Parliamentary Liberal Party, showing that divisions on foreign policy could be found in the party as whole, rather than just in the parliamentary elite.

CONCLUSION

International policy played an important part at 'low' levels of Liberal politics. Without further evidence, it is difficult to be sure exactly *why* this was the case. However, we can be sure that Liberals campaigning throughout the country gave a high priority to their internationalist case. Even at times other than the Munich Crisis, international policy was, therefore, a significant aspect of the discourse of inter-war politics in Britain.

NOTES

1. *The Times*, 22 May 1919, p. 14; 26 May 1919, p. 9.
2. NLC Archives, DM668: London Liberal Federation, *The London Liberal Programme of 1920* (London: London Liberal Federation, June 1920). LLF, 34th–36th Annual Reports, 1936–38.
3. University of Bristol, NLC Archives, DM1172: Western Counties Liberal Federation Executive Minutes, 1927–66.

4. University of Bristol, NLC Archives, DM 668: Home Counties Liberal Federation, Executive Committee Reports.
5. University of Bristol, NLC Archives, DM668: *The Liberal Agent*, 30, 134 (July 1929), p. 12.
6. E.A. Rowe, 'The British General Election of 1929' (Oxford BLitt. thesis, 1959).
7. The author was given access to the minute book by Mrs Nelia Penman, who responded to his letter in *Liberal Democrat News* (No. 448, 14 Feb. 1997, p. 7), asking to be contacted by people who were active in the Liberal Party in the 1920s and 1930s. Mrs Penman (as Nelia Muspratt) was active in the 8.30 Club, and had recently obtained the minute book from the Club's former honorary secretary, Valerie Borthwick. The minute book has subsequently been deposited with the archives of the National Liberal Club, at the University of Bristol Library.
8. Examples of diverse views amongst members were: A.J. Irvine, who joined the Labour Party in 1943 (having been a Liberal candidate in 1935 and 1939), and was a Labour MP in 1947–78; and E.H. Garner Evans, who served as a Conservative and National Liberal MP in 1950–59.
9. Two Conservative speakers achieved some prominence in later life: J.A. Boyd-Carpenter served in the Cabinet as paymaster-general in 1962–4, while Derek Walker-Smith was a junior minister in the late 1950s.
10. The existing membership list begins on 25 Feb. 1936, at the 8.30 Club's inception. By 3 May 1938, it had recorded 154 people having joined, with a further six names deleted from the list. However, either a page is missing or it was never made, as the accounts of debates include reference to 31 people joining at debates later in 1938 and 1939, so real figures were nearer 200.
11. 8.30 Club Minute Book: ff. 10a, and b, Account of Debate, 31 Mar. (1936); ff. 28a, and b, Account of Debate, 16 Mar. (1937).
12. 8.30 Club: f. 14, Account of Debate, 26 May 1936.
13. 8.30 Club: f. 18a–c, Account of Debate, 27 Oct. 1936.
14. 8.30 Club: ff. 22a, and b, Account of Debate, 12 Jan. 1937.
15. 8.30 Club: ff. 50a, and b, Account of Debate, 8 Nov. 1938.

Conclusion: Liberal Politics and Liberal Ideology

T HIS CONCLUDING chapter examines the place of inter-war Liberal international policy and the development of a distinctive Liberal ideology. It also draws together the main themes of Liberal international policies in the inter-war period to examine how far they were practical, and how far they made an impact on Liberal policy after the Second World War.

THE LEAGUE OF NATIONS, MILITARY DISARMAMENT AND TREATY REVISION: LIBERAL INTERNATIONALISM IN THE 1920s

Liberal international policy in the 1920s was defined by a commitment to the League of Nations, military disarmament and treaty revision. This was in particular contrast to the arms-length approach to the League of both Labour and the Conservatives. It stemmed partly from the experience of the First World War, which illustrated the necessity of developing an international body to remedy grievances, and then reducing armaments to a low level. Meanwhile, Liberal international policy was strongly influenced by the belief that there must be a 'clean peace', as argued by Asquith from 1917, and put more clearly by Keynes in his *The Economic Consequences of the Peace*. This persuaded Liberals (and many in other parties) that the Treaty of Versailles was unjust and that, consequently, it was likely to lead to another conflict if its excesses were not remedied.

How practical were Liberal policies in these areas? First, on treaty revision, at all levels of the party, the idea of reducing reparations was popular and widely argued. It was, moreover, a policy which was likely to meet with a favourable response in Germany. However, other German grievances, such as territorial questions, were not tackled in any detail in the 1920s, and at no point did the party ever consider exactly what Germany should be entitled to, and whether this might satisfy the Germans. For the Liberal policy of treaty revision to have been genuinely practical, it should have had some idea of the nature of any future territorial settlement. One might also ask why the Liberal Party was not more outspokenly critical of government policy on treaty revision in the 1920s? One clear answer to this is that for much of the decade this important aspect of British foreign policy was conducted along lines with which most Liberals could agree. Governments run by Labour and the Conservatives all accepted that the Versailles settlement needed to be revised, and that Germany needed to be brought into the League of Nations. Because this Liberal orthodoxy was pursued by Conservative and Labour politicians in office, not only did the Liberal Party not need to formulate new policies, but it was not able to criticise many of the principles underlying government policy.

What though of the League and disarmament – important rallying cries for Liberals in the 1920s? On the latter issue, there is no doubt that Liberals had clear ideas on how Britain could disarm, and we have seen that the party put forward detailed proposals on, for example, sizes of ships and numbers of soldiers. This issue was also the one on which the Liberal Party differed most from the Conservative government of 1924–29, and so it was particularly vocal on disarmament. It was similarly vocal against Labour's 1924 programme to build more cruisers for the Royal Navy. There is also no doubt that, had a Liberal government taken office in Britain in the mid/late 1920s, specific and ambitious proposals would have been made to the other major world powers. The answer that these powers would have given to Liberals would have depended on how secure they felt. The view that disarmament could only follow a security settlement was a constant refrain of the French in the 1920s, and this depended on making the League a body which could genuinely settle important international disputes.

Much, then, hung on the Liberal Party's ability to develop the League and, at first glance, one might say that the party had only the beginnings of a League policy in the 1920s, with few specific proposals. But this would miss the point of Liberal policy. While it is true to say that the party simply believed that nations should make a leap of faith and submit all of their disputes to the League, it is not fair to dismiss this as naïve and idealistic. It was a cogent view of international affairs, in which obedience to international law was paramount. If nations adopted the simple principle of abiding by League decisions, then all else would follow. Moreover, the leap of faith was backed up by the view that resistance to aggression could only be made a reality if all nations in the League agreed to take part in sanctions. Though it was not a complicated plan, it was a policy which contained in it the seeds of a new world order, and provided the party with both principles and a policy. Winning the argument for universal international law was thus at the heart of Liberal international policy in the 1920s.

INTERDEPENDENCY, ECONOMIC DISARMAMENT AND COLLECTIVE
SECURITY: LIBERAL INTERNATIONALISM IN THE 1930s

Even if Liberal international policy had been cogent in the 1920s, it
would not be correct to say that Liberals had strongly thought out the
principles underlying their policies. These had not advanced much
beyond the Gladstonian idea that nations could be made to behave as
individuals did, by agreeing to abide by laws. In the 1930s, however,
Liberals articulated a new principle, that of 'interdependency'.

The main originator of interdependency was Walter Layton. The first
occasion on which this idea was discussed in Liberal circles was at the
1931 Liberal Summer School, on 2 August, when Walter Layton said that
the global economic crisis had given the world 'an object lesson on the
interdependence of nations such as it has never had before'. But Layton
had himself raised the idea in an editorial in *The Economist* in April 1929,
in the context of defending free trade, and throughout 1929–31 it had
gained a wide audience through the pages of the journal. The idea was
soon given further publicity by Ramsay Muir's book *The Interdependent
World and its Problems* (1932), and in the same year that this book was
published, Muir and Lady Acland moved a resolution at the NLF which
declared that, 'All the peoples of the earth have become politically and
economically interdependent.' Ever since the 1930s, interdependency
has remained at the heart of the Liberal approach to international policy.
Today, the belief in the 'interdependence of the world's peoples' stands
in the Liberal Democrats' party constitution as proof of that.

By the early 1930s, the Liberal belief in interdependency was accompanied by the view that governments throughout the world had
declared an 'economic war' on each other, through erecting tariff barriers
and seeking to exclude other nations from the colonies that they controlled. Liberals came to believe that this was at the root of many of the
grievances of the expansionist powers, and they argued that 'economic
disarmament' was necessary in order to place the world on a more stable
footing. This involved passing a number of resolutions at the NLF in
the mid-1930s, calling for a World Economic Conference which would
re-establish free trade; but it reached its fruition in 1937, at the Assembly,
which urged international agreement on 'the control of colonial territories, the distribution of raw materials, the stabilisation of exchanges
and the accessibility of markets'. Though the Liberal Party did not accept
radical calls for international control of all colonies until 1942, it was
clear that any settlement of international grievances would involve a
marked change in the way colonies were managed. This represented
the integration of foreign and imperial policies into one 'international
policy'.

But the policy did not simply depend on there being an economic conference at which all powers would happily come to agreement, making some gains, and making some concessions. The idea of economic disarmament was underpinned by 'collective security'. In its first version, this meant developing the League of Nations so that it could settle grievances, while at the same time being able to resist any acts of aggression that might be made by a country or group of countries. Later, Liberals came to accept that alliances might have to replace the League. The origins of the Liberal conception of collective security are to be found in the realisation, after the Japanese attack on Manchuria in 1931, that the League must show that it was capable of preventing challenges to international law by the resolute imposition of sanctions. By 1934, Liberal policy was to investigate the establishment of an international air force under the control of the League. By the time of the Liberal Party Council meeting in December 1936, with the Rhineland remilitarised, and Mussolini secure in Abyssinia, the party was talking more openly about the need for collective security to be backed up by military force, and it had accepted that the League had been weakened. The party thus entered 1937 with a policy firmly in favour of showing the dictators that aggression would be resisted militarily. By mid-1938, it was recognised that if this could not happen through the League, it might need to take place through an alliance system. From then until the outbreak of war in September 1939, the vast bulk of the Liberal Party stuck to this line, especially in parliament under the leadership of Archibald Sinclair, with only one-fifth of Liberal MPs supporting the government on Munich.

One problem for the Liberals was that the idea of collective security did not find much favour in the country. As we have seen, Sinclair was roundly and regularly denounced as a warmonger, as were the other anti-appeasers such as Churchill. Moreover, there was not even support from every section of the Liberal Party, as a small group, including people such as J.A. Spender and Lord Lothian, never accepted that the League should be abandoned, and argued that an alliance system would plunge the world into war. However, every writer on alternatives to appeasement accepts that they were not universally popular. So if one assumes that a Liberal government would have behaved differently had one been in power, the most important question to ask is whether an alternative would have worked?

This question, of course, depends in part on indulging in some counter-factual history, and it is never possible to come up with firm answers. We can, however, make an attempt to do so, based on what we know actually did happen. If we do this, we can be fairly sure that the Liberal view that a colonial settlement would prevent the dictators from advancing was fraught with difficulties. In the first place, we know with a fair degree of certainty that Hitler's main ambitions lay in eastern Europe, and that one of his most important targets was the conquest of the Soviet Union. If he did intend to regain colonial possessions as part of a plan for world domination (and this is hotly contested),[1] then it came much lower in his order of priority. Though colonial questions were probably more important for the Italians and the Japanese, these two countries were at least as much interested in controlling territories themselves, as sharing resources with the world.

What though, of collective security? This was the mainstay of Liberal international policy in the mid-to late-1930s, and it was only by showing the dictators that aggression would be resisted that Liberals believed Hitler and the others would even come to the conference table. Could it have worked? This question has been argued over by historians for decades now, and much depends on whether it would have been possible to induce France and the Soviet Union to join with Britain in an anti-Nazi alliance. There is clear evidence that France would have been prepared to join with Britain in an alliance after the *Anschluss*, and this may well have made it clear to Germany that aggression would be met with stern resistance. The Soviet Union's position is less clear, but it is certain that they offered Britain and France a triple alliance in April 1939, and that Chamberlain rejected it because he was staunchly anti-Soviet. As Parker says, clear alternatives to appeasement were on offer in 1938 and 1939, and they were all rejected by the government.[2] The Liberal Party had been prominent in arguing for these in public, and it is clear that if it had been in office, the policy of appeasement would have been dropped long before Hitler presented terms to Czecho-slovakia in the summer of 1938.

Any discussion of alternatives to appeasement has to come back, at some point, to an understanding of what Hitler actually intended to do. Was he a uniquely evil leader, who would have tried to dominate Europe whatever the other European powers did? Or was he, as Taylor argued, an opportunist, who exploited weaknesses in British and French diplomacy? One does not need to adopt a position on this dispute to say that there was at least as much chance of the Liberal policy working as there was of appeasement maintaining peace. For if Hitler was an opportunist, then it was necessary to adopt collective security, showing him that aggression was futile, and that through diplomacy he could make significant gains where his grievances were just. However, if Hitler intended to dominate Europe, then it was necessary to arm and resist his claims for territory in Czechoslovakia. In the long term, concessions alone could never prevent Hitler from expanding throughout eastern Europe, and they ultimately only made it easier for him to concentrate on his real goals in the Soviet Union.

A LIBERAL PHILOSOPHY OF INTERNATIONAL RELATIONS

In the introduction to this book, Martin Ceadel's analysis of inter-national relations was discussed as a useful starting point when thinking about this general area. It was said there that in Ceadel's typology, most Liberals of the 1920s and 1930s would be categorised as pacific-ists, in that they believed that war could be prevented and eventually abolished by reforms, with defence justified as a way to protect reforms. In the proverbial 'ideal world', there is little doubt that this would be true. As we have seen, for much of the inter-war period, Liberals argued that peace could best be achieved through developing the international law of the League of Nations, with the law backed up by economic/military sanctions.

However, the evidence of the years following the announcement of German rearmament, makes such a categorisation problematic. In these years most Liberals placed far more emphasis on more 'defencist' or even 'crusading' types of international policy such as collective security. This does not mean though, that Ceadel's typology is invalid. All it suggests is that, in practice, distinctions between different types of international thought can be difficult to make. Liberals were far more pragmatic than we might have believed in the past, and 'events' had a major influence on their views.

To truly understand the nature of debates in the Liberal Party at this time, an alternative typology can be developed. In this, two terms which are already in use for this period as a whole can be appropriated, and by slightly altering each of them, they can be made relevant to the Liberal Party. These terms are 'collective security' and 'appeasement'. By prefacing both with the term 'internationalist', one can make them appropriate for Liberals. Thus, we have the bulk of the party favouring 'internationalist collective security': this is defined as support for the internationalism of the League of Nations, underpinned by economic disarmament, but backed up by collective security when a crisis threat-ened and the negotiating procedures of the League had clearly failed. Implicit in that was a rejection of the nineteenth-century Liberal belief in the supremacy of the nation state. Most of the figures discussed in this book fall into this category, but among its most enthusiastic advocates were Archibald Sinclair, Megan Lloyd George and Ramsay Muir. Overwhelmingly, this approach informed party policy until mid-1938. After that point, with the League in tatters, internationalist col-lective security refocused on a Grand Alliance centred on Britain, France and the Soviet Union to provide the ballast for a tough diplomatic stance against Hitler.

In the second category we have the 'internationalist appeasers'. They were far less influential than other Liberals, but included prominent figures such as Lord Lothian, F.W. Hirst and, in the late 1930s, Herbert Samuel. In the final years before the war, there was little in what they said to distinguish them from the bulk of appeasers in the Conservative Party, but underpinning their approach lay a belief that international law should be at the heart of foreign policy. This gave them much in common with the Liberal Party, but their belief that Hitler could be trusted separated them from their Liberal colleagues. With internationalist collective security dominating the party, it is important to reflect further on what that meant, and how it differed from previous Liberal attitudes to international relations.

One important line of continuity was from the party's long-established commitment to free trade. In the context of Ottawa, Anthony Howe has argued that, 'If Cobdenite ideas retained any substantial influence after 1932, it was within the gamut of instincts and principles that informed the "idealist" strand in British foreign policy and public opinion on issues of war and peace.' As with pre-First World War Radicalism, inter-war Liberalism went beyond Cobden's view that free trade itself was the best weapon against war. In both periods, international law was key, but it was equally true that policy in both periods placed much emphasis on free trade as a part of an overall peace package. For Liberals in the 1930s that meant that economic disarmament was a vital part of their alternative to appeasement.[3]

One of the most important aspects of free trade was that it led Liberals to develop a distinctive view of the relationship between nations. In Edwardian Britain, and even before, Liberals believed that the economic interdependence of states through trade gave them shared interests. That meant that they formed, as Bernstein has argued, 'a community with a common interest, just as domestic society did'.[4] For Edwardian Liberals, that could best be protected by agreement between the European powers, resolving differences between themselves in concert and acting jointly against sources of trouble from elsewhere – although, practically, there were no major non-European threats to stability other than Japan.

This view of the world as a community continued to inform the inter-war Liberal mind. But there were important changes. In the first instance, the idea of European Concert was seen as deeply flawed. That view arose from the belief that the pre-war system of diplomacy had failed due to 'secret diplomacy', and the lack of clear procedures for solving disputes. No Concert could tackle those problems as the diplomacy that it involved tended to be secret, and did not seek to create international law or internationally accepted structures for conflict resolution. So inter-war Liberals invested their hope in the League of Nations, which it was hoped would be far more effective at securing international stability, because it would be rules-based and transparent. Crucially, it was hoped that the League would be universal. Obviously, in a way that the Concert of Europe never could be, it would be extra-European. But it would also include representation for all nations, with the result that disputes between small powers could be resolved through the League, rather than dragging in Great Powers in the way that the Balkans had prior to 1914.

If the pre-war view of international community changed, it also developed. In particular, the very idea of community became more sophisticated in the inter-war years. Prior to 1914, interdependence had been based solely on economic considerations. But the interdependency of which Walter Layton and Ramsay Muir wrote was of a different order entirely. In particular, it included the dominance of Western values in trade, films and sport. Meanwhile, the existence of the League of Nations both stemmed from and fed political interdependency, as politicians found that decisions made by an international body had the potential to supersede the authority of national parliaments.

All of this was accompanied by a development in Liberal attitudes to empire. Prior to 1914, Liberals had no interest in expanding the Empire. In the inter-war years, it became far more consensual to embrace self-government enthusiastically. No longer was it a Radical position. This, combined with the commitment to the League, contributed to an approach to international relations in which Liberals looked well beyond the Empire in terms of defining the political community to which Britain belonged.

A further aspect of internationalist collective security was the Liberal attitude to weaponry. In contrast to the pre-war Liberal approach, Liberals of the inter-war period saw international regulation of military force as crucial. That took several forms. In the first instance, they pursued the cause of disarmament, believing that the existence of armaments was a cause of war, and that the British government should push harder for international agreements. So throughout the 1920s, criticisms of the government record on disarmament were a feature of Liberal politics, and showed some similarity to pre-war Radical critiques of government policy, which had seen excessive military expenditure as both dangerous and a distraction from social priorities. The difference in the inter-war Liberal case is found partly in the view that international disarmament agreements were a priority. A further difference is also seen in the belief that private manufacture of armaments might be incompatible with the goals of peace. So at the same time as a degree of internationalisation of disarmament, there might have to be a measure of nationalisation of arms production.

The major difference between the pre-war and inter-war Liberal approach to weaponry, however, was the growing realisation that an international military force might be necessary. Having recognised from 1918 onwards that the League might have to rely at some point on military cooperation between its members as the ultimate sanction (Murray's 'crushing war'), they came to see that a force under the League's control might be the only way of achieving this. So in the 1930s, Liberals looked towards an international police force, usually focusing on the need for an international air force. That stemmed from two dominant features of the 1930s mindset. The first was the fear of aerial bombing, which, it was believed, could be devastating to civilian populations. Control of the air, therefore, would protect civilians against that danger. But, second was the realisation that the League might only work if it had some kind of force to use against a disobedient and disruptive nation. For the same reason that air power was seen as such a terrible offensive weapon, a significant League air force was seen as an effective deterrent.

It was hoped, of course, that such action would not be necessary if bodies for resolving international conflicts were effective. So the inter-war years also saw the development of Liberal thought on international cooperation. At the heart of this was the League of Nations, which represented a leap forward in terms of Liberal attitudes to international cooperation. Before 1914, Liberals had tended to see treaties and law as the focus of collaboration between nations. But, after 1918, their thought was institutionally focused, believing that an all-inclusive institution was far more likely to be effective than the essentially random development of international law. Thus, in the 1920s and 1930s, Liberal international thought exhibited universalist and institutionalist dimensions that had not been apparent before the First World War.

This all meant that a passionate belief in the League of Nations was the *leitmotif* of inter-war Liberal internationalism, before it became apparent in 1938 that it had failed. Until that point, the institution of the universal League was believed to be the answer to all international disputes. When it was seen merely as weak or needing development – as it was on several occasions – Liberals simply argued for a stronger commitment to the League, or sought further universal institutions, such as an International Equity Tribunal and an International Police Force. That approach lay at the heart of internationalist collective security in the 1920s and 1930s.

LIBERAL INTERNATIONALISM DURING AND AFTER THE SECOND WORLD WAR

Liberal policy in the 1930s aimed at preventing war, perhaps through a show of force; perhaps through actually using force. When war actually broke out, though, there was no Liberal strategy on how the war should be fought, although Lloyd George, in the first months of the war, favoured a negotiated peace, and he was widely accused of defeatism.[5] However, as the First World War had led to the League of Nations, an important outcome of the Second World War for Liberals was the creation of the United Nations. Indeed, early in the war, Liberals in the League of Nations Union had argued that a new organisation would be vital after the war.[6]

As we saw in Chapter 4, many of the more radical ideas discussed within the party in the late 1930s became Liberal policy during the war. These included the establishment of an international police force, and the international control of colonies, and they had obvious roots in inter-war Liberalism. So too did the post-war Liberal commitment to European Union[7] when it became an issue after 1945. By the 1950s, the party's internationalist hue on Europe and other issues was an important part of its platform and it was often given as a reason by members for joining the party.[8] It was certainly not the case that all Liberals took a pro-European view – some (Dingle Foot, Gilbert Murray) had broader internationalist horizons than just Europe: they believed that membership of Europe would harm Britain's Commonwealth and Atlantic interests. Some (Dingle Foot again, and Lady Megan Lloyd George) were anxious about surrendering sovereignty on vital national interests. But, broadly, Liberals were enthusiasts for Europe, especially people such as Lord Layton and F.L. Josephy. The Liberal Assembly passed pro-European motions in 1947 and 1948, and in 1956 it called for Britain to be active in establishing a common market. There was some wavering in 1958–59, when Jo Grimond preferred EFTA to the EEC, and there is some evidence to suggest that the pro-EEC policy represented a victory for the Liberal Parliamentary Party against the more free-trade rank-and-file Liberal Party Organisation.[9] In any case, from 1959, the Liberal Party was resolutely pro-EEC.

Prior to 1939, schemes for European federalism had fallen on deaf ears in Liberal ranks: the League offered all that Liberals wanted in international cooperation, and the Empire made it problematic for Britain to forge links with European countries. But with the collapse of the League, and the onset of decolonisation, Europe became a more attractive prospect. A belief in a legal or institutional basis to European unity was also a logical development of the Liberal belief that nations must be organised into a wider international body in order to promote peace and prosperity. This begins from a belief that it is possible to have a moral order as the basis of international peace, and that nations can be made to behave like individuals if the correct laws are in place. Strong roots of this are found in the idea of interdependency that became such an important part of Liberalism in the 1930s.

Even though the structure of the British electoral system, and the legacy of the Asquith–Lloyd George feud, kept the Liberal Party out of office in the 1920s and 1930s by preventing a major Liberal revival, there was a constant and thriving third-party debate on international politics. The inter-war years were genuinely a time of three-party politics in a two-party system. Liberalism survived, even if countless able Liberal MPs and candidates experienced electoral defeat. With support for internationalism being so important to Liberal Democrats in British politics today, the spirit of the defeated yet gallant crusaders of the 1920s and 1930s lives on.

NOTES

1. See, for example, Philip Bell, 'Hitler's War? The Origins of the Second World War', in Paul Hayes (ed.), *Themes in Modern European History, 1890–1945* (London: Routledge, 1992). Alan Bullock, 'Hitler and the Origins of the Second World War', in E.M. Robertson (ed.), *The Origins of the Second World War* (London: Macmillan, 1971). Milan Hauner, 'Did Hitler Want a World Dominion', *Journal of Contemporary History*, 13 (1978), pp. 15–32. Keith Robbins, 'Fifty Years On: Recent Scholarship on the Origins of the Second World War', *German History*, 8, 3 (1990), pp. 339–45.
2. Parker, *Chamberlain and Appeasement*, pp. 136–7, 224, 347.
3. Anthony Howe, *Free Trade and Liberal England, 1846–1946* (Oxford: Clarendon, 1997), pp. 295, 302.
4. George L. Bernstein, *Liberalism and Liberal Politics in Edwardian England* (Boston, MA: Allen & Unwin, 1986), p. 166.
5. Wrigley, *Lloyd George*, pp. 141–2. Frank Owen, *Tempestuous Journey: Lloyd George, His Life and Times* (London: Hutchinson, 1954), p. 745.
6. Birn, *League of Nations Union*, pp. 201–2.
7. The term EU is only strictly appropriate after the Maastricht Treaty, but it is used here to refer to the general idea of European integration, rather than specific forms such as EEC or EFTA.
8. Jorgen Scott Rasmussen, *The Liberal Party: A Study of Retrenchment and Revival* (London: Constable, 1965) pp. 245–7.
9. Ibid., p. 142. Malcolm Baines, 'The Survival of the British Liberal Party, 1932–59' (Oxford DPhil., 1990), pp. 96, 116–19, 136–8.

Appendix 1:
General Elections, 1918–45

	Seats	Candidates	Votes	% votes
1918 (December):				
Coalition Unionist	335	374	3,504,198	32.6
Coalition Liberal	133	158	1,455,640	13.5
Coalition Labour	10	18	161,521	1.5
(Coalition)	(478)	(550)	(5,121,359)	(47.6)
Conservative	23	37	370,375	3.4
Irish Unionist	25	38	292,722	2.7
Liberal	28	253	1,298,808	12.1
Labour	63	388	2,385,472	22.2
Irish Nationalist	7	60	238,477	2.2
Sinn Fein	73	102	486,867	4.5
Independent and others	10	197	572,503	5.3
1922 (November):				
Conservative	345	483	5,500,382	38.2
National Liberal	62	162	1,673,240	11.6
Liberal	54	328	2,516,287	17.5
Labour	142	411	4,241,383	29.5
Others	12	59	462,340	3.2
1923 (December):				
Conservative	258	540	5,538,824	38.1
Liberal	159	453	4,311,147	29.6
Labour	191	422	4,438,508	30.5
Others	7	31	260,042	1.8
1924 (October):				
Conservative	419	552	8,039,598	48.3
Liberal	40	340	2,928,747	17.6
Labour	151	512	5,489,077	33.0
Communist	1	8	55,346	0.3
Others	5	16	181,857	1.1

	Seats	Candidates	Votes	% votes
1929 (May):				
Conservative	260	590	8,656,473	38.2
Liberal	59	513	5,308,510	23.4
Labour	288	571	8,389,512	37.1
Communist	0	25	50,614	0.3
Others	8	31	293,880	1.0
1931 (October):				
Conservative	473	523	11,978,745	55.2
National Labour	13	20	341,370	1.6
Liberal National	35	41	809,302	3.7
Liberal	33	112	1,403,102	6.5
(National Government)	(554)	(696)	(14,532,519)	(67.0)
Independent Liberal	4	7	106,106	0.5
Labour	52	515	6,649,630	30.6
Communist	0	26	74,824	0.3
New Party	0	24	36,377	0.2
Others	5	24	256,917	1.2
1935 (November):				
Conservative	432	585	10,922,827	49.7
Liberal National	33	44	887,331	4.0
Liberal	21	161	1,422,116	6.4
Labour	154	552	8,325,491	37.9
Ind. Lab. Party	4	17	139,577	0.7
Communist	1	2	27,117	0.1
Others	4	31	272,595	1.2
1945 (July):				
Conservative	213	624	9,988,306	39.8
Labour	393	604	11,995,152	47.8
Liberal	12	306	2,248,226	9.0
Communist	2	21	102,780	0.4
Common Wealth	1	23	110,634	0.4
Others	19	104	640,880	2.0

Sources: David Butler and Gareth Butler, *British Political Facts, 1900–1994* (London: Macmillan, 1994); Rif Winfield, *Liberals in Parliament: An Electoral History, 1924–1994* (Aberystwyth: University of Wales, 1994).

Appendix 2:
The Liberal Summer School
(dates and speakers on international relations)

This list indicates who spoke on international relations at Liberal Summer Schools. Opening and closing speeches by party leaders usually referred to some aspect of the issue, but their speeches have only been listed when it was a substantial part of their address.

1921, 26 September–c. 2 August, Grasmere

Walter Layton (International Finance and Reparations)

1922, 1–9 August, Oxford

J.M. Keynes (Reparations and Rhineland)
Robert Cecil (League of Nations and Europe)
Frederick Maurice (Disarmament)
Hamilton Grant (India)
J.A. Spender (Egypt)
Viscount Grey (Anglo-American Relations and Europe as part of closing address)

1923, 2–9 August, Cambridge

Walter Layton (Arms Reduction as part of a 'Budget for 1933')

1924, 30 July–6 August, Oxford

Lord Meston (India)
Gilbert Murray (League of Nations as part of opening address)
Edward Grigg (Empire Consultation in Foreign Policy)

1925, 29 July–5 August, Cambridge

Francesco Nitti (Liberty and Italy)
Albert Milhaud (French Liberalism)
Moritz Bonn (German Liberalism)

1926, 23–30 July, Oxford

Viscount Grey (Locarno, the League, and Europe)
Walter Layton (League of Nations Economic Conference and Anglo-
American Debts)
J.A. Spender ('The Contentions of East and West' – travel surveys)
Walter Runciman (Anglo-American Debts)

1927, 28 July–4 August, Cambridge

No discussion of international relations: LSS entirely devoted to
industrial policy.

1928, 2–9 August, Oxford

Sheldon Amos (Egypt)
Philip Kerr (India and East Africa)
Wilson Harris (The Future of the League (read by Walter Layton))
J.A. Spender (Anglo-American Relations)
Ramsay Muir (League of Nations in closing address)
Herbert Samuel (Nationalism and Internationalism in closing address)

1929, 1–8 August, Cambridge

J.W. Garner (Anglo-American Naval Disarmament)
S.K. Ratcliffe (Anglo-American Naval Disarmament)
Philip Kerr (Anglo-American Relations)
Geoffrey Mander (Disarmament)

1930, 31 July–6 August, Oxford

Robert Hamilton (East Africa)
Walter Layton (India)
Srinivasa Sastri (India)
Ameer Ali (India)
Lord Lothian (Russia)
Walter Layton (Tariffs and International Relations)
Arthur Salter (Anglo-American Debts)

1931, 30 July–5 August, Cambridge

Lord Lothian (Russia)
Walter Layton (European Crisis and Interdependency)
E.M. Patterson (American Foreign Policy)

1932, 28 July–3 August, Oxford

Ramsay Muir (Tariffs)
Lord Astor (Tariffs)
C.R.S. Harris (Tariffs)
Robert Cecil (Disarmament)
R.B. MacCallum (Disarmament)
Dingle Foot (Patriotism)
Frederick Whyte (Far East)

1933, 3–9 August, Cambridge

Kingsley Griffith (Economic Nationalism as part of opening
   address)
Lord Lothian (Economics, Sovereignty, and Federalism)
Frederick Whyte (International Police Force)
Sir John Hope Simpson (Situation in China)
Walter Layton (Tariffs)

1934, 2–8 August, Oxford

Herbert Samuel (Intervention as part of opening address)
Geoffrey Mander (Disarmament)
Walter Layton (Tariffs)

1935, 1–7 August, Cambridge

Norman Angell (Collective security)
Ramsay Muir (Colonies and Tariffs)

1936, 30 July–5 August, Oxford

Rachel Crowdy (Japan in the Far East)
Lady Layton (Sanctions and Treaty Revision)
Ivan Maisky (USSR and the League)
P.S. Mumford (Air Bombing)
Edward Thompson ('For what shall I fight?')
Walter Layton (Anti-pacifism)
Karl von Abshagen (German Colonial Claims)
Arthur Salter (German Colonial Claims)
George Paish (World Economic Conference as part of closing
   address)

1937, 29 July–4 August, Cambridge

Archibald Sinclair (Economic Disarmament as part of opening
  address)
Herbert Richmond (British Empire)
Lord Allen of Hurtwood (Remedy of International Grievances)
H. Horsfall Carter (League of Nations)
Wickham Steed (Czechoslovakia)

1938, 28 July–3 August, Oxford

Jules Menken (War and Economics)
Frederick Whyte (Far East)
Herbert Samuel (Germany)
Ramsay Muir (Appeasement)
George Edinger (Appeasement)
Miss Wellington Koo (China)
Peter Chalmers Mitchell (Spain)
Elizabeth Wiskemann (Czechoslovakia)
Walter Layton (Mobilisation in War)
William Brown (Psychology of Nationalism)

1939, 3–9 August, Cambridge

Graham Hutton (Economic Resources of Axis Powers)
Lionel Curtis (Federalism)
Ramsay Muir (Federalism)
Herbert Samuel (Conscientious Objectors)
Arthur Willert (US Foreign Policy)
Arthur Salter (British Foreign Policy)
Eduard Beneš (Science and Art)
Walter Layton (Germany)
Ramsay Muir (International Control of Colonies)

Appendix 3:
Dates of Liberal Conferences, 1918–39

National Liberal Federation

1918, 26 & 27 September, Manchester
1919, 27 & 28 November, Birmingham
1920, 25 & 26 November, Bradford
1921, 24 & 25 November, Newcastle
1922, 17–19 May, Blackpool
1923, 30 May–1 June, Buxton
1924, 23 & 24 May, Brighton
1925, 14 & 15 May, Scarborough
1926, 17 & 18 June, Weston-super-Mare
1927, 26 & 27 May, Margate
1928, 11 & 12 October, Great Yarmouth
1929, 3 & 4 October, Nottingham
1930, 16 & 17 October, Torquay
1931, 14 & 15 May 1931, Buxton
1932, 28 & 29 April 1932, Clacton-on-Sea
1933, 18 & 19 May 1933, Scarborough
1934, 3 & 4 May 1934, Bournemouth
1935, 23–25 May 1935, Blackpool

Liberal Party Assembly

1936, 18 & 19 June 1936, London
1937, 27–29 May 1937, Buxton
1938, 19 & 20 May 1938, Bath
1939, 11 & 12 May 1939, Scarborough

Appendix 4:
Policy Statements[1]
(Reproduced by kind permission of the Liberal Democrats)

1. **Resolution on the League of Nations, passed at the National Liberal Federation, 27 November 1919[2]**

Resolution adopted by the NLF

Proposed: Prof. Gilbert Murray
Seconded: Lady Bonham Carter

This Council heartily endorses the resolutions of its general Committee and its Executive Committee welcoming the establishment of the League of Nations. The Council expresses its disappointment that the practical work of the League of Nations has not yet begun, that there are important nations still outside the League and that war is still being waged in many parts of the world. It appeals to all Liberals to take an active part in the task of informing and moulding public opinion in support of the ideals upon which the League is based, and declares its deepened conviction that it is only through this method of enlightened international cooperation that the peace of the world can be made secure.

Amendment rejected by the NLF

Proposed: J.M. Kenworthy, MP
Seconded: A.E. Newbould, MP

This Council heartily endorses the resolutions of its general Committee and its Executive Committee welcoming the establishment of the League of Nations.

The Council maintains that the primary interest of the British Empire and the world is immediate, general, and permanent peace, to secure which the League, elected on a democratic basis, should at once be brought into effective operation; and its first duty should be to enlarge its membership so that it may cease to be an alliance of victors, and become in fact a genuine League of Peoples.

The League should also speedily revise those terms of the Peace

Treaties which are obviously provisional in character, and which, unless modified so as to secure general assent, will be a continuous source of friction and the certain cause of future wars; also more effective provision should be made by the League to prevent those undeveloped countries which are under its tutelage from becoming spheres of economic exploitation by mandatory Powers.

This Council is of opinion that the League should insist upon the general abolition of conscription, the limitation of armaments, and the creation of an international force to ensure its decision; and that all contracts between constituent Powers must in the first instance be submitted to their respective parliaments, and shall be invalid unless approved by the League.

It appeals to all Liberals to take an active part in the task of informing and moulding public opinion in support of the ideals upon which the League is based, and declares its deepened conviction that it is only through this method of enlightened international cooperation that the peace of the world can be made secure.

2. **Resolution on 'The Washington Conference, Armaments, and the League of Nations', passed at the National Liberal Federation, 24 November 1921**[3]

Proposed: Violet Markham
Seconded: Trevelyan Thomson, MP

That this Council of the National Liberal Federation expresses its satisfaction that the Government has sent delegates to the Washington Conference on Disarmament, and cordially welcomes and endorses the proposals made by the Government of the United States of America for a ten years 'Naval Holiday'. The Council heartily approves of the acceptance of these proposals by the British representatives at the Conference, and the suspension of the orders recently given out for large and costly additions to the British Navy.

At the same time, the Council deeply deplores the fact that, although this country is not threatened by any conceivable military combination, and the German Navy has been utterly destroyed, the Government is spending on the Army, the Navy, and the Air Force in the present financial year nearly three times as much as the amount spent before the War.

The Council urges the Government to give specific instructions to its representatives, both at the Washington Conference and on the League of Nations, to support all practical projects for a progressive disarmament of all Nations, and for the maintenance of the Article of the League of Nations Covenant which insists upon open Treaties.

3. Extract on 'Liberal Foreign Policy', from the 1923 Liberal general election manifesto[4]

Liberal Foreign Policy

Liberal policy stands for the prompt settlement of Reparations, with due consideration for the position of inter-Allied debts, and for an earnest endeavour to cooperate with the great American Commonwealth in bringing peace to the world. Liberals hold that the economic restoration of Europe is the necessary condition of the revival of our industries and the establishment of peace. They would welcome the reopening of full relations with Russia.

The whole force of the Liberal Party will be thrown into the support of the League of Nations. Our foreign policy should aim at making full use of the League, and enlarging its scope and power, until all nations are included within it, and in substituting international cooperation for the perpetuation of national enmities and the piling up of the means of destruction.

4. Resolutions on 'Peace and Disarmament' and 'The British Commonwealth', passed at the National Liberal Federation, 11 October 1928[5]

Proposed: Mrs W. Runciman
Seconded: Dr E. Leslie Burgin

(a) Peace and Disarmament

The foundation of all national well-being lies in the establishment of settled peace and mutual confidence between nations. The British Empire ought always to be in the forefront of every effort for real peace, whether associated with the League of Nations, or, like the recent proposals of the United States, originating outside that League. It should be our aim not to act as a brake on the efforts of the League but to stimulate them. We should strive for the conclusion of complete arbitration treaties with all Powers ready to make them, and should sign forthwith the Optional Clause of the Permanent Court of International Justice. We should regain the lead which has been lost by the hesitancy and irresolution of the Government in the movement towards disarmament, both by mutual agreement and by an immediate and substantial reduction of our own armaments in accordance with the spirit of our undertaking in the Covenant of the League of Nations, the Locarno Treaty, and the Kellogg Pact.

(b) The British Commonwealth

The maintenance and improvement of close and friendly relations with the other members of the British Empire is one of the supreme interests of this country. In particular it is important that more effective arrangements should be made for continuous consultation on foreign affairs and defence, with a view to avoiding misunderstandings such as have already arisen. Inter-imperial migration should be more systematically encouraged; the flow of capital for the needs of the Empire should be better regulated, while steady encouragement should be given to the development of free institutions in the dependent regions of the Empire, and primitive peoples should be protected against unfair exploitation. It is as a fellowship of free nations that the British Empire has held together. This, and not any system of fiscal bonds (such as once led to the disruption of the Empire) is the true cement of our commonwealth. A system of Imperial Preference, such as advocated by Protectionists, would dislocate the tested economic system under which this country has thriven, and would impose upon our already burdened people, and more particularly upon the poorer classes, a serious increase in the cost of living. It would, therefore, have the effect not of strengthening, but of weakening, the Empire.

5. **Extract from a pamphlet on 'The Foreign Policy of the Liberal Party', published prior to the May 1929 general election**[6]

The Nine Points of Liberal Foreign Policy

The policy of the Liberal Party is:

(a) To use and strengthen the existing Treaties for the prevention of war and the pacific settlement of international disputes, so that whenever there is any threat of war anywhere the nations may immediately take counsel together to prevent resort to hostilities, or where hostilities have broken out, to stop them in order that the issues may be settled by pacific means. It is to the progressive substitution of law for war that the Liberal Party looks as the primary means of outlawing war upon earth.

(b) To maintain a vigorous initiative at Geneva in promoting those political and humanitarian activities which the League has so conspicuously fostered, and which contribute so much to international justice and good will. Also to strengthen and expand the work of the International Labour Office for uplifting the standards of living of the workers of all nations. Such British initiative has been painfully lacking in the last few years.

(c) To work for an early, large and all-round reduction of armaments. It is a cynical betrayal of the ideals of the peoples that the Governments of the nations should pledge themselves to renounce war altogether as an instrument of national policy and yet continue to maintain the bloated and dangerous armaments they now possess. The all round reduction of armaments will be the acid test of the Nation's faith in the treaties for the pacific settlement of disputes which they have signed. There could be no danger to national security if all nations were to effect simultaneous and equivalent reductions on a large scale. The Treaties for the renunciation of war have altered the basis of national armaments. The British Government should take a fearless lead in bringing about such disarmament agreements and in cutting down its own expenditure on armaments. It ought also to do all in its power to prohibit the use of poison gas, aerial bombs, submarines, or other methods of attacking the civilian population, as being both inhuman and unjustifiable in a world which has renounced war as a lawful instrument of national policy.

(d) To sign the 'Optional Clause' by which all 'justiciable' disputes are referred to the Court of International Justice at the Hague, with the necessary reservation regarding differences between members of the British Commonwealth of Nations.

(e) To accept and apply the principle of the peaceful settlement of international disputes of every kind by conciliation, arbitration, or reference to the Permanent Court of International Justice.

(f) To accept naval parity with the United States in the spirit and in the letter, to work out an agreement to limit and reduce naval armaments on the basis put forward by Mr Gibson at Geneva, and – most important of all – to consider what changes should be made in international law relating to neutral and belligerent rights at sea, as a result of the ratification of the Covenant of the League of Nations, the Bryan Treaties, the Washington Pacific Treaties, and the Pact of Paris.

(g) To develop pacific procedure, through the League of Nations, whereby defects in the Treaties of Peace or in other international treaties can be raised without imputation of unfriendliness, and fairly considered with a view to their revision by agreement. The Liberal Party has no desire to see the treaty system of the world thrown into the melting pot, but it is clear that it will be impossible permanently to prevent war unless international grievances which command the sympathy of world opinion, can be removed peacefully and in time.

(h) To re-establish normal political and economic relations with Russia at the earliest possible date, on the basis of the non-interference of each country in the domestic affairs of the other.

(i) To do all in its power to reduce tariff and other hindrances to international trade to the absolute minimum, in the conviction that the only lasting basis for prosperity in Great Britain, and full employment at high wages, is the freest possible trade between all the nations of the world.

The policy of the Liberal Party is thus one which seeks peace and prosperity for all nations through international cooperation, the League of Nations, disarmament, and freer trade. It is only by moving forward resolutely to these ideals, and not merely by giving lip service to them, that they will effectively be realised.

6. Resolution on 'Peace and Disarmament', passed at the National Liberal Federation, 29 April 1932[7]

Proposed: Gerald Bailey
Seconded: Captain Reginald Berkeley

(a) Peace:
This Council of the National Liberal Federation believes that the course of events in the Far East has seriously imperilled the development of a just and peaceful international order, which is the greatest of British interests. It recognises that War in everything but name has been in progress, and that it is essential that no policy of violence in contravention of the Covenant of the League, the Pact of Paris and the Nine-Power Treaty should be permitted to accomplish anything (though the fairest and most radical consideration should be given to the peaceful satisfaction of the genuine needs of both Japan and China in a changing world). It urges the Government to maintain the fullest support of the policy of the League of Nations resolution of March 11th, and to recognise no situation in Manchuria, or elsewhere, created by means contrary to Pact or Covenant or Nine-Power Treaty; and it assures the Government that, should a policy of protest against the breach of international obligations continue to prove ineffective to secure peace and justice, this Council would support such measures of united collective constraint as may be best fitted to achieve that essential public purpose with the minimum of injury and delay.

(b) Disarmament:
This Council affirms its profound concern that the World Disarmament Conference should result in a general and voluntarily accepted Treaty providing for substantial reduction and comprehensive limitation of the armaments of all nations; notes with satisfaction that the first stage of the Conference has shown, inter alia, considerable agreement as to the desirability of abolishing primarily 'aggressive' weapons, such as were prohibited for certain Powers in the Peace Treaties; and, believing that

this would be a useful and practicable contribution towards disarmament and towards full application of the principle of equality of status, it urges the Government to declare in more definite terms its support of this policy, and, in particular, to support:

    (i)   the abolition, or failing that, the non-replacement and reduction of numbers of warships over 10,000 tons;

   (ii)   the abolition of tanks;

 (iii)   the prohibition of preparations of chemical warfare (as well as prohibition of use in war-time);

 (iv)   the abolition of naval and military aviation, and the international control of civil air transport.

The Council regards limitation of expenditure on armaments as an essential counter-check to direct limitation; it urges the Government to maintain in the Conference the support given to this principle by the British delegation in the Preparatory Commission, and to be forward in applying the principle themselves.

7. Resolutions on Free Trade and Foreign Policy, passed at the National Liberal Federation, 18 May 1933[8]

The Return to Free Trade

Proposed: Sir Francis Acland
Seconded: Sir George Paish

This Council re-affirms its conviction that unfettered freedom of trade is essential to the restoration of prosperity to this country, and pledges itself to work without respite or compromise for the abolition of all protective duties, quotas, subsidies, and other restrictions of any kind whatsoever and for the re-establishment of a complete free trade system in this country.

This Council further affirms that not only is free trade the first economic interest of this country, but that its extension throughout the world is a vital condition of world prosperity and of international peace.

The Council calls upon His Majesty's Government to use every effort to bring about, at the earliest possible moment, the meeting of the World Economic Conference, as the only means by which in an interdependent world, the currents of international trade can be set flowing again, and the world's abundance be made available for the world's peoples. The primary aim of such a Conference must be to bring about the abolition or drastic reduction of the artificial obstacles to world-trade – tariffs, quotas, subsidies[,] prohibitions and exchange restrictions – and the establishment of a stable monetary system, which cannot exist in a tariff-ridden world. If it is to play its part in world-reconstruction, this country must be prepared to give a lead by reversing its present tariff policy, and by cancelling all commitments (such as those of Ottawa) which stand in the way; by abolishing its quotas; and by sweeping away its costly subsidies on wheat, sugar, etc. The Economic Conference should also be asked to adopt an Economic Covenant, whereby all signatory states would agree not to impose new tariffs or other trade restrictions without consultation with other countries affected thereby.

Failing a general agreement on these necessary measures, for the restoration of world-trade, this Council strongly urges that Britain should take the lead in the formation of a union of free trade and Low Tariff countries, which would be open to all nations. Every member of such a Union would pledge itself at its discretion either to admit the goods of other members untaxed, as we maintain this country should do, or not to charge against them any tariff exceeding (say) 10 per cent with exception only for revenue tariffs where the customs duty was balanced by an equivalent excise. They would be free to levy whatever tariffs they might think fit, or none at all, against goods coming from countries not members of the Union. In this way, even if Empire countries did not join the Union, when formed, Britain would retain freedom to admit their products without duty. Such a Union, offering to its members greatly enlarged opportunities of trade, would be so attractive to other countries that its orbit might be expected steadily to enlarge. The adoption of this plan would necessitate a revision of the most-favoured-nation clause in all treaties, which, as it now stands, requires member-countries to give the same terms to non-members without their conceding anything in return.

Peace and Disarmament

Proposed: Dr F.W. Norwood
Seconded: Geoffrey Mander MP

This Council of the National Liberal Federation deplores the fact that the forces which make for war are stronger to-day than at any time since 1918, and that hopes of peace have been weakened by repeated dis-appointments. Therefore a more virile peace-policy is the supreme need of the time.

The Council views with the greatest concern the present position of the League of Nations in respect of the dispute between Japan and China. Means must be found to ensure that decisions are given in future with much less delay, and in the present case practical steps must be taken to convince the parties to the dispute that a decision of the League is a matter of importance. The Council views with distrust the attitude of the Foreign Offices of the Great Powers towards the League, and hopes to see in the future representation of this country a greater measure of accord with public opinion and a greater measure of loyalty to the League.

The Council is in favour of drastic reductions in armaments, but is not unaware of the danger that disarmament discussions which are governed by competitive strategic policies, ultimately envisaging war, cannot have satisfactory results. The war machine cannot be used for the prevention of war. Heavy armaments do not scare it away, and lessened armaments do not mitigate the war spirit.

For economic reasons also, the ruinous and ever-increasing burden of war costs must be lightened. In particular, the deadly new methods with which science is providing the Nations must either be forsworn or brought under international control, and this especially applies to air forces.

The Council pledges the Liberal Party to a more determined Peace Policy, as distinct from a prevention-of-war policy. The Governments of the World are guilty of a suicidal contradiction when they prepare for war while professing that war is legally renounced as an instrument of policy.

8. Resolution on 'Peace and the League of Nations', passed at the National Liberal Federation, 4 May 1934[9]

[This was part of a broad debate throughout the 1934 NLF meeting, which attempted to define an overall Liberal policy statement. The results were published as *The Liberal Way: A Survey of Liberal Policy, Published by the Authority of the National Liberal Federation* (London: George Allen & Unwin, 1934).]

Do we really mean to outlaw war, and to make it possible to trust for our safety to international cooperation through the League of Nations? Or are we still to trust to armaments and alliances, abandoning hope of an organised system of world peace?

Proposed: Mrs Corbett Ashby
Seconded: Geoffrey Mander MP

The Liberal Party believes whole-heartedly and without qualification in the League system. But it recognises that the League cannot do its work, or create the confidence which will lead the nations to disarm, unless the principal countries clearly define beforehand, as they have not yet done, what action they will take to call to account any country which breaks its pledges. Their failure to do this is the cause of the present weakness of the League.

The Liberal Party therefore demands that this country should take the lead by adopting an Act of Parliament empowering the Government to deny financial and trade facilities to an aggressor State; such Act to be brought into operation by a simple resolution of parliament if and when other Nations are ready to cooperate. Other countries can then justly be urged to take the same steps.

The Liberal Party also urges the consideration of the establishment of an International Aerial Police Force under the League of Nations as part of a plan for the abolition of Military Aviation and the international control of civil aircraft as well as generally with a view to increased security and the better maintenance of world order.

9. Resolution on 'Peace and Security', passed at the National Liberal Federation, 25 May 1935 [10]

Proposed: Geoffrey Mander MP
Seconded: J.C. Smuts
Amended by: Hendon & Newcastle Central local parties as indicated in italics

This Council further affirms that the foundations of a healthy social order are peace, security and freedom, all of which are to-day gravely endangered. It reaffirms its conviction that peace and security can no longer be achieved by our own strength, or by means of alliances, but only by a world system of collective guarantee *followed by immediate and general reduction of Armaments*. It deplores the present trend of events, the weakening of the collective system, and the increasing readiness of the nations to trust to *national* armaments for security. This state of things, in a world all of whose peoples hate war and long for secure peace, is mainly due to the failure of governments, including our own, to give adequate and effective support to the League of Nations. *It therefore advocates the strengthening of the League of Nations by the creation of an International Equity Tribunal for the Settlement of non-justiciable disputes, and of an International Police Force to repel aggression and to enable the cooperating States' Members to give effect to* their solemn pledges regarding disarmament. *It also urges the substitution of National control of the Arms Industry, with International publicity and supervision in place of the present system of trade in Armaments for private profits; and an embargo of the export of Arms to States violating the Covenant of the League of Nations.*

10. *Constitution of the Liberal Party, Adopted by the Liberal Party Convention June 18th and 19th, 1936* **(London: Liberal Party Publication Department, 1936)**

Constitution of the Liberal Party

Preamble

1. The Liberal Party exists to build a Liberal Commonwealth, in which every citizen shall possess liberty, property and security, and none shall be enslaved by poverty, ignorance or unemployment. Its chief care is for the rights and opportunities of the individual, and in all spheres it sets freedom first.

Through the League of Nations it aims at a world freed from the fear of war, whose peoples, enjoying free access to the earth's abundance and trading freely to their mutual benefit, cooperate in the tasks of peace.

In Imperial relations its objectives are to increase cooperation between the self-governing members of the British Commonwealth, without aiming at Imperial self-sufficiency; to collaborate with the people of India in their political and economic advancement; to develop the Crown Colonies in their own interests; to insist on the principle of trusteeship with respect to the less developed peoples; and to make and keep the Colonial Empire free to the trade of the world.

At home its goal is a country in which the powers of the State will be steadily used to establish social justice, to wage war against poverty, to ensure that the country's resources are wisely developed for the benefit of the whole community, and to create the positive conditions which will make a full and free life possible for all citizens – a country in which, under the protection of law, all citizens have the right to speak freely, write freely, and vote freely; power through a just electoral system to shape the laws which they are called upon to obey; an effective voice in deciding the conditions in which they live and work; liberty under free trade to buy, sell, and produce; guarantees against the abuse of monopoly whether private or public; opportunity to work at a fair wage; decent homes and healthy surroundings; good education and facilities for training; access to land and an assurance that publicly created land values shall not be engrossed by private interests; and, as a safeguard of independence, the personal ownership of property.

These are the conditions of liberty, which it is the function of the State to protect and enlarge.

2. The Party is a Society of men and women banded together to achieve these aims. All who subscribe to the Party as a whole, or to any of its recognised units, and are in general agreement with its aims, are members of the Party.

11. Resolution on 'Foreign Policy', passed at the Liberal Assembly, 27 May 1937[11]

Proposed: Ramsay Muir
Seconded: Aline Mackinnon

This Assembly of the Liberal Party, recognising the present dangerous condition of the world, believes that the armaments of the loyal Members of the League must be adequate for collective defence against aggression, but holds that, if war is to be avoided, it is urgently necessary that this country and the other States [*sic*] Members of the League should make it unmistakably clear, not only that their armaments will never be used inconsistently with the Covenant of the League, but also that, if the necessity should arise, they would be used in loyal cooperation for the maintenance of the common peace. This Assembly, convinced that the scale and character of British armaments must be determined by the requirements of this policy, and that an extension of armaments without a clarification of policy is in the highest degree dangerous, views with profound apprehension the variable and incoherent policy which the Government is pursuing and is convinced that a continuance of this course will lead to disaster.

The true object of international policy should be the restoration of the influence and authority of the League of Nations, which cannot be established if its primary function is conceived to be merely the prevention of aggression, and the preservation of the *status quo*. Its primary function should be the creation of the conditions of peace, and the removal of the grievances from which wars arise.

At this moment the subjects which most urgently call for solution by international agreement are the control of colonial territories, the distribution of raw materials, the stabilisation of exchanges and the accessibility of markets. It is the duty of the British Government to make it clear that it is willing to do everything in its power to meet genuine grievances, provided that this is a part of a general settlement which will include the return to the League of the countries which have left it, and an agreement upon all-round disarmament.

12. Resolution on 'Foreign Policy', passed at the Liberal Assembly, 19 May 1938[12]

Proposed: Ramsay Muir
Seconded: Harcourt Johnstone

That this Assembly of the Liberal Party earnestly desires peace and friendship with all nations, whatever their forms of Government, and condemns efforts to divide the nations into ideological camps. It nevertheless recognises that our security and the defence of freedom, and the rights of small nations against those governments which are now using war as an instrument of national policy, require an expansion of British armaments. But it believes that the present policy of His Majesty's Government, involving as it does the sacrifice of sound principles of world order, is a danger to the security of the British Empire, and to the peace of the world.

While ready to welcome every effort to reduce the causes of misunderstandings between Nations it is constrained to condemn the Rome agreement in its present form on the ground that it involves the recognition of the Italian annexation of Abyssinia and implies the connivance of His Majesty's Government in the continuance of Italian intervention in Spain contrary to the Non-Intervention Agreements, to which both the Italian and British Governments are parties.

It considers that the failure of the Non-Intervention Agreements should be frankly recognised; that the Non-Intervention Committee should be dissolved; and that, while any direct intervention by the British Government in Spain should be confined to the relief of the sufferings of the Spanish people and the promotion of peace, it should no longer prevent the constitutional government of Spain from purchasing the supplies which it needs to defend itself from rebellion at home and invasion from abroad.

The Assembly finally declares that peace can only be preserved and adequate protection afforded to the world-wide interests of Great Britain if His Majesty's Government will resolutely pursue the policy of Collective Security and the Collective enforcement of Justice. It therefore urges the Government to bring about cooperation in mutual defence among as many States as possible and to announce publicly its readiness to join with any other States willing to take part in an open discussion of the steps necessary for the redress of legitimate grievances and the removal of the political and economic causes of war.

13. Resolution on 'Foreign Affairs', passed at the Liberal Assembly, 12 May 1939[13]

Proposed: Gwilym Lloyd George MP
Seconded: Mrs Denis Browne

This Assembly reaffirms its previous resolutions on foreign affairs and declares that the inexcusable misdirection by the Prime Minister of the foreign policy of this country is destroying democracy abroad and endangering our liberties at home and that the grave danger in which our country finds itself is directly due to our Government's betrayal of the principles of collective security in the past and has no confidence that their apparent and belated conversion to the collective system represents a permanent change of policy.

The Assembly thanks President Roosevelt for the courage and clarity of the lead he has given to the world and the hope he has inspired that the forces favourable to an organised system of peace will achieve their ends.

The Assembly earnestly hopes that the distrust which the Government's Foreign Policy has inspired abroad will not impede the formation of a powerful and permanent combination of peace-loving powers, which is the only security against war. In particular, it urges the extreme importance of a full agreement with Russia.

NOTES

1. Full versions of manifestos can be found in Iain Dale (ed.), *Liberal Party General Election Manifestos, 1900–1997* (London: Routledge, 2000).
2. *Proceedings in Connection with the Thirty-Sixth Annual Meeting of the National Liberal Federation Held at Birmingham, November 27th and 28th, 1919* (London: LPD, 1919), pp. 50–9.
3. *Liberal Magazine*, XXIX, 339 (Dec. 1921), p. 688.
4. *Proceedings in Connection with the Forty-First Annual Meeting of the National Liberal Federation Held at Brighton, May 22nd, 23rd and 24th, 1924* (London: LPD, 1924), p. 27.
5. *Proceedings in Connection with the 45th Annual Meeting of the Council, Held at Great Yarmouth, October 10th to 12th, 1928* (London: LPD, 1928), pp. 18–23.
6. LPD, *Pamphlets & Leaflets*, 1929 (London: LPD, 1930).
7. *Report of the Forty-Ninth Annual Meeting of the Council of the National Liberal Federation, Clacton-on-Sea, April 27th–30th, 1932* (NLF, 1932), p. 78.
8. National Liberal Federation, *Report of the Fiftieth Annual Meeting of the Council of the National Liberal Federation, Scarborough, May 17th–19th, 1933* (NLF, 1933), pp. 279–81.
9. *Report of the Fifty-First Annual Meeting of the Council of the National Liberal Federation, Bournemouth, May 2nd–5th, 1934* (NLF, 1934), pp. 56–60.
10. *Liberal Magazine*, XLIII, 501 (June 1935), pp. 304–5.
11. *Liberal Magazine*, XLV, 525 (June 1937), p. 294.
12. *Liberal Magazine*, XLVI, 537 (June 1938), p. 296.
13. *Liberal Magazine*, XLVII, 549 (June 1939), p. 286.

Appendix 5:
Liberal MPs and Munich

On 6 October 1938, the House of Commons voted on two questions. The first of these was on a resolution opposing government policy and calling for a world conference to settle all grievances, accompanied by support for collective security through the League. The second question proposed support for the government's foreign policy. The voting record of the Liberal MPs was as follows:[1]

For the government (4)

Herbert Holdsworth (Bradford South)[2]
D. Owen Evans (Cardiganshire)
Henry Haydn Jones (Merionethshire)
F. Kingsley Griffith (Middlesbrough West)

Against the government (14)

Richard Acland (Barnstaple)
James de Rothschild (Isle of Ely)[3]
Ernest Evans (University of Wales)
Dingle Foot (Dundee)
David Lloyd George (Caernarvon Boroughs)[4]
Megan Lloyd George (Anglesey)[5]
Gwilym Lloyd George (Pembrokeshire)[6]
Percy Harris (Bethnal Green South-West)
Geoffrey Mander (Wolverhampton East)
Goronwy Owen (Caernarvonshire)[7]
Wilfred Roberts (North Cumberland)
Hugh Seely (Berwick-upon-Tweed)
Archibald Sinclair (Caithness & Sutherland)
H. Graham White (Birkenhead East)[8]

Did not vote (2)

Francis Dyke Acland (North Cornwall)
Joseph Paton Maclay (Paisley)

NOTES

1. Hansard, *339 HC Deb. 5s*, cols. 554–62.
2. Following the Munich vote, Holdsworth joined the Liberal Nationals.
3. de Rothschild only voted on the first question. It is not clear why.
4. Although the members of the Lloyd George family group were elected as Independent Liberals in 1935, they rejoined the Liberal Party in parliament 11 days after the election. One Liberal elected in 1935, Robert Bernays, joined the Liberal Nationals in October 1936 and is not included in these figures.
5. Ibid.
6. Ibid.
7. Ibid.
8. White (who spoke against the government on 6 October) only voted on the first question. It is not clear why.

Appendix 6:
8.30 Club Debates[1]

25 February 1936: 'The manufacture of armaments should be a State monopoly.'
Proposed: Roger Fulford and Aline Mackinnon. Opposed: Ronald Haylor and Christopher Smuts. Nine other speakers. Defeated 15 to 12.

31 March 1936: 'That the present situation demonstrates the immediate need of an International Police Force under the control of the League.'
Proposed: (Mr) Goddard and Nelia Muspratt. Opposed: Alan Campbell Johnson and (Mr) Dimont; 15 other speakers. Motion won by a large majority (over 50 present).

28 April 1936: 'That this House advocates the censorship of the Press.'
For: W. Fordham and Eric Walker. Against: George Edinger and Frank Milton; 15 other speakers. Defeated.

26 May 1936: 'That this House prefers to support France rather than Germany.'
Proposed: Christopher Smuts and Margaret Layton. Opposed: J.D. Bateman and (Ivor?) Phillips. Nine other speakers. Carried 25 to 13.

27 October 1936: 'That this House deplores the Government's policy of non-intervention in the Spanish struggle.'
Proposed: F.L. Josephy and A.J. Irvine. Opposed: (Mr) Boyd Carpenter and Mr Sharp. Nine other speakers. Defeated.

24 November 1936: 'That this House supports the Euthanasia Bill.'
Proposed: Betty Arne and J. Crawshay Williams. Opposed: Dr Taylor and Dr Hudson; 14 other speakers. Defeated 25 to 12.

12 January 1937: 'That in view of the spread of militarism throughout the world this House is prepared to acquiesce in conscription in England to defend democracy.'
Proposed: E. Collieu and (Mr) Collingridge. Opposed: R.H. Walton and J.H. Black. Eight other speakers. Defeated 22 to 6.

23 February 1937: 'That a Popular Front Government is the only possible alternative to the present National Administration.' (Joint debate with Younger Member's Circle of the National Liberal Club.)
Proposed: Donald M. Smith (NLC) and (Miss) Bliss (8:30). Opposed: J.D. Bateman (8.30) and Stephen Bach (NLC). Eight other speakers. Defeated 20 to 17.

16 March 1937: 'That the present distribution of colonies among World powers is inequitable.'
Proposed: W. Fordham and Betty Arne. Opposed: D. Walker-Smith and J. Grimond; 11 other speakers. Carried 22 to 16.

4 May 1937: 'On a raft in mid-ocean are four survivors of a shipwreck; a Bishop, a famous Cricketer, a Judge and a psychologist. One of them has to be thrown overboard that the other three may survive.'
Judge: Eric Walker. Psychologist: George Chubb. Cricketer: Alan Campbell Johnson. Bishop: Roger Fulford; 19 spoke. Psychologist sacrificed on casting vote of chairman, ahead of cricketer.

26 October 1937: 'That this House advocates the suppression of Fascist and Communist propaganda.'
Proposed: H.E.S. Bryant Irvine and Nelia Muspratt. Opposed: J.D. Bateman and J. Parker; 12 other speakers. Defeated 22 to 8.

30 November 1937: 'That a Nation's "need for expansion" is always fictitious.'
Proposed: A.J. Irvine and W. Fordham. Opposed: Aubrey Herbert and Edward Bach; 12 other speakers. Carried 21 to 19.

25 January 1938: 'That this House is of opinion that in the interests of World Peace the provisions of the League Covenant should not be invoked in the present dispute between China and Japan.'
Proposed: Alan Campbell Johnson and Hugh Gosschalk. Opposed: Anthony Moore (League of Nations Union) and J. Comyns Carr. Eight other speakers. Carried 21 to 15.

22 February 1938: 'That in the opinion of this House the cinema is a degrading influence.'
Proposed: H. Hodgkinson and Donald M. Smith. Opposed: Eric Walker and Stephen Mason. Four other speakers. Defeated by 16 to 15.

29 March 1938: 'That in the opinion of this House, the Prime Minister by exercising publicly his right to over-ride our Foreign Office has weakened our prestige abroad for some years to come.'

Proposed: Frank Milton and T.C. Fraser. Opposed: Harold Marnham and Michael Lambert; 12 other speakers. Carried 37 to 14.

3 May 1938: 'That this House supports the Government's present physical fitness campaign.'
Proposed: J.M. Ahern and Stephen Bach. Opposed: J.A. Brown and Alice Strickland; 11 other speakers. Defeated 20 to 17.

8 November 1938: 'That this House considers that Mr Chamberlain acted wrongly in the recent crisis.'
Proposed: Sheila Grant-Duff and Eric Walker. Opposed: John Gardiner and Stephen Mason; 12 other speakers. Carried 26 to 15.

6 December 1938: 'That this is the best of all possible ages.'
Proposed: Ronald Haylor and H. Gosschalk. Opposed: George Chubb and H. Tanner. Six other speakers. Defeated 20 to 11.

31 January 1939: 'That in the opinion of this House Great Britain should give a lead in assuming responsibility for European refugees.'
Proposed: Frank Byers and Margaret Layton. Opposed: Ian Campbell and T. Chambers. Seven other speakers. Carried 21 to 5.

28 February 1939: 'That the Labour Party has no future in our country'.
Proposed: Aubrey Herbert and Ruth Kitching. Opposed: (Mr) Willis (Chairman of the League of Youth) and Alice Strickland. Eight other speakers. Defeated 16 to 15.

28 March 1939: 'That in the opinion of this House the admission of women to the House of Commons and to the suffrage was a mistake.'
Proposed: J.D. Bateman and George Chubb. Opposed: Nelia Muspratt and S. Hidden; 12 other speakers. Defeated 24 to 6.

NOTE

1. 8.30 Club Minute Book. Formerly in the possession of Mrs Nelia Penman, but now deposited in the National Liberal Club Archives, University of Bristol.

Bibliography

Note: Unless otherwise stated, place of publication is London

MANUSCRIPT COLLECTIONS

Individuals

H.H. Asquith: Bodleian Library, Oxford
William Wedgwood Benn (Stansgate Papers): House of Lords Records
    Office
David Lloyd George: House of Lords Records Office
Donald Maclean: Bodleian Library, Oxford
Gilbert Murray: Bodleian Library, Oxford
Herbert Samuel: House of Lords Records Office
Archibald Sinclair (Thurso Papers): Churchill College, Cambridge

Liberal organisations

Home Counties Liberal Federation: University of Bristol Library
London Liberal Federation: University of Bristol Library
National Liberal Club: University of Bristol Library
Western Counties Liberal Federation: University of Bristol Library
Women's Liberal Federation: University of Bristol Library

Government bodies

CAB 16/102: Committee of Imperial Defence Sub-Committee on the Disarmament Conference (Three Party Committee), Reports, Proceedings, and Memoranda: Public Record Office, Kew
CAB 16/103: Committee of Imperial Defence Sub-Committee on the Disarmament Conference (Three Party Committee), Agenda Sub-Committee: Public Record Office, Kew
CAB 23 & 24, Cabinet Minutes and Memoranda: Public Record Office, Kew

CAB 27/476, Cabinet Committee on Preparations for the Disarmament Conference, 1931: Public Record Office, Kew
CAB 27/505, Ministerial Committee on Disarmament Conference, 1932: Public Record Office, Kew
FO 371, Foreign Office Papers: Public Record Office, Kew
FO 800/226, Miscellaneous Correspondence of Lord Reading, 1931: Public Record Office, Kew
FO 800/285-91, Miscellaneous Correspondence of John Simon, 1931–35: Public Record Office, Kew

CONTEMPORARY NEWSPAPERS AND PERIODICALS

Contemporary Review
Daily Chronicle
Daily News
Economist, The
Fortnightly Review
Forward View
Lloyd George Liberal Magazine
Manchester Guardian
Nation
New Outlook
News Chronicle
New Statesman
Saturday Westminster Gazette
Sunday Express
The Times
Weekly Westminster
Weekly Westminster Gazette
Westminster Gazette

LIBERAL PARTY PUBLICATIONS

Liberal Agent
Liberal Magazine
National Liberal Federation Proceedings
Pamphlets & Leaflets

REFERENCE MATERIAL

Annual Register (Longmans Green, 1919 et seq.).
Dictionary of National Biography, 1941–1950 (Oxford: Oxford University Press, 1959).

Dictionary of National Biography, 1951–1960 (Oxford: Oxford University Press, 1971).

Dictionary of National Biography, 1961–1970 (Oxford: Oxford University Press, 1981).

MANIFESTOS

Dale, Iain (ed.), *Liberal Party General Election Manifestos, 1900–1997* (Routledge, 2000).

MEMOIRS

Asquith, H.H., *Memories and Reflections* (2 volumes) (Cassell, 1928).

Hodgson, Stuart (ed.), *Ramsay Muir: An Autobiography and Some Essays* (Lund Humphries, 1943).

Macmillan, Harold, *Winds of Change, 1914–1939* (Macmillan, 1966).

Samuel, Viscount, *Memoirs* (Cresset Press, 1945).

Spier, Eugen, *Focus: A Footnote to the History of the Thirties* (Oswald Wolff, 1963).

BIOGRAPHIES AND BIOGRAPHICAL STUDIES

Butler, J.R.M. *Lord Lothian (Philip Kerr), 1882–1940* (Macmillan, 1960).

Campbell, John, *Lloyd George: The Goat in the Wilderness, 1922–31* (Jonathan Cape, 1977).

Casser, George H., *Asquith as War Leader* (Hambledon, 1994).

Charmley, John, *Churchill: The End of Glory, A Political Biography* (Hodder & Stoughton, 1993).

De Groot, Gerard J., *Liberal Crusader: The Life if Sir Archibald Sinclair* (Hurst, 1993).

Dutton, David, *Simon: A Political Biography of Sir John Simon* (Aurum, 1992).

Fry, Michael G., *Lloyd George and Foreign Policy, Volume One: The Education of a Statesman, 1890–1916* (Montreal: McGill-Queen's University Press, 1977).

Gilbert, Martin, *Prophet of Truth: Winston S. Churchill, 1922–1939* (Heinemann, 1976).

Harris, Kenneth, *Attlee* (Weidenfeld & Nicolson, 1982; 1995 edn).

Hinde, Wendy, *Richard Cobden: A Victorian Outsider* (New Haven, CT: Yale University Press, 1987).

Hubback, David, *No Ordinary Press Baron: A Life of Walter Layton* (Weidenfeld & Nicolson, 1985).

Jenkins, Roy, *Asquith* (Collins, 1964).
Jenkins, Roy, *Gladstone* (Macmillan, 1995).
Judd, Dennis, *Lord Reading* (Weidenfeld & Nicolson, 1982).
Koss, Stephen, *Asquith* (Allen Lane, 1976).
Macleod, Iain, *Neville Chamberlain* (Frederick Muller, 1961).
Owen, Frank, *Tempestuous Journey: Lloyd George, His Life and Times* (Hutchinson, 1954).
Pugh, Martin, *Lloyd George* (Longman, 1988).
Robbins, Keith, *Sir Edward Grey: A Biography of Lord Grey of Falloden* (Cassell, 1971).
Rowland, Peter, *Lloyd George* (Barrie & Jenkins, 1975).
Skidelsky, Robert, *John Maynard Keynes: Hopes Betrayed, 1883–1920* (Macmillan, 1983).
Skidelsky, Robert, *John Maynard Keynes: The Economist as Saviour, 1920–1937* (Macmillan, 1992).
Smith, Patricia Anne, *Lord Lothian and British Foreign Policy, 1918–39* (Carleton University, Ottawa, unpublished M.A. thesis, April 1968).
Stocks, Mary, *Ernest Simon of Manchester* (Manchester: Manchester University Press, 1963).
Taylor, A.J.P., *Lloyd George: Twelve Essays* (Hamish Hamilton, 1971).
Trevelyan, G.M., *Grey of Falloden* (Longman, 1937).
Turner, John (ed.), *The Larger Idea: Lord Lothian and the Problem of National Sovereignty* (The Historians Press, 1988).
Wasserstein, Bernard, *Herbert Samuel: A Political Life* (Oxford: Clarendon, 1992).
West, Francis, *Gilbert Murray: A Life* (Croom Helm, 1984).
Wilson, Duncan, *Gilbert Murray OM, 1866–1957* (Oxford: Clarendon, 1987).
Wilson, John, *CB: A Life of Sir Henry Campbell-Bannerman* (Constable, 1973).
Wilton, Iain, *C.B. Fry: An English Hero* (Richard Cohen, 1999).
Wrigley, Chris, *Lloyd George* (Oxford: Blackwell, 1992).

DIARIES AND LETTERS

Ball, Stuart (ed.), *Parliament and Politics in the Age of Baldwin and MacDonald: The Headlam Diaries, 1923–1935* (Historians Press, 1993).
Pottle, Mark (ed.), *Champion Redoubtable: The Diaries and Letters of Violet Bonham Carter, 1914–45* (Weidenfeld & Nicolson, 1998).
Taylor, A.J.P. (ed.), *Lloyd George: A Diary by Frances Stevenson* (Hutchinson, 1971).
Taylor, A.J.P. (ed.), *My Darling Pussy: The Letters of Lloyd George & Frances Stevenson, 1913–41* (Weidenfeld & Nicolson, 1975).

CONTEMPORARY PUBLICATIONS

Acland, Richard, *Only One Battle* (Victor Gollancz, 1937).

Asquith, H.H., *The Paisley Policy* (Cassell, 1920).

Cato, O., *Guilty Men* (Gollancz, 1940).

Clay, Henry (ed.), *The Inter-War Years and Other Papers: A Selection from the Writings of Hubert Douglas Henderson* (Oxford: Clarendon, 1955).

Davies, David, *The Problem of the Twentieth Century* (Ernest Benn, 1930).

George, David Lloyd, *Is It Peace?* (Hodder and Stoughton, 1923).

George, David Lloyd, *The Truth about Reparations and War Debts* (Heinemann, 1932).

George, David Lloyd, *Spain and Britain* (The Friends of Spain, 1937).

George, David Lloyd, *The Truth About the Peace Treaties, in two volumes* (Gollancz, 1938).

Grey, Edward, *Lord Grey on Present-Day Politics* (Liberal Publication Department, 1922).

Grey, Edward *et al.*, *The League of Nations* (Oxford: Oxford University Press, 1918).

Hirst, Francis W., *Safeguarding and Protection* (Richard Cobden-Sanderson, 1926).

Hirst, Francis W., *Armaments: The Race and the Crisis* (Richard Cobden-Sanderson, 1937).

Hirst, Francis W., Murray, Gilbert and Hammond, J.L., *Liberalism and the Empire: Three Essays* (R. Brimley Johnson, 1900).

Hobhouse, L.T., *Liberalism* (Oxford: Oxford University Press, 1911).

Hobson, J.A., *Imperialism – A Study* (Constable, 1902).

Kerr, Philip and Curtis, Lionel, *The Prevention of War* (New Haven, CT: Yale University Press, 1923).

Keynes, John Maynard, *The Economic Consequences of the Peace* (Macmillan, 1919).

Liberal Industrial Inquiry, *Britain's Industrial Future: Being the Report of the Liberal Industrial Inquiry of 1928* (Ernest Benn, 1928).

Liberal Summer School, *Essays in Liberalism: Being the Lectures and Papers which were delivered at the Liberal Summer School at Oxford, 1922* (Collins, 1922).

Lothian, Marquess of, *Liberalism in the Modern World* (Lovat Dickson, 1934).

Lothian, Marquess of (Philip Kerr), *Pacifism is Not Enough (Nor Patriotism Either)* (Oxford: Clarendon, 1935).

Lothian, Marquess of, 'The Demonic Influence of National Sovereignty', in Marquess of Lothian *et al.*, *The Universal Church and the World of Nations* (George Allen & Unwin, 1938), pp. 1–23.

Lothian, Marquess of, *et al.*, *The Family of Nations* (New York: Carnegie Endowment for International Peace, 1937).

Mathews, Basil (ed.), *The League of Nations* (Oxford: Oxford University Press, 1919).

Maurice, Frederick, *Disarmament* (*Daily News*, 1924).

Meston, Lord, *India and the Empire* (*Daily News*, 1925).

Muir, Ramsay, *Peers and Bureaucrats: Two Problems of English Government* (Constable, 1910).

Muir, Ramsay, *Britain's Case Against Germany: An Examination of the Historical Background of the German Action in 1914* (Manchester: Manchester University Press, 1914).

Muir, Ramsay, *The National Principle and the War* (Oxford: Oxford University Press, 1914).

Muir, Ramsay, *The Making of British India, 1756–1858* (Manchester: Manchester University Press, 1915).

Muir, Ramsay, *The Expansion of Europe: The Culmination of Modern History* (Constable, 1st edn 1917 to 6th edn 1939).

Muir, Ramsay, *The Character of the British Empire* (Constable, 1917).

Muir, Ramsay, *National Self-Government, its Growth and Principles: The Culmination of Modern History* (Constable, 1918).

Muir, Ramsay, *Nationalism and Internationalism: The Culmination of Modern History* (Constable, 1916, and 2nd edn 1919).

Muir, Ramsay, *Liberalism and Industry: Towards a Better Social Order* (Constable, 1920).

Muir, Ramsay, *A Short History of the British Commonwealth: Volume I, The Islands to the First Empire (To 1763)* (George Philip & Son, 1920).

Muir, Ramsay, *A Short History of the British Commonwealth: Volume II, The Modern Commonwealth (1763 to 1919)* (George Philip & Son, 1922).

Muir, Ramsay, *Politics and Progress: A Survey of the Problems of To-day* (Methuen, 1923).

Muir, Ramsay, *The New Liberalism* (*Daily News*, n.d., but was received in Bodleian Library Jan. 1924).

Muir, Ramsay, *America the Golden: An Englishman's Notes and Comparisons* (Williams & Norgate, 1927).

Muir, Ramsay [An Impenitent Politician], *Robinson the Great: A Political Fantasia on the Problems of To-day and the Solutions of To-morrow, Extracted from the Works of Professor Solomon Slack, LL.D.* (Christophers, 1929).

Muir, Ramsay, *Political Consequences of the Great War* (Thornton Butterworth, 1930).

Muir, Ramsay, *Protection versus Free Imports* (Liberal Publication Department, 1930).

Muir, Ramsay, *How Britain is Governed: A Critical Analysis of Modern Developments in the British System of Government* (Constable, 1930, and 3rd edn 1933).

Muir, Ramsay, *The Interdependent World and its Problems* (Constable, 1932).

Muir, Ramsay, *Faith of a Liberal* (Lovat Dickson, 1933).

[With a Foreword by Muir, Ramsay], *The Liberal Way: A Survey of Liberal*

Policy, Published by the Authority of the National Liberal Federation (George Allen & Unwin, 1934).

Muir, Ramsay, *Is Democracy a Failure?* (Lovat Dickson, 1934).

Muir, Ramsay, *A Brief History of Our Own Times* (George Philip & Son, 1934, and 3rd edn 1940).

Muir, Ramsay, *The Record of the National Government* (George Allen & Unwin, 1936).

Muir, Ramsay, *Future for Democracy* (Nicholson & Watson for the Liberal Book Club, 1939).

Muir, Ramsay, *Civilization and Liberty* (Jonathan Cape, 1940).

Muir, Ramsay, *The British Empire: How it Grew and How it Works* (Jonathan Cape, 1940).

Muir, Ramsay, *A Better Britain in a Better World: In the Form of Letters from an Uncle to a Nephew an [sic] the problems ahead, and the Nephew's reactions* (King and Staples, 1943).

Murray, Gilbert, *Foreign Policy of Sir Edward Grey* (Oxford: Clarendon, 1915).

Murray, Gilbert, *The Way Forward* (George Allen, 1917).

Murray, Gilbert, *The League of Nations and the Democratic Idea* (Oxford: Oxford University Press, 1918).

Murray, Gilbert, *Faith, War, and Policy* (Oxford: Oxford University Press, 1918).

Murray, Gilbert, *The League and its Guarantees* (British Periodicals, 1920).

Murray, Gilbert, *The Problems of Foreign Policy: A Consideration of Present Dangers and the Best Methods for Meeting Them* (George Allen & Unwin, 1921).

Murray, Gilbert, *The Future of the British Empire in Relation to the League of Nations* (Sheffield: J.W. Northend, 1928).

Murray, Gilbert, 'Revision of the Peace Treaties', in Leonard Woolf, *The Intelligent Man's Way to Prevent War* (Victor Gollancz, 1933), pp. 67–153.

Murray, Gilbert, *Cult of Violence* (Lovat Dickson, 1934).

Murray, Gilbert, *Liberality and Civilisation* (George Allen & Unwin, 1938).

The Next Five Years: An Essay in Political Agreement (Macmillan, 1935).

Phillips, Hubert, *The Liberal Outlook* (Chapman and Hall, 1929).

Phillips, Hubert; Holgate, Arthur; Hughes, R. Moelwyn; Jones, T. Elder; Lloyd, Ifor; Menken, Jules and Sainsbury, Alan, *Whither Britain? A Radical Answer* (Faber & Faber, 1932).

Streit, Clarence, *Union Now* (Jonathan Cape, 1939).

SECONDARY PUBLICATIONS: BOOKS

Adams, R.J.Q. and Poirier, Philip P., *The Conscription Controversy in Great Britain, 1900–18* (Macmillan, 1987).

Beckett, Francis, *Enemy Within: The Rise and Fall of the British Communist Party* (John Murray, 1995).

Beddoe, Deirdre, *Back to Home and Duty: Women between the Wars, 1918–1939* (Pandora, 1989).

Bell, P.M.H., *The Origins of the Second World War in Europe* (Harlow: Longman, 1986).

Bentley, Michael, *The Liberal Mind, 1914–1929* (Cambridge: Cambridge University Press, 1977).

Bernstein, George L., *Liberalism and Liberal Politics in Edwardian England* (Boston, MA: Allen & Unwin, 1986).

Biagini, Eugenio F., *Liberty, Retrenchment and Reform: Popular Liberalism in the Age of Gladstone, 1860–1880* (Cambridge: Cambridge University Press, 1992).

Birn, Donald S., *The League of Nations Union, 1918–1945* (Oxford: Clarendon, 1981).

Buchanan, Tom, *Britain and the Spanish Civil War* (Cambridge: Cambridge University Press, 1997).

Bullock, Alan, *The Liberal Tradition from Fox to Keynes* (Oxford: Oxford University Press, 1967).

Caputi, Robert J., *Neville Chamberlain and Appeasement* (Associated University Presses, 2000).

Ceadel, Martin, *Thinking About Peace and War* (Oxford: Oxford University Press, 1987).

Charmley, John, *Chamberlain and the Lost Peace* (Hodder & Stoughton, 1989).

Clarke, Peter, *Liberals and Social Democrats* (Cambridge: Cambridge University Press, 1978).

Cook, Chris, *A Short History of the Liberal Party, 1900–88* (Macmillan, 1989).

Dangerfield, George, *The Strange Death of Liberal England* ([1935] MacGibbon & Kee, 1996).

Dockrill, Michael L. and Goold, J. Douglas, *Peace without Promise: Britain and the Peace Conferences, 1919–23* (Batsford, 1981).

Douglas, Roy, *The History of the Liberal Party, 1895–1970* (Sidgwick & Jackson, 1971).

Edwards, Ruth Dudley, *The Pursuit of Reason: 'The Economist', 1843–1993* (Hamish Hamilton, 1993).

Freeden, Michael, *Liberalism Divided: A Study in British Political Thought, 1914–1939* (Oxford: Clarendon, 1986).

Gatzke, Hans W., *Stresemann and the Rearmament of Germany* (New York: Norton, 1969; first published, Baltimore, MD: Johns Hopkins University Press, 1954).

Goldsworthy, David, *Colonial Issues in British Politics, 1945–61: From 'Colonial Development' to 'Wind of Change'* (Oxford: Clarendon, 1971).

Grayson, Richard S., *Austen Chamberlain and the Commitment to Europe: British Foreign Policy, 1924–29* (London: Frank Cass, 1997).

Hamer, D.A., *Liberal Politics in the Age of Gladstone and Rosebery: A Study in Leadership and Policy* (Oxford: Clarendon, 1972).

Harris, Sally, *Out of Control: British Foreign Policy and the Union of Democratic Control, 1914–1918* (Hull: University of Hull Press, 1996).

Hinsley, F.H. (ed.), *British Foreign Policy under Sir Edward Grey* (Cambridge, Cambridge University Press, 1977).

Hobsbawm, Eric J., *Nations and Nationalism since 1780: Programme, Myth and Reality* (Cambridge: Cambridge University Press, 1992).

Howard, Michael, *The Continental Commitment: The Dilemma of British Defence Policy in the Era of the Two World Wars* (Temple Smith, 1972).

Howard, Michael, *War and the Liberal Conscience* (Oxford: Oxford University Press, 1981).

Howe, Anthony, *Free Trade and Liberal England, 1846–1946* (Oxford: Clarendon, 1997).

Howe, Stephen, *Anticolonialism in British Politics: The Left and the End of Empire, 1918–1964* (Oxford: Clarendon, 1993).

Iriye, Akira, *The Origins of the Second World War in Asia and the Pacific* (Harlow: Longman, 1987).

Jacobson, Jon, *Locarno Diplomacy: Germany and the West, 1925–29* (Princeton, NJ: Princeton University Press, 1972).

Joyce, Peter, *Realignment of the Left? A History of the Relationship between the Liberal Democrat and Labour Parties* (Macmillan, 1999).

Kirchner, Emil Joseph, *Liberal Parties in Western Europe* (Cambridge: Cambridge University Press, 1988).

Koss, Stephen (ed.), *The Pro-Boers: The Anatomy of an Antiwar Movement* (Chicago, IL: University of Chicago Press, 1973).

Koss, Stephen, *Nonconformity in Modern British Politics* (Batsford, 1975).

Koss, Stephen, *The Rise and Fall of the Political Press in Britain, Volume 2: The Twentieth Century* (Hamish Hamilton, 1984).

Lee, Marshall and Michalka, Wolfgang, *German Foreign Policy, 1917–1933: Continuity or Break?* (Leamington Spa: Berg, 1987).

Lentin, A., *Guilt at Versailles: Lloyd George and the Pre-history of Appeasement* (Methuen, 1985).

Lewis, John, *The Left Book Club: An Historical Record* (Victor Gollancz, 1970).

Long, David and Wilson, Peter (eds), *Thinkers of the Twenty Years' Crisis: Inter-War Idealism Reassessed* (Oxford: Clarendon, 1995).

Madariaga, Salvador de, 'Gilbert Murray and the League', in Jean Smith and Arnold Toynbee (eds), *Gilbert Murray: An Unfinished Autobiography* (George Allen and Unwin, 1960), pp. 176–97.

Matthew, H.C.G., *The Liberal Imperialists: The Ideas and Politics of a Post-Gladstonian Elite* (Oxford: Oxford University Press, 1973).

McKercher, B.J.C., *The Second Baldwin Government and the United States, 1924–1929: Attitudes and Diplomacy* (Cambridge: Cambridge University Press, 1984).

Morgan, K.O., *Consensus and Disunity: The Lloyd George Coalition Government, 1918–22* (Oxford: Clarendon, 1979).

Morris, A.J. Anthony, *Radicalism Against War: The Advocacy of Peace and Retrenchment* (Longman, 1972).

Parker, R.A.C., *Chamberlain and Appeasement: British Policy and the Coming of the Second World War* (Macmillan, 1993).

Parker, R.A.C., *Churchill and Appeasement: Could Churchill Have Prevented the Second World War?* (Macmillan, 2000).

Porter, Bernard, *Critics of Empire: British Radical Attitudes to Colonialism in Africa, 1895–1914* (Macmillan, 1968).

Pugh, Martin, *The Making of Modern British Politics, 1867–1939* (Oxford: Blackwell, 1982).

Rasmussen, Jorgen Scott, *The Liberal Party: A Study of Retrenchment and Revival* (Constable, 1965).

Richardson, Dick, *The Evolution of British Disarmament Policy in the 1920s* (Pinter Publishers, 1989).

Rothwell, V.H., *British War Aims and Peace Diplomacy, 1914–18* (Oxford: Clarendon, 1971).

Russell, Conrad, *The Liberal Cause: The Three Century-Long Tradition of the Liberal Democrats* (Hebden Bridge: Hebden Royd, 1990).

Russell, Conrad, *An Intelligent Person's Guide to Liberalism* (Duckworth, 1999).

Searle, G.R., *The Liberal Party: Triumph and Disintegration, 1886–1929* (Macmillan, 1992).

Semmel, Bernard, *Liberalism and Naval Strategy: Ideology, Interest, and Sea Power during the Pax Britannica* (Boston, MA: Allen & Unwin, 1986).

Semmel, Bernard, *The Liberal Ideal and the Demons of Empire: Theories of Imperialism from Adam Smith to Lenin* (Baltimore, MD: Johns Hopkins University Press, 1993).

Smith, Adrian, *The New Statesman: Portrait of a Political Weekly, 1913–1931* (London: Frank Cass, 1996).

Steiner, Zara, *The Foreign Office and Foreign Policy, 1898–1914* (Cambridge: Cambridge University Press, 1969).

Stewart, Graham, *Burying Caesar: Churchill, Chamberlain and the Battle for the Tory Party* (Weidenfeld & Nicolson, 1999).

Swartz, Marvin, *The Union of Democratic Control in British Politics During the First World War* (Oxford: Clarendon, 1971).

Taylor, A.J.P., *The Trouble Makers: Dissent Over Foreign Policy, 1792–1939* (Hamish Hamilton, 1957; 1993 Pimlico edn).

Taylor, A.J.P., *The Origins of the Second World War* (Hamish Hamilton, 1961).

Taylor, A.J.P., *English History, 1914–1945* (Oxford: Clarendon, 1965; 1976 edn).

Taylor, Miles, *The Decline of British Radicalism, 1847–1860* (Oxford: Clarendon Press, 1995).

Thompson, Neville, *The Anti-Appeasers: Conservative Opposition to Appeasement in the 1930s* (Oxford: Oxford University Press, 1971).

Thorpe, Andrew, *The British General Election of 1931* (Oxford: Clarendon, 1991).

Vincent, John, *The Formation of the British Liberal Party, 1857–1868* (Constable, 1966, and 2nd edn, Hassocks: Harvester, 1972).

Walters, F.P., *A History of the League of Nations* (Oxford: Oxford University Press, 1952; 1960 edn).

Wilson, Trevor, *The Downfall of the Liberal Party, 1914–35* (Collins, 1966).

Winfield, Rif, *Liberals in Parliament: An Electoral History, 1924–1994* (Aberystwyth: University of Wales Press, 1994).

SECONDARY PUBLICATIONS: ARTICLES

Baines, Malcolm, 'The Liberal Party and 1945 General Election', *Contemporary Record*, 9, 1 (Summer 1995), pp. 48–61.

Bell, Philip, 'Hitler's War? The Origins of the Second World War', in Paul Hayes (ed.), *Themes in Modern European History, 1890–1945* (Routledge, 1992).

Birn, Donald S., 'The League of Nations Union and Collective Security', *Journal of Contemporary History*, 9, 3 (1974), pp. 131–59.

Bosco, Andrea, 'Lothian, Curtis, Kimber and the Federal Union Movement (1938–40)', *Journal of Contemporary History*, 23 (1988), pp. 465–502.

Boyce, Robert, 'British Capitalism and the Idea of European Unity between the Wars', in Peter M. Stirk, *European Unity in Context* (Pinter, 1989), pp. 65–83.

Bullock, Alan, 'Hitler and the Origins of the Second World War', in E.M. Robertson (ed.), *The Origins of the Second World War* (Macmillan, 1971).

Ceadel, Martin, 'The First British Referendum: The Peace Ballot, 1934–5', *English Historical Review*, 95 (1980), pp. 810–39.

David, Edward, 'The Liberal Party Divided, 1916–18', *Historical Journal*, 13 (1970), pp. 509–33.

Dunbabin, J.P.D., 'British Rearmament in the 1930s: A Chronology and Review', *Historical Journal*, 18, 3 (1975), pp. 587–609.

Durran, P.J., 'Liberal Attacks on Disraelian Imperialism', *Journal of Imperial and Commonwealth History*, 10 (1982), pp. 262–84.

Goodlad, Graham D., 'The Liberal Nationals, 1931–1940: The Problems of a Party in "Partnership Government"', *Historical Journal*, 38, 1 (1995), pp. 133–43.

Hauner, Milan, 'Did Hitler Want a World Dominion?', *Journal of Contemporary History*, 13 (1978), pp. 15–32.

Laybourn, Keith, 'The Rise of Labour and the Decline of Liberalism: The State of the Debate', *History*, 80, 259 (June 1995), pp. 207–26.

Lentin, Antony, '"A Conference Now": Lloyd George and Peacemaking, 1929: Sidelights from the Unpublished Letters of A.J. Sylvester', *Diplomacy and Statecraft*, 7, 3 (Nov. 1996) pp. 563–88.

Moradiellos, Enrique, 'Appeasement and Non-Intervention: British Policy during the Spanish Civil War', in Peter Catterall and C.J. Morris (eds), *Britain and the Threat to Stability in Europe, 1918–45* (Leicester: Leicester University Press, 1993).

Philip, Alan Butt, 'The Liberals and Europe', in, Vernon Bogdanor (ed.), *Liberal Party Politics* (Oxford: Clarendon, 1983), pp. 217–40.

Philip, Alan Butt, 'Europeans First and Last: British Liberals and the European Community', *Political Quarterly*, 64, 4, Oct.–Dec. 1993, pp. 447–61.

Pinder, John, 'Federalism in Britain and Italy: Radicals and the English Liberal Tradition', in Peter M. Stirk (ed.), *European Unity in Context: The Interwar Period* (Pinter, 1989), pp. 201–23.

Robbins, Keith, 'Fifty Years On: Recent Scholarship on the Origins of the Second World War', *German History*, 8, 3 (1990), pp. 339–45.

Schreuder, D.M., 'Gladstone and Italian Unification, 1848–70: The Making of a Liberal?', *English Historical Review*, 85 (1970), pp. 475–501.

Watt, Donald Cameron, 'Churchill and Appeasement', in Robert Blake and Wm. Roger Louis (eds), *Churchill: A Major New Assessment of His Life in Peace and War* (Oxford: Oxford University Press, 1993).

SECONDARY PUBLICATIONS: UNPUBLISHED THESES

Baines, Malcolm, 'The Survival of the British Liberal Party, 1932–59' (Oxford D.Phil., 1990).

Hart, Michael, 'The Decline of the Liberal Party in Parliament and in the Constituencies' (Oxford D.Phil., 1982).

Markwell, D.J., 'John Maynard Keynes and International Relations: Idealism, Economic Paths to War and Peace, and Post-war Reconstruction' (Oxford D.Phil., 1995).

May, Alexander C., 'The Round Table, 1910–66' (Oxford D.Phil., 1995).

Rose, Inbal A., 'The Conservative Dimension of Foreign Policy During the Lloyd George Coalition, 1918–22' (Oxford DPhil., 1994).

Index

DATE DUE

4SI-05			

#47-0108 Peel Off Pressure Sensitive